FROM
PARTICIPATION
TO
PARTNERSHIP

FROM PARTICIPATION TO PARTNERSHIP

A JOURNEY TO SAFETY AT THE FRONT LINE

SCOTT GADDIS

PALMETTO

PUBLISHING

Charleston, SC
www.PalmettoPublishing.com

Paperback ISBN: 979-8-8229-4550-0
eBook ISBN: 979-8-8229-4551-7

In memory of my mother, who recently passed. Her life was a testament to unconditional love and facing adversity with determination and an unyielding passion to prevail.

To Connie, my greatest advocate and supporter, who navigated our life challenges with unparalleled grace.

To my children, Matthew, Nicholas, Jonathan, and Taylor, for their understanding and patience as I missed countless milestones, ball games, performances, and, too often, their birthdays during my business travels.

Table of Contents

Foreword

By: Sandy Smith

If this were any other book about safety, it would start one of two ways: either with some shocking safety statistics to show you the seriousness of the subject matter—some high-level numbers about workplace deaths and injuries each year—or a personal anecdote about a friend or colleague who died from a preventable incident and how that changed and motivates the author's safety vision.

And if Scott were simply another safety influencer looking to enhance his credibility and increase his social media following, this book would be filled with pithy anecdotes and meme-able chunks of wit that would make excellent social posts while saying nothing particularly helpful to everyone in health and safety who actually crave guidance to help them succeed at the very difficult job they have to do every day.

Having known Scott for nearly twenty years and having had the pleasure of collaborating with him for five of those years, I can assure you that this book is quite different from other books about occupational safety and health that you might have read. While it's a story about Scott's life in safety, as told by a masterful storyteller and practitioner who has served a long career on the front lines, it is so much more.

This book is not a candy-coated fairy tale full of empty platitudes and worthless, untested advice. This is the work of a man who has had a career spent in safety in the real world of work, where people really get hurt and lives change forever as a result of a moment of inattention or years of persistent neglect.

There is a lot of wisdom here, as anyone who knows Scott would expect, but there's also honesty, humility, and introspection. Wisdom is the product of reality's tempering expectations and ambitions. Even in a life dedicated to keeping people safe, incidents still happen, people get hurt, and plans go awry. If every plan came off as intended every time, no one would learn anything new and we wouldn't need this book.

This is a book written by someone who knows the world is changing quickly and understands the vital importance of keeping up. When Scott started his safety career, most recordkeeping and analysis was done on paper spreadsheets. There were no armies of sensors collecting data, no tablets or mobile phones for capturing observations, and no artificial intelligence for crunching massive amounts of data to uncover trends that support leading indicators that could prevent incidents from happening. Most critically, the US-based Occupational Safety and Health Act (OSH Act) and Occupational Safety and Health Administration were not yet even a generation old.

While a generation certainly sounds like a long time, if we consider the fact that the Industrial Revolution that transformed capitalism began in the eighteenth century, and that during much of that time workers were considered disposable, less valuable than the commodities they produced, we realize that occupational health and safety as a practice still had the training wheels on when the OSH Act was signed into existence.

Today, we've come a long way. The young practitioner Scott describes at the beginning of this book couldn't have dreamed of the technology he would be able to bring to bear on his work by 2024. AI was something like Hal in *2001: A Space Odyssey*, not an easily accessible application that can eliminate months of work crunching numbers in spreadsheets. Handheld communication devices were something one saw in Star Trek movies, not something workers carried around in their pockets to capture observations and report incidents as they occur.

Scott has been at the forefront of all these developments in health and safety. But more than that, he has been and continues to be a champion of growing, learning, and adapting to what technology can do for us. As every safety leader knows, even workers themselves can resist these changes. Scott shows us what it means to be a change agent who helps workers see how embracing these new technologies can save their lives. It's not easy to make reluctant workers change their behavior, even when it's in their best interest to do so. But true leaders, like Scott, know how to do it, and he's willing to help the rest of us learn how to do it as well.

Change, therefore, is a constant and critical theme throughout this book. Scott's career spans more than thirty years at this point, but he practices safety like it's 2024, not 1994. No one in the business of keeping people safe in 2024 and beyond can remain stuck in their favorite methodologies, using tools that served them well in the past. However, Scott never discards a method merely to replace it with a new one. He believes that a good process is invaluable, regardless of its age. In this book, Scott highlights some of those solid frameworks that have stood the test of time, reintroducing them to some and reaffirming their value to others.

The workplace has changed, our tools have changed, and we must change as well to adapt not only to technology but also to the way we think about safety culture. In days past, organizations were often strict hierarchies in which authority flowed down and workers did as they were told. Today, safety is a partnership, or at least it should be, where workers at the front line are critical contributors who are providing incident and observation data, receiving and acting on data-based analytics to improve their situational awareness, and leading safety initiatives for the entire organization.

So, while this is a story of a lifetime spent in safety, it's not the story of an idealist who has stuck to his original truth. It's the story of a realist who has grown, evolved, and adapted his approach to safety to serve today's workers and the workplace. It's about growth, partnership, and hard work.

This is a book of valuable lessons for everyone, including safety practitioners, organizational leaders, and even workers on the front line who want to better understand the way safety ought to work and the role they can play in making it happen. It's a book people will want to keep in the workplace so they can refer to it when needed. It's a compelling story and a critical reference guide all in one.

I've read many books about safety and safety management systems over the years, and I can honestly say it's been a pleasure reading Scott's book and I was honored when he asked me to write this foreword. Scott and this book are valuable resources, and I'm delighted he's sharing his knowledge with all of you. I'm looking forward to the impact it will have on the world of workplace safety.

Preface

Safety is not an intellectual exercise to keep us at work.
It is a matter of life and death. It is the sum of our
contributions to safety management that determines
whether the people we work with live or die.

—Sir Brian Appleton

Sir Brian Appleton was one of three technical assessors and an investigator in the aftermath of the Piper Alpha disaster. The Piper Alpha disaster was a catastrophic offshore oil and gas platform explosion and fire that occurred on July 6, 1988, in the North Sea, off the coast of Scotland. The tragedy resulted from a series of safety management failures, including inadequate maintenance and safety procedures, a lack of proper communication, an inability to assess and manage the risks associated with maintenance work properly, and a poor work culture that excluded the contributions and value of those working at the front line. The disaster claimed the lives of 167 people, with only sixty-one survivors, making it the deadliest offshore oil platform disaster in history.

The Piper Alpha disaster led to a significant overhaul of safety regulations and procedures in the oil and gas industry. The investigation into the incident revealed systemic issues and latent errors that the industry needed to address to prevent future tragedies. The lessons from this disaster have helped to improve safety standards in the offshore oil industry and influenced changes in how many manage safety today. The memory of those who lost their lives on that fateful day serves as a reminder of the importance of prioritizing safety more than anything else in hazardous industries.

This event is burned in my memory, possibly because it occurred just weeks after I graduated with my bachelor of science in occupational safety and health. Indeed, since then, there have been other significant disasters in the workplace. Still, I tend to go back to this event repeatedly because it was my first real-life example of an actual catastrophe happening adjacent to the start of my career. The devastating event showed me my future: every work detail, every idea, every plan, and every program or process mistake could be the difference between life and death. This one event and its findings would underscore the critical importance of safety in the workplace and how I would lead safety throughout my career. I would be part of a work system, and my work would influence getting people home to their families daily. The event taught me that safety is a shared responsibility that requires a robust safety management system, self-awareness, contributions from the front-line workers who are closest to the risks, and leadership support to remove the barriers that inhibit a strong safety culture.

While writing this book, I drew inspiration from the many safety practitioners I have studied and admired, and from whom I have gained incredible insights during my career. Each has had a part in making me better. I often question whether I have anything new or valuable to add. However, my experiences are unique, and they can offer a fresh perspective on leading safety. By sharing my journey and the lessons I've learned, I hope to inspire others in the field and contribute to the ongoing conversation about improving safety in the workplace. Every voice matters in this critical discussion, and I am excited to add my voice to the chorus of safety advocates. Throughout my career, especially over the past few years, when I have counseled and consulted younger safety practitioners, spoken at conferences, and even led webinars during the COVID years, I have often been asked if I could recommend a book that summarizes the things I discuss. I have indeed published environmental, health, and safety content over the years, but this is my first attempt to combine some of it.

The world of safety is changing rapidly. Some may know about Safety I and Safety II. Over the past few years, both have become popular conversation starters and have drawn fervent debate from many of my safety colleagues. Some are firmly planted in one camp or the other. Each approach offers a unique perspective on identifying and mitigating risks and promoting safety in operations. Each approach has strengths and weaknesses, and it is important to understand the nuances of each approach to implement them in a practical setting.

Safety I, the traditional model, focuses on preventing mishaps by recognizing and managing risks and emphasizing adherence to established procedures and standards. It operates on the principle that accidents stem from deviations or failures in normal operations, focusing on root cause analysis and reducing human interactions. It is where I began my work as a safety practitioner long ago.

Safety II considers what goes right, advocating a better understanding of how safety emerges from the successful interaction of people, processes, and technology under varied conditions. It values adaptability, resilience, and the role of human operators as integral to maintaining safety, suggesting that success in everyday operations offers valuable insights for safety enhancement. This sounds like how I have learned to leverage the many things I will share throughout this book.

My question is: Why not simply SWIPE (Steal With Integrity and Pride from Everywhere), blend the strengths of both, and adopt strategies that acknowledge the prevention of failures and the promotion of successful practices? As you read this book, you will see that it is critical to learn from adverse events and routine operations to glean comprehensive safety insights. Promoting a just culture where workers can report errors, near-misses, and operational successes without fear of reprisal fosters transparency and continuous improvement, eventually creating an environment of learning and empowerment that enhances the entire safety management system. It creates a positive and supportive workplace where everyone is committed to upholding the highest standards of safety and excellence by proactively addressing potential risks and ensuring the well-being of their employees and stakeholders. Resilience is critical, and designing robust processes against known risks while remaining flexible enough to adapt to unforeseen challenges is vital.

At the end of this book, I will look at what I think will be the future of health and safety. I think we will see a lot of aggressive changes in how we manage and lead safety with challenges and areas of focus that will be new to many practitioners. We will see safety integrated even further into the overall operational and strategic fabric of many organizations as environmental, social, and governance and diversity, equity, and inclusion continue to be elevated in the workplace. Technology will lead a revolution in enhancing organizational learning and promoting an even more profound cultural shift toward safety that encompasses not just the prevention of bad outcomes through the application of data and analytics, but also the proactive creation of value through safety as a core organizational principle. The safety practitioner will have much to contend with going forward.

My lesson to you is this: with new ideas, the refreshment of some old ones, and adopting broad business management approaches, you can achieve a more nuanced and compelling safety management process. Simple approaches work best at the front line and even in the boardroom. Front-line workers must balance productivity, efficiency, quality, and safety, among other concerns, so keeping safety processes simple and straightforward is essential. Complexity adds too much to the mental load of most workers, so I advocate simple, proven practices that facilitate faster decision making and better problem solving. Your management system must move; it must leverage itself with process strength as it grows more mature, and that requires focusing on simple, accurate, and valuable program elements. Similarly, front-line workers must move from simply participating in the safety work I care about to building partnerships in the safety work we all care about. It is about genuinely collaborating for better safety at the front line.

I wrote the book thinking not about the seasoned safety practitioner who has years of experience, but about the person who has not experienced the safety performance he or she desires, about someone who is possibly newer to safety management or organizational leadership, and even about the worker from the front line who has a passion for health and safety and wants to grow into a leadership role. Granted, there is learning for everyone, but my initial thinking has been a look back at my career and asking myself what I wish I knew when I began my professional journey. The book's title encompasses everything I have ever wanted to do as a safety practitioner. *From Participation to Partnership, A Journey to Safety at the Front Line* means I want to share with you my ideas for getting a group of people to join as owners of a safety process in a way that is real, alive, and personal and gets everyone home to their loved ones safe and healthy every single day.

The book is divided into four parts: Learning to Lead Safety, Laying the Safety Foundation, Leveraging the Front Line for Transformational Safety Change, and Looking Forward in Occupational Safety and Health. This is how I think about my safety practice in general, meaning that I need to understand how to be the best version of myself, I need to be able to influence the management system positively, and I need to partner with people to do it well while keeping an eye on the future and the things that will likely challenge or benefit me going forward.

I also note that I am not an academic. Academic work is incredibly valuable in safety practice, as it has provided critical research and teaching in the field. I, however, am a practitioner. My job has been to learn and apply safety concepts at the front lines. I commonly refer to myself as a safety generalist whose work has always been multifaceted and with many competing priorities. I am the guy in the trenches who, for many years, woke up taking some of what I learned and, with hands-on experience, tried to make it work at the front lines. I take new ideas, refresh old ones and combine them with traditional principles, and then adapt them to the appetites of the organizations I have led. It is a different journey for us all, but this has been my path, and I expect it will be similar for many of you reading this book.

It feels like I've been working on this book for thirty-five years. It is the culmination of some things I've learned. I will share things that helped me improve my own safety processes and provide better leadership to the front line. I hope that you will find something of value.

Reflections

Reflective thinking turns experience into insight.

– JOHN MAXWELL

I have had a lengthy career. I am celebrating more than thirty-five years of work in safety and health, as well as at times leading environment and sustainability programs. I have worked at General Electric (GE), Kimberly Clark Corporation, Bristol Myers Squibb, and Coveris High-Performance Packaging, in that order. I have also served as a senior leader with an Environment, Health, Safety and Quality technology company called Intelex, as a key thought leader, adviser, mentor, coach, and safety and health practitioner, consulting with our teams on how EHSQ practitioners want to use our technology solutions. For the first time in my career, I am part of a large team, with a sizable portion of my colleagues being millennials and members of Gen Z. I spend most days answering questions, listening to ideas, vetting work plans, and just being me because the team looks to me as the chief safety and health practitioner. They want to know and understand my experiences leading safety and health. They want to learn everything it will take to serve our clients as best we can. A phrase I hear almost daily is "how can we." How can we build a better product? How can we serve our customers better? How can we market to practitioners with higher value? Every single day, I take the "how can we" call.

I want to acknowledge my team because their values are incredibly high for developing software solutions that help protect people's lives and support sustainable solutions for the environment. It is an orchestra of people who come to work without preconceptions, where everyone works together without worrying about where the final credit lands. In many respects, they do what much of what this book is dedicated to helping you do. They are looking at the collective effort of the whole because it exceeds the individual efforts of the few. They are helping with technology to move safety, quality, and environmental partnerships to the front lines.

I want to recognize Megan Petracco for the book illustrations. I also want to acknowledge two former work colleagues and good friends: Sandy Smith, who wrote the foreword in my book, and Graham Freeman, who wrote the afterword. Both have challenged me and helped me open the years of my professional journey and share them with a broader audience.

I spent the first part of my career in site-level manufacturing facilities learning and leading safety, health, and, at times, environmental programs. The latter part of my career has been taking what I learned, leading people-based processes, and redistributing those learnings through various corporate-level roles. The following chapters will bring out some of what I discovered and employed. Looking back, working in the site-level manufacturing facilities was the most rewarding part of my career. Regardless of how frustrating they could be at times, it was me and, usually, 500–600 people trying to do remarkable things, with the only thing standing between success and failure being ourselves.

I cut my safety practitioner teeth when I began at GE, where corporate environmental, health, and safety (EHS) oversight was heavy. I was fortunate to start a career straight out of college in the town where I grew up. My first role was at the GE Motors plant, where I was hired as an entry-level practitioner, but I soon learned that regardless of my level, I would lead a lot of EHS work. The plant manufactured large, heavy, industrial AC/DC motors with a highly skilled front-line workforce that did most of its work by hand. I still remember walking through the expanse of large buildings, looking and listening to the large stamping presses, mallets pounding coils of wire into stator cores, and heavy materials being transported by hoists and fork trucks to their various workstations for their next assembly operation. Every day, I would come home with black cast iron dust embedded in my clothing, as we all did. It was a heavy, dirty, labor-intensive operation. When I joined, we had over 150 OSHA recordable injuries and illnesses and astronomically high workers' compensation costs, and, in the beginning, I had no idea that we were awful. Much of my work was compliance-driven, employing mandated programs supported by strict guidelines. I sometimes thought I had better, simpler, more straightforward approaches to the same end goals. Still, I am thankful that the rigor of working within a well-designed management system and a solid safety framework gave me clear guardrails to perform. Looking back, it was a necessary part of my learning. Over the course of a few short years of collaborating with people differently, we had more than halved the injury rate and significantly reduced the workers' compensation costs to the business, which today seems incredibly high. Still, during my tenure, it was viewed as a significant turnaround. I left the plant before my work was done, but I felt good about the progress that had been made.

Most of my professional life was spent at Kimberly Clark Corporation. When I started there, it was still the Scott Paper Company, but within a few years, we had merged with Kimberly-Clark, so I often refer to it all as the latter. The first third of my eighteen-year tenure was spent at a local paper manufacturing facility in Owensboro, Kentucky. For lack of a better way to describe it, it was a magical place where I got to employ everything I knew about safety. I learned from the other leaders, adapted ideas from forward-thinking safety thinkers through their books, and applied what I thought would work.

We were a Greenfield manufacturing site where different people from various walks of professional and private life came together to support the idea that the organization could achieve remarkable success through talent, skill diversity, and pure constructive collaboration from a group of people who shared a lofty vision of doing incredible things together. I will talk specifically about my time there in this book. However, even when I do not identify this facility as the place I am writing about, there is a good chance I am writing about my experiences there. Looking back on our differences there compared to other places I have worked, every worker, even those from the front line, had a computer, a telephone with a personalized phone extension, a specific desk space within an office area, and a personal mailbox. There was no time clock to punch in or out, nor were supervisors hovering over the workforce. I am not sure every worker ever needed all those things. However, in hindsight, all of it sent a simple message: that every worker who walked into the facility was valued for the contributions he or she would make. We were building an organization and a culture that had trust from the senior leader's office to the front line by applying simple but meaningful work principles that governed it all. We had the best and brightest group, who wore the same uniforms, shared the same capability development plans, and were treated as partners in leading a portion of Kimberly-Clark's manufacturing business. We were a team of people who erased our organizational titles and regarded each other as partners.

To give you a taste of our achievements, within a few years of the facility's opening, we had achieved best-in-class safety performance in a company of over 160 facilities and world-class control of workers' compensation costs, which is always the final test of how I personally judge safety success. The Owensboro Kimberly Clark facility's success trajectory has never changed, and they have continued to reach new heights in safety. At my departure, I gave my role to a new safety coordinator who had previously worked in manufacturing and shipping as an operating technician without much formal safety training at all.

She was far less equipped than I was, but she had a passion for learning and the determination to take safety even further, and she did. The facility has achieved OSHA's VPP Star Status, ISO certifications, and numerous national and state safety awards recognizing their achievements. Their lagging and leading safety performance indicators paint a picture of process control and world-class safety in many respects. It is not a perfect place, but it is a place that lives its values, and I am glad safety was and has remained a chief value there. I was a small part of that, but I was fortunate to be part of its early beginnings, and that molded much of how I have led safety and health ever since.

It is important that I recognize specific people, many of whom were my bosses who had a hand in helping me become a better safety practitioner and leader. My first boss, Mike Wright, hired me directly from college. He knew I was incredibly green, but he threw me into the deep end to see how well I could learn to swim. He always had a life ring available if needed, but he knew I would be successful if I could learn safety by collaborating with people on the front lines and solving their challenges. I gained most of my knowledge and leadership competence in my second role, as the safety and health leader for the Owensboro Kimberly-Clark paper manufacturing facility. Names that come to mind are Mike Lerch, Tim Gardner, Rae Hill, and Connie Gaddis. Each person played an important part in helping me develop my skills and my thinking on how to lead occupational safety and health effectively. As I was promoted, Drew Barfoot, Todd Visscher, Larry Nedrow, and Randy Kates were pivotal because they all knew I worked rather unconventionally. Still, each mentored me and provided a clear runway or removed the hurdles necessary for me to be successful. I was probably not very easy to manage, but I am thankful they all had patience. All these people are leaders from whom I learned how to do my work. This book has their fingerprints on many of its pages.

In addition, I have worked bi-vocationally in a local church ministry for almost forty years. I mention it because leading occupational safety and health and leading a faith-based ministry have been very similar paths for me. My faith drives much of my work as a practitioner simply because I know, based on my faith, that I need to care deeply for others. I vividly remember an episode when I had just taken leadership for EHS at Bristol Myers Squibb. During my first week there, my boss introduced me to a large crowd at a company meeting and asked me to say a few words. After sharing my EHS vision and ninety-day work plan, I ended with what I wake up daily to do. I told the audience that I loved my work and that I loved them enough to protect them. As we returned to our offices from the meeting, my boss looked over at me and asked, "Did you just tell three hundred people that you loved them?" It is humorous now as I think about that episode. Still, I just looked at him and said, "Love is a verb," and everything I do is assessed against the idea that my job is showing people through taking necessary actions to protect them that I want to get them home safe to those who also love them.

I am sure I have caused a few eyes to roll, and you now possibly believe this is a bit soft coming from an "in-the-trenches safety guy," but think with me for a moment. Look backward in your life. Think about that one person you felt genuinely cared for you, wanted the best for you, gave you constructive feedback when you needed to improve, celebrated your accomplishments, and was simply there for your journey. Many of those people and organizations in my life are listed above during the various stages of my story. They built me this way.

This book will not dive any further into my faith-based journey other than to tell you that I learned to be an authentic leader from relationships with people around me and the faith that guides me, and both have taught me to better care for the people in the organizations I have served. I will challenge you to be an authentic leader and to care deeply about the people in your care. In many ways, what separates good safety practitioners from great ones is that the great ones genuinely care for the workers at the front line. I want you to be a great one.

Part I:
Learning to Lead Safety

Chapter 1:

Safety at the Front Line

Don't forget where you came from.

— IDA CARR

Worker safety and collaborating with individuals on the front lines have been the most essential parts of any success I have experienced as a safety practitioner. I grew up in a blue-collar, working-class family. Listening to many well-told stories throughout my life, I discovered a lengthy tradition of a family that worked hard with their hands as construction workers, union insulators, machine operators – and one family member was even a steel mill worker. Most were exceptional leaders wherever they worked, even if many led from the front lines. My grandmother, Ida Vanell Carr, was no different. She worked at General Electric (GE) as a utility line worker, producing mostly radio tubes for almost thirty years. Her job demanded a high level of skill and knowledge. They regularly relied on her to resolve issues, fill vacant positions, and suggest improvements to work processes. The management team knew her, appreciated her, and counted on her front-line leadership. As a young child, I sometimes saw my grandmother leave the house in a clean, white, starched uniform and return home exhausted in a dirty, sweat-stained garment at the end of the day. I saw firsthand how hard she worked.

I was the first person in my immediate family to graduate from college. My first job out of college was with GE, the same company and in the same town where my grandmother had worked. Before my first workday, she imparted the most significant lesson I would learn, and it has been how I have approached my work throughout my career. "Don't forget where you came from, as the people you work with are much like me," she said. "Don't get above your raisin'" may be a better way to interpret what she was saying. She understood workplace safety and, at times, the lack of good safety management because she had witnessed it firsthand for much of her adult life. My grandmother was telling me this: I should approach my safety work as if she were on the factory floor. This idea has stayed with me throughout my career—imagining workers as if they were family members. Yes, you and I have been called to protect the front line and engage them in building a safety partnership.

WORKER ENGAGEMENT

When we look into the idea of worker engagement, we frequently discover that it refers to how much employees are passionate about, invested in, and motivated by the work they do and the employer they work for. Workers' wholehearted commitment is vital for the company's success. Knowing the organization's safety goals, and believing that everyone has a role to play, is critical for safety success.

What does your intuition tell you about the front line, and do you think they have the same goals as you do for safety success?

WORKER PARTNERSHIP

The transition from participation to a safety partnership is a collaborative effort involving the safety practitioner, the members of the management team, and the workers on the front lines. Within an organization, a genuine relationship between organizational members connects each level. I often discuss transitioning workers from participation to partnership, and in the upcoming chapters, I will share ideas to help you move in that direction. You should know that workers will participate with you. They do so because they value their safety and the job's success. Large groups of people are readily willing to join me and achieve what needs to be done. However, I want them to work together, take ownership of the safety process with me, and eventually take some of the responsibility for leading safety without me. I believe in their abilities to do this. It would be best if you did the same.

Ask yourself, "Do I have confidence in my workforce's ability to make the right decisions when I am not there?" If you cannot answer "yes," it is likely that worker partnership has not yet reached a degree of cultural maturity.

BRADLEY CURVE

The Bradley Curve is useful for understanding this idea. The curve is the work of Berlin Bradley, who was a plant manager at DuPont and came up with the curve in the 1990s, and it remains quite relevant today. This concept builds on the idea that human behavior contributes to accidents and incidents on the job.

Figure 1 below shows the curve as a roadmap, illustrating the progression of a company's safety culture through four distinct phases:

- Reactive
- Dependent
- Independent
- Interdependent

Each phase represents a different level of safety awareness and cultural maturity supported by the organization's behaviors, providing insights into how its members perceive and manage safety.

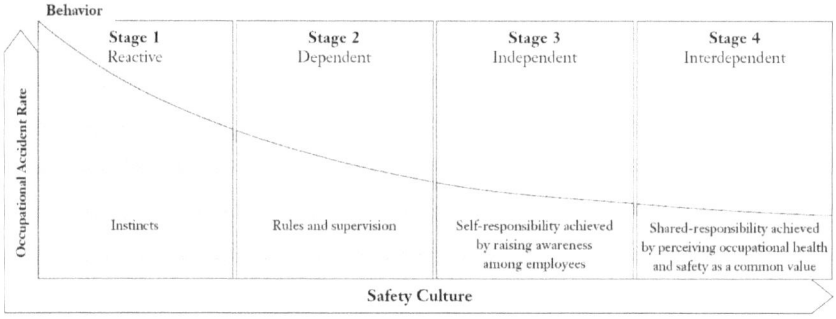

Figure 1

Here is how each stage is defined:

Reactive

Workers at this stage deny responsibility and believe accidents are inevitable because of the dangerous nature of the job or the inherent risks involved. Workers frequently misinterpret and misrepresent safety as a matter of chance. Attending to loss after it has occurred is a symptom of a management approach that lacks definition. The emphasis is on avoiding detection, and workers do not accept responsibility for workplace safety. As a result, safety is overwhelmingly a question of luck.

Dependent

Workers perceive safety by adhering to rules and procedures. Management's commitment is clear, but applying rules and regulations enforces the process. At this stage, workers believe that strictly following instructions guarantees a safe workplace. If the rules and procedures are done well, the accident rates will decline, which is a significant driver of success at this stage of thinking. Another characteristic is the pressure to perform and using rewards or punishments to influence behavior.

Independent

Workers accept responsibility and believe they can make a difference with their activities. This stage shows that workers believe in personal accountability and place a high value on safety. Their participation and proactive actions are proof of this. The workers actively value the organization's requests and engage in the safety processes.

Interdependent

Workers see safety as a shared duty and work vigorously to improve the workplace culture. This stage includes collaboration, problem-solving, resource allocation, and team accountability. The safety practitioner, management team, and front line are all on board and working together to ensure safety. The workers partner with safety leadership to achieve the desired success.

Understanding the Bradley Curve helps organizations identify their current safety culture stage and gives solid indicators for moving toward a more proactive and collaborative safety environment. This model emphasizes that advancing through these phases requires procedural compliance and a fundamental shift in attitudes, behaviors, and organizational values toward safety.

Looking back at the numerous facilities I was part of, I found many of them stuck in the dependent stage of the Bradley Curve, a stage that significantly hindered our safety performance. Many frontline workers and most of the management team relied on me and my teams to be their answer for everything related to safety. I learned quickly that I would never have enough time or dedicated safety resources to be everything to everyone in their moment of need. What I did know was that this dilemma would stall my efforts to reach the safety performance I desired. I needed to move a group of people to a deeper cultural maturity level where they actively cared for one another.

CURVE MATURITY

There are specific attributes of the Bradley Curve that help with a deeper understanding of cultural maturity. Each stage, supported by Chart 1 below, paints a picture of where you are today to help you better understand your organization's approach to managing safety and the logical steps toward a more robust work culture as you advance.

Here are the definitions of each attribute:

Prevailing Opinion

This attribute is the prevailing mindset within an organization regarding the certainty and acceptability of accidents and incidents. It reflects whether accidents are viewed as unfortunate but usual occurrences or as events you can avoid through proper safety measures and practices. This attitude significantly influences how safety is prioritized and managed across all levels of the organization.

Overarching Behavior

This refers to the underlying actions and safety behaviors of workers in the organization. It encompasses how workers proactively identify, report, and mitigate hazards and how they participate in safety. The organization's overarching behaviors reflect the group's approach to safety, ranging from reactive (responding to incidents after they occur) to proactive (preventing accidents through continuous engagement and improvement).

Leadership Style

Leadership style is the approach leaders, managers, and supervisors take in guiding, influencing, and engaging their teams, especially in safety. It can range from reactive—leaders rarely enforce safety rules and procedures—to transformational—leaders coach and mentor to inspire and motivate workers to internalize safety values and work collectively toward a safer workplace. The leadership style is pivotal in shaping the safety culture and driving the evolution from a reactive to an interdependent safety culture.

Safety Activity

These are the specific actions, programs, and initiatives that promote safety in the workplace. Occupational safety activities can include training sessions, safety audits, risk assessments, safety meetings, and even safety technologies. The scope and effectiveness of these activities are broad but indicate an organization's commitment to safety and its stage of cultural maturity on the Bradley Curve.

Personal Responsibility

This is how individuals and groups acknowledge and accept their role in ensuring workplace safety. In the earlier stages of the Bradley Curve, responsibility rests primarily with management or the safety practitioner. As the organization progresses along the Bradley Curve, there is a shift toward a collective recognition of shared and owned responsibility; every worker feels accountable for their safety and that of their colleagues.

Each of these characteristics plays a significant part in moving safety forward, and their associated attributes are crucial in determining an organization's position along the Bradley Curve. Look again at Chart 1 below at the attributes found in the chart to further your understanding.

	Reactive	Dependent	Independent	Interdependent
Prevailing Opinion	Loss-producing incidents are a regular part of doing work. The prevailing opinion is that accidents happen.	Acknowledgment that loss-producing incidents should be minimized mainly to meet external expectations.	A belief that accidents are preventable through individual actions and awareness.	A shared conviction that safety is integral to operational success and that all accidents can be prevented through teamwork.
Overarching Behavior	There are minimal to no proactive safety measures; accidents are responded to rather than prevented.	Beginning to comply with safety regulations due to external pressures, safety measures are rule-based.	Individuals take personal responsibility for safety, proactively identifying and mitigating risks.	Collective responsibility for safety, with high levels of collaboration and mutual care.
Leadership Style	Laissez-faire or autocratic, with little to no emphasis on safety from leadership.	Directing, with leaders and managers enforcing safety rules and procedures.	Participative, with leaders encouraging personal accountability and involvement in safety initiatives.	Transformational leadership fosters a partnering culture where safety is a core value and a shared responsibility.
Safety Activity	Ad-hoc and minimal, primarily focused on compliance after incidents occur.	Implementation of basic safety training and compliance protocols.	Comprehensive safety training, employee-led safety audits, and proactive risk assessments.	Advanced safety systems, continuous improvement processes, and cross-functional safety teams.
Personal Responsibility	Limited awareness or acceptance of safety responsibilities at any level.	Safety responsibilities are acknowledged by management but not fully embraced by employees.	Employees at all levels recognize and embrace their role in ensuring workplace safety.	Safety responsibilities are deeply ingrained and collectively owned, with everyone actively partnering in safety.

Chart 1

As you review the above, ask yourself these questions.

- Where do I see my organization fitting into one of these stages?
- Considering the attributes described, do I see attributes that contribute to adverse events in my workplace?
- Are incidents still a part of our routine? Are there repeats of the same type of incident?
- Where can we make improvements as an organization?

These are a few beginning questions as you consider using the Bradley Curve.

As a safety practitioner, you should carefully consider the work, the workers, and your desired culture. Where are you now, and where do you want to go?

Some people criticize the Bradley Curve for oversimplifying causation, disregarding intuition, downplaying rule compliance, lacking deeper influential contexts such as organizational or human factors, oversimplifying complex activities, and neglecting human fallibility. Further, most events do not happen linearly, and there is much for you to consider. With all that said, I have never used this model in the manner that the critics identified. Nevertheless, I agree that the model will not prevent every accident from taking place. However, it is a simple and effective way to promote healthy conversations and cultural progress.

Keeping things simple is vital when discussing culture and systems, especially with those on the front lines. As a practitioner, I can make better decisions driven by data based on what I find at each stage, enabling me to plug any holes in the process and move forward. The model shows the relationship between occurrences and the capacity to assess the culture along the way to make improvements. I still find much use in the Bradley Curve, and I continue to find new ways to improve on what it offers.

The Bradley Curve will reliably determine your stage of safety maturity and help you understand the improvements you need to make. You can also add new characteristics or attributes to suit your organization. It is essential to note that behavior alone does not determine the safety process's effectiveness. However, substandard actions can demolish every attempt to control bad outcomes, and worker behavior should be a priority in your plan to prevent loss.

Do you want your safety culture to grow toward interdependence in the future? Is that happening? If not, your program may lack process strength, or maybe you are not taking steps to achieve your program's desires. Do you believe that simply aiming for a target is enough for you to hit it successfully? Achieving cultural excellence requires the safety practitioner to address many questions. You need to discuss the details of the cultural journey you plan to embark on with management and the front-line teams. I also do not believe the Bradley Curve qualifies as a methodology. Consider using the Bradley Curve to assess your present condition and where you desire to go. Judging each stage's performance indicators and how the workers actively participate in each stage are markers of such growth. It is enough to get you effectively headed in the right direction.

WORKER ENGAGEMENT IS KEY

As shared earlier in the chapter, worker engagement frequently refers to how invested, motivated, and passionate workers are about their work and employer. Your first question is, to what degree are workers engaged in safety where I work, and why? Engaged workers view the company's success as a personal accomplishment and contribute positively. They understand the organization's established safety goals and believe their role contributes to success. A meta-analysis by Gallup, which examined more than 82,000 business units and 1.8 million employees in 230 organizations, across forty-nine industries and in seventy-three countries, shows that companies with high worker engagement have 62 percent fewer safety incidents than those with lower worker engagement. The most significant indicator for judging engagement may be the front line's value in ensuring the organization accomplishes its safety goals (Rigon, 2016).

Can you see it demonstrated in your organization? What is your gut telling you about the front line? Are they invested in your values as a safety practitioner?

I have used the Bradley Curve as a safety practitioner most effectively when I have thought deeply about how I felt about our cultural journey, where we were at the time, and where I wanted to go. I then pulled small groups separately from the front line, middle management, and senior leadership, reviewed each stage of the Bradley Curve, and asked where they believed we were.

Reflecting on the organizations I have led; my guess is that you will find significant disparity between distinct groups and levels in the organization. You will also find that not every group is at the same stage of the curve. There will be parts of your safety process that might be doing very well, but other parts that are not performing and need help getting to the next stage. The magic occurs when you combine all the groups I have described and discuss where the organization is today and if you have the appetite to move forward.

In principle, the curve works very simply. Suppose you find yourself in the reactive stage. To reach the next step, you must make changes within your work system reflective of the characteristics and attributes listed in the next phase of the curve. Each stage is further characterized by a worker's desire to engage in safety differently from the previous.

Certain safety activities and measures can establish a specific behavioral basis for each stage, which is crucial for mitigating incidents and improving occupational safety. As a result, different people and groups recognize, accept, and own varying degrees of responsibility, which are always based on the culture's maturity.

PERCEPTIONS MATTER

Our perceptions influence our reality. Perceptions are essential for implementing safety measures and controlling workplace losses. Workers' feelings about safety relate to their understanding of it and how their employer responds to their concerns. Many attributes influence safety perceptions, including worker attitude, involvement, communication, policy and procedures, training, risk control, investigation, corrective actions, reporting, recognition, and management support, to name a few. How a worker perceives workplace safety is an important indicator. It goes further than safety. Elevated levels of safety engagement at work have a positive effect beyond the safety practitioners' area of responsibility. Workers who value safety also work at a higher level to deliver services and produce quality products. I spent a career leading safety and health and watching maintenance, quality, and operations improve because we established robust safety management systems and strong approaches to doing things well.

If you lead safety correctly, it can be a lever in the integrated success of your whole organization. Considering the powerful influence of how workers feel about their role, it is up to you to link the actual level of safety, your organization's place along the Bradley Curve, and how the front-line workers perceive where they are along its path.

SAFETY PERCEPTIONS SURVEY

Surveys can help you understand where your organization is on its safety journey. Use the statements below as a starting point to decide whether more safety measures are needed.

- I am never asked to do unsafe things.
- I am not concerned about my workplace safety.
- My job never requires me to do unsafe or substandard tasks.
- I have a complete understanding of my responsibilities for safety at my workplace.
- I have the necessary knowledge of all safety hazards in my workplace.
- I have the necessary skills to do my job safely.
- My impression is that my organization values my health and safety.
- My immediate supervisor cares about my safety and takes action to keep me safe.
- I have a good understanding of my rights and obligations regarding safety.
- I am not afraid to report safety issues to management even if I am at fault.
- There is consistent communication between management and workers regarding safety matters.
- The organization addresses safety concerns with the highest priority.
- All incidents are investigated quickly to improve safety and health.

In addition to the above, I would encourage you to think about your own work system and add additional statements if necessary to understand better where to focus your attention going forward.

You should also consider measuring each safety perception to better understand the priorities of the work ahead of you. Here is a scale to consider as a starting point for the statements above.

- **0 - Strongly Disagree**: The individual strongly disagrees with the statement. They perceive significant threats and believe that safety measures are either absent or completely ineffective, leading to a constant sense of danger and vulnerability.
- **1 - Disagree**: The individual disagrees with the statement. They acknowledge some efforts towards safety but find them largely ineffective, resulting in frequent feelings of unsafety and exposure to potential harm.
- **2 - Somewhat Disagree**: The individual somewhat disagrees with the statement. They see some safety measures in place but consider them insufficient, leading to occasional concerns and a general feeling of being somewhat unsafe.
- **3 - Neutral**: The individual neither agrees nor disagrees with the statement. They recognize that there are safety measures but doubt their adequacy and effectiveness, resulting in a balanced perception with concerns and reassurances.
- **4 - Agree**: The individual agrees with the statement. They believe safety measures are generally effective and well-implemented, with only minor concerns about potential risks, leading to a mostly secure feeling.
- **5 - Strongly Agree**: The individual strongly agrees with the statement. They have full confidence in the safety measures and believe their environment is free from significant risks, leading to a strong sense of security and well-being and a collaborative work culture.

FRONT-LINE PARTNERSHIP

Safety on the front lines involves interdependence and a true partnership. This does not mean workers lose their personal or professional identities. Still, people at every organizational level and rank seeking a partnership deliberately decide to join and contribute to safety excellence. This ensures that the operation remains safe, from the boardroom to the front line, where products are made or services are delivered. Taking responsibility for each other's safety is a logical step for workers, like caring for a neighbor. Everyone equally values protection, as it is a collective concern and responsibility.

Here are some qualities I believe are present when you have interdependence:

- Safety becomes a core integrated value in the organization. It is a commitment not just for a few workers but for everyone in the organization. Safety is a factor in all decisions, such as quality, operations, finance, and other functional support elements that could negatively affect workplace safety. Safety is the litmus test for going forward in the decision-making process in every area of the business management system.
- Everyone has the authority to take ownership of safety initiatives, provide suggestions for improvement, and participate in—even lead—safety-related activities such as safety audits and inspections. They also stop and ask questions when things seem wrong without fear of retaliation.
- All workers' voices are crucial. They are encouraged and valued for raising concerns about substandard conditions or practices. Everyone is constantly aware of the organization's inherent risks and is trained to identify potential hazards, knowing their actions are integral to the workplace's safety.
- The organization embraces a learning and continuous improvement culture in which workers learn, develop skills, and share their knowledge.

- Teamwork is a requirement to work, and the team is active in their input in a way that increases safety through more effective loss control efforts, policies and procedures, and rule development.
- The management team is deeply committed to safety and understands the importance of creating a safe work environment. They provide equal and shared equity from the boardroom to the front line for continuously improving safety culture, ensuring that everyone feels secure and supported in their efforts.
- The organization consistently moves from externally applied discipline through dependence to self-discipline and through independence to a state of interdependency in which everyone helps each other perform better.

CLOSING

I have often shared with my teams over the years that we will succeed, even if we sometimes stumble. Still, we will own it together, which I believe is the ultimate level of partnership. Getting to a stage of interdependence and authentic partnership on the front lines is messy. You will make mistakes, and that is okay. At the end of a long, arduous road, you ensure safety on the front lines by partnering with workers, implementing process controls, embracing sound management systems, developing effective programs, and fostering a safety-focused work culture.

Getting you closer to those partnerships is why I wrote this book.

The purpose of this chapter is to help you understand where you believe your organizational safety culture is now and where you want it to go. Overall, I know that partnering with the front line significantly reduces at-risk behaviors and lowers the number of loss-producing events. It promotes an increased sense of care for oneself and one another, and it supports an actively caring work community that helps everyone return home safe every day.

Chapter 2

Safety Knowledge is a Partnering Need

I am still learning.

— MICHELANGELO, AGE 87

Recognizing the fundamental aspects of safety leadership and management is a significant move toward ensuring a safer work environment. Before college, I had the fortunate experience of working in farm operations and construction. My experiences as a front-line worker helped me understand why I wanted to become a safety practitioner. You may be a new safety practitioner or someone with limited education and experience who is taking on safety leadership or has joined a safety team. Regardless, you are learning to lead because of your passion, motivation, interest, or industry knowledge. In my career, I have seen that some of the most exceptional people I have employed and worked with in safety had limited formal education but a strong dedication to protecting their colleagues at work and a deep desire to learn. You may be reading this book because you are looking for insights, ideas, or methods to help you do your job better.

I have held nine professional titles throughout my career, each representing my position within a different organization. Nevertheless, I have always considered myself purely an occupational safety and health practitioner. Reflect on this for a moment: What do you consider yourself to be? Are you striving to be a safety practitioner? Practitioners grow into experts and employ their knowledge and skills in a profession. Learning, absorbing information, and applying it for a result is a constant process for practitioners. Physicians are practitioners because they diagnose, evaluate, analyze, treat, and monitor patients until recovery. Safety and health practitioners share many of the same aspects. We find problems and then analyze and mitigate risks associated with hazardous conditions, materials, and practices. After that, we closely observe everything to ensure the sustainability of our treatment plans. Please do not discount the fact that we are indeed professionals and leaders, but what excites me most is applying scientific discipline to real problems and eliminating or lessening the chance of harm to people, the work process, and the production process. Effective execution of the safety practitioner's role yields enhanced controls in numerous organizational areas.

SAFETY CAPABILITY NEEDS

Clear expectations are the foundation of effective safety partnerships, but it all begins with the practitioner's technical and program capabilities. The role of safety practitioners has transformed over the years, but it remains vital in ensuring the safety of workers in various industries. In the past, practitioners bore most of the decision-making burden. Nevertheless, from my experience, I have realized that it is impossible to have complete control over everything that happens on the front lines each day. Your safety practice capabilities are essential, but how you champion your expertise and enlist others to help is paramount to delivering success. It is critical to understand that you may be the front line's most valuable ally in preventing significant injury or death, so what you know and how you apply it is a big part of the role.

Given the vast knowledge practitioners need, the following areas of expertise are critical to helping you perform your duties effectively as a safety practitioner:

Occupational Safety Laws and Regulations

One of the basic principles of working in occupational safety is understanding regulatory frameworks and laws governing workplace safety at the local, state, and federal levels. This includes a deep knowledge of safety and health specific to the regulations in the geographic region where you work. Some regulations are the Occupational Safety and Health Administration (OSHA) in the US, the UK Health and Safety at Work Act, and European health and safety laws based on Article 137 of the EU Treaty.

Key aspects include:

- Learning about the laws and regulations that affect your organization and having a clear understanding of how the essential standards apply to your industry.
- Keeping informed about any changes or updates to regulations for compliance. This requires analyzing regulatory agencies' websites, conducting internet searches, engaging with trade groups and practitioner associations, and participating in seminars or training sessions on regulatory changes.
- Interpreting and applying regulations to ensure compliance with workplace safety policies.

Hazard Identification and Risk Assessment

The safety practitioner must identify potential workplace hazards and assess associated risks. Hazard identification aims to systematically analyze the workplace and identify conditions or practices that could lead to accidents, injuries, or illnesses. Hazard identification and risk assessment are inseparable. It helps prioritize corrective actions by quantifying the likelihood and severity of potential loss-producing events. The better you quantify risk, the greater your chance of sustainable loss control. Identifying hazards, conducting practical risk assessments, and mitigating work system risks are essential skills for the safety practitioner.

Key aspects include:

- Building the skill to identify potential workplace dangers, including physical hazards, hazardous substances, and unsafe practices. Recognizing these risks involves experience, analysis of past losses, inspections, audits, and benchmarking with similar industries.
- Becoming familiar with risk assessment tools like risk matrices or methods used for job safety analysis to quantify and prioritize risks is essential.
- Investigating historical incident data and near-miss reports to identify the latest trends and areas of concern. It is also worth considering a system that can adapt to changing work conditions or processes for ongoing hazard identification and risk assessment.

Safety Management Systems

A comprehensive safety management system is crucial for achieving long-term success in occupational safety. You should know about safety management systems such as ISO 45001 and ANSI Z10, which offer a structured approach to risk management. The framework design of the safety management system should be comprehensive to manage workplace safety and address all identified threats through audits.

Key aspects include:

- Identifying the ideal management system for your organization and familiarizing yourself with the components of safety management systems, such as policies, procedures, risk assessment processes, incident reporting, and continuous improvement.
- Tailoring the safety management system to fit your organization's needs and risks. Considering every organization's distinct nature, this may necessitate prioritizing certain elements of the management system or giving preference to certain aspects.

- Establishing procedures to audit and evaluate the safety management system's effectiveness, adjusting as necessary.
- Demonstrating leadership in applying safety management principles to promote a safety culture within the organization.

Safety Training

Workplace safety programs must include safety training. Developing and delivering effective training programs for workers is the role of safety practitioners. These programs should address diverse topics such as regulatory compliance, hazard recognition, safe work practices, regulatory requirements, proper use of personal protective equipment (PPE), and emergency response procedures.

Key aspects include:

- Conveying complex safety concepts clearly and concisely to diverse audiences within the organization.
- Assessing training needs by considering workers' roles, workplace hazards, and regulatory requirements.
- Creating training materials and curricula that are engaging, informative, and customized for the target audience.
- Delivering training in various formats, such as classroom sessions, hands-on demonstrations, online modules, and microlearning to ensure workers comprehend and retain the information.
- Assessing training program effectiveness through testing, evaluations, and feedback and making necessary improvements.

Accident Investigation

Unfortunately, accidents and incidents will happen in the workplace. Safety practitioners must be able to conduct thorough investigations. The investigation aims to establish the immediate causes, root causes, and system factors responsible for the incident. Strong analytical skills and attention to detail are necessary for effective accident investigations. Safety practitioners who become proficient in investigation skills can create lasting corrective actions that reduce the likelihood of future incidents.

Key aspects include:

- Understanding the individuals, equipment, materials, and environment involved and where to find and collect the best data to understand the event that leads to control.
- Collecting data by gathering evidence, witness statements, and relevant documents to reconstruct the events leading to an accident.
- Analyzing immediate causes, which are frequently considered the most visible and direct causes of an incident, as they are the symptoms of more significant underlying problems.
- Analyzing root causes that serve as the reasons why underlying causes exist. These are the main factors that generate a work environment where safety incidents are more likely to happen if you cannot eliminate or mitigate them to a reasonable level.
- Identifying and implementing corrective actions to prevent similar incidents in the future, which may include changes in procedures, equipment, or training.
- Creating comprehensive accident reports that document findings, causes, and recommendations for prevention.

Safety Audits and Inspections

Maintaining a safe work environment requires regular workplace inspections and safety audits. Skilled safety practitioners conduct thorough inspections to identify safety deficiencies and areas for improvement. These inspections provide valuable information for evaluating the management system, assessing the effectiveness of safety programs, and implementing corrective actions. The key to success in this work lies in attention to detail, organizational knowledge, and a suitable understanding of inspection protocol and the difference between auditing and inspection.

Key aspects include:

- Developing a comprehensive audit plan that outlines the scope, objectives, and schedule for safety audits.
- Creating checklists and procedures for conducting audits and inspections, ensuring no critical safety aspects are overlooked.
- Documenting findings and observations during audits and inspections and generating detailed reports that include recommendations for improvement.
- Monitoring the implementation of corrective actions resulting from audit findings and ensuring that deficiencies are addressed promptly.

Culture

A safe culture is essential for a healthy work environment. The safety practitioner should recognize that culture is fundamental to an organization's health and performance. The first step is a commitment from management. Leaders in an organization must not only speak about safety but also back it up with their actions. The other critical element is worker involvement. Workers at every level need to engage actively in safety activities. This can encompass risk assessments, safety meetings, incident investigations, etc. Workers participating in these processes are more likely to assume ownership of safety and contribute to a positive safety culture.

Key aspects include:

- Reporting safety concerns and near misses without fear of retaliation and as an open dialogue to help identify potential hazards before they lead to incidents.
- Viewing incidents and other events as improvement opportunities rather than failures. Learning from these events allows

organizations to prevent similar incidents and improves worker perceptions of safety.

- Actively identifying, evaluating, and mitigating workplace risks. Effective risk management helps organizations prevent incidents and enhance safety performance.
- Embracing the value of training ensures that workers have the necessary skills and knowledge to perform their jobs safely. Competence extends beyond training and encompasses the practical application of knowledge and skills.
- Monitoring of audits and inspections to identify areas for improvement and measure the effectiveness of safety initiatives. Organizations can use performance monitoring to ensure progress in error control at work.

Document Control

Occupational safety relies on accurate recordkeeping. Safety practitioners ensure the maintenance of records for safety inspections, incident reports, training documentation, and compliance with safety regulations. These records are essential for compliance and can be crucial in legal matters or regulatory audits. The safety practitioner is also responsible for ensuring that documents are complete, up-to-date, and readily accessible.

Key aspects include:

- Establishing and maintaining organized and accessible records of safety inspections, incidents, training, and compliance documentation.
- Analyzing safety data to identify trends, areas of concern, and opportunities for improvement.
- Reporting incidents, injuries, and safety performance data to relevant authorities.
- Ensuring the confidentiality, security, and integrity of safety-related documents and data.

Emergency Response and Evacuation

The importance of preparing for unexpected emergencies cannot be overstated. Understanding emergency response protocols, including evacuation plans, fire safety procedures, and first-aid practices, is crucial for safety practitioners. These plans must be effectively coordinated and communicated to ensure appropriate worker responses in crises. Worker safety relies on preparedness for emergencies.

Key aspects include:

- Developing comprehensive emergency response plans that cover various scenarios, such as fires, chemical spills, natural disasters, and medical emergencies.
- Organizing and conducting regular emergency drills and training sessions to ensure workers know their roles and responsibilities during emergencies.
- Establishing effective communication systems to notify and coordinate workers during emergencies.
- Ensuring that necessary resources, such as first-aid kits, firefighting equipment, and evacuation routes, are readily available and well-maintained.

Crisis Management

Crisis management is a strategic and systematic approach to responding effectively to unexpected events that can harm an organization's stability, safety, and reputation. It requires proactive planning, quick decision-making, effective communication, and resource allocation to minimize crises and ensure a speedy recovery. The core of crisis management is recognizing risks, preparing response plans, and assembling crisis teams. Effective crisis management helps protect the well-being of workers and stakeholders and an organization's reputation and longevity.

Key aspects include:

- Preparedness for all probable crises that may cause harm, including natural disasters, chemical spills, and other emergencies.
- Creating comprehensive plans that outline actions for diverse emergencies, including evacuation routes, communication protocols, and resource allocation.
- Establishing and training emergency response teams to address crises quickly and effectively.
- Developing crisis communication strategies to keep workers, stakeholders, and the public informed during emergencies.
- Conducting post-crisis debriefings and analyses to identify areas for improvement in emergency response procedures.

Ergonomics

Ergonomics ensures occupational safety by designing workspaces, tasks, and equipment that match workers' abilities. Practitioners need knowledge of ergonomic principles to avoid musculoskeletal disorders and improve comfort and efficiency in the workplace.

Key aspects include:

- Conducting ergonomic assessments of workstations to ensure they are designed to minimize physical strain and reduce the risk of musculoskeletal disorders.
- Training workers on proper ergonomic practices, including adjusting chairs, keyboards, and monitors for comfort and efficiency.
- Recommending ergonomic solutions such as ergonomic chairs, keyboard trays, and adjustable desks to improve worker comfort and productivity.

Chemical Safety

Many industries face significant concerns regarding exposure to hazardous chemicals. Safety practitioners must comprehensively understand hazardous chemicals, their properties, safe handling practices, storage requirements, and disposal methods. Compliance with chemical safety regulations is crucial. Practitioners must conduct chemical risk assessments, implement control measures, and ensure workers know about the chemicals they work with and have access to safety data sheets to understand chemical hazards.

Key aspects include:

- Identifying hazardous chemicals in the workplace and understanding their potential health effects.
- Ensuring that safety data sheets are readily available for all chemicals and that workers are trained in interpreting them.
- Implementing safe storage and handling procedures for chemicals, including proper labeling, ventilation, and segregation.
- Conducting exposure monitoring to assess worker exposure levels and implementing controls to reduce exposure if necessary.

Personal Protective Equipment

Personal protective equipment (PPE) is vital to workplace safety when higher control efforts cannot eliminate or mitigate the risk to an acceptable level. This work requires careful selection, use, and maintenance when engineering controls cannot minimize a worker's risk level. Safety practitioners must know how to select the correct PPE for different tasks and must ensure proper training for workers. This requires understanding PPE standards, evaluating effectiveness, and establishing inventory tracking systems. Knowing the significance of PPE is vital for safety practitioners to prevent injuries and illnesses.

Key aspects include:

- Choosing the appropriate PPE for different tasks and conducting assessments to ensure it adequately protects workers.
- Ensuring workers are trained in correctly using and caring for PPE and conducting fit testing for items such as respirators.

- Establishing procedures for regular PPE inspection and maintenance to ensure it remains in good working condition and provides the intended level of protection.
- Managing PPE inventory to ensure an adequate supply is always available and that replacements are procured when necessary.

Safety Software and Tools

Safety software and tools are fundamental assets in managing occupational safety in modern times. These digital solutions provide a streamlined approach to collecting, analyzing, and managing safety data, enabling organizations to proactively identify and address workplace hazards. Safety software includes incident reporting systems, audit tools, and data analytics platforms, enabling safety practitioners to monitor performance, detect trends, and create detailed reports. Mobile apps and cloud-based software improve accessibility by enabling real-time data entry and reporting from the field. Integrating safety software helps organizations strengthen workplace safety and promote a culture of transparency and continuous improvement in safety practices.

Key aspects include:

- Using safety software solutions for incident reporting, hazard notification, risk management, observations, safety job procedures, corrective action tracking, and generating reports and analytics.
- Employing data analysis tools to identify safety trends and opportunities for improvement.
- Using mobile apps for safety inspections, audits, and incident reporting to streamline data collection and reporting and enlarge data capture.

- Integrating safety software with other organizational systems, such as HR or ERP systems, to ensure data consistency and accuracy.

Health and Industrial Hygiene

Health and industrial hygiene focus on identifying and handling workplace factors that affect worker health. This involves exposure to hazards such as noise, chemicals, biological agents, and physical stressors. Safety practitioners need a firm grasp of industrial hygiene principles and the ability to assess workplaces for potential health hazards. Developing and implementing control measures, such as ventilation systems, personal monitoring, and hygiene practices, is vital for safeguarding worker health.

Key aspects include:

- Conducting exposure assessments to evaluate workplace hazards such as noise, chemicals, dust, and biological agents.
- Implementing control measures to reduce exposure, which includes engineering controls (e.g., ventilation systems), administrative controls (e.g., scheduling), and personal protective equipment.
- Using monitoring equipment and air sampling techniques to quantify exposure levels and assess compliance with permissible exposure limits (PELs) or threshold limit values (TLVs).
- Promoting overall worker health by advocating wellness programs and providing guidance on healthy practices within the workplace.

Environmental Management

Often, safety practitioners have a crucial role in environmental management, ensuring the protection of ecosystems and communities from industrial impacts. Safety practitioners must learn about environmental regulations and how they affect workplace safety in industries with ecological concerns.

Key aspects include:

- Understanding environmental laws and regulations that pertain to the industry, such as those governing air quality, water pollution, hazardous waste, and land use.
- Integrating environmental and occupational safety practices to ensure that workplace activities do not harm the environment or violate environmental regulations.
- Familiarity with environmental management systems (e.g., ISO 14001) and their alignment with safety management systems.
- Promoting sustainability practices within the organization to minimize environmental impact while maintaining workplace safety.

CLOSING

The journey as a safety practitioner is long, and the longer you are on it, the more you need to learn. Indeed, you will not know everything as you begin. Even after leaving college with my occupational safety and health degree, I had much to learn. I have mentioned many technical skills you should master to improve your knowledge and skills as a safety practitioner, and you will need to learn them to succeed in the industry.

Competence is a necessary attribute for a safety practitioner. It is the combination of training, skills, experience, and knowledge you must acquire and your ability to apply it in the right place. Workplace safety relies heavily on the involvement of safety practitioners. The responsibilities I have written about in this chapter demonstrate that safety is a complex field requiring technical expertise, practical abilities, and a dedication to continuous improvement. Excelling in these areas will help you protect worker well-being and create a safer work environment.

Chapter 3:

The Attributes of Safety Leadership

A leader is one who sees more than others see, who sees farther than others see, and who sees before others see.

— Leroy Eimes

Overseeing safety and health requires more than technical knowledge. It requires specific leadership qualities. Successful leaders are not born with inherent leadership skills. They develop through study, experience, and adapting to circumstances. Throughout my career, I have focused on enhancing safety and health processes and performance in local and corporate settings. It's important to realize that if you are a safety and health practitioner, you are a leader, or at least you should strive to be one.

Think about our work for a moment. We believe in sharing our vision, mission, strategy, and objectives to achieve and maintain regulatory compliance. However, we also recognize that this is a minimum requirement. It is our day job and really what most of us were hired to do. The rest is everything we learn on the job or absorb from others. I learned much after my formal education. I took on uncharted territory in my career to improve company culture, communication, management, and crisis handling, as you will. Many challenges lie ahead, demanding various leadership attributes. However, what should be clear is that these challenges present opportunities for personal growth.

Taking charge during an unexpected crisis gave me some of my earliest leadership lessons. I was a staff safety and health specialist early in my career. I hadn't been out of college long, and most of my knowledge at that time had come from a book or a professor standing before me. During my morning commute to work on a Friday, I saw a yellow haze outside and adjacent to the manufacturing building of my workplace.

Without thinking about it, I headed to the building entrance. There, I heard workers calling for me through the intercom system. When I reached them, the yellow haze I'd seen outside had drifted into the building through open doors and windows. I saw the haze and picked up a distinct acrid, chemical smell. I immediately called my manager, who also led the safety and health program. We both agreed that we needed to evacuate that part of the building. He effectively managed all the organizational responsibilities and tasked me with investigating the origin of the yellow haze and providing feedback. I found a chemical drum emitting the substance in our hazardous waste storage area. As I got closer, I saw that the contents inside the drum were bubbling and appeared to be getting hotter as time elapsed. Later, we learned that a worker caused an exothermic chemical reaction by using too much hardener to solidify the drum's varnish material. The worker was at the end of their shift and thought they needed to complete the task before leaving. I did not have that information then. All I knew was that we had a dangerous drum of chemicals that seemed ready to explode.

Following instructions, I informed my manager, and the senior leadership team promptly evacuated the facility and contacted emergency services. When emergency services arrived, they were unsure how to deal with the situation. In the early 1990s, hazmat teams were not common in our area, so most of their expertise was managing fire situations. What I did notice, however, was that the situation was getting worse, and I had little help in dealing with the problem. Some colleagues, including higher-ranking staff and the manufacturing workers, left during the evacuation while I remained at the back of the plant. I had to use a Motorola two-way radio to communicate between the fire department and a few plant leaders who stayed behind. I felt isolated and alone. Even then, as a young safety practitioner, I knew I would wait and deal with the problem because I thought it came with my role. I was committed to using every ounce of knowledge and skill to help do my part in bringing about a successful conclusion to the crisis.

An important lesson from this is that leading is about more than having followers. This situation thrust me into leading from the level of an individual contributor. Still, because I knew enough about our chemical processes, had supporting chemical safety data sheets, and was brave and bold enough to stay in proximity to the crisis, I could be a commanding voice that said what needed to be said. Even then, I knew I had enough subject expertise to deal with the situation and was not afraid to take on a leadership position. However, I am sure I made mistakes as the crisis unfolded. A few months after this event, they promoted me to lead the plant environment, safety, and health team. Senior leadership noticed and appreciated my willingness to stand up and be direct, even when it was incredibly uncomfortable.

This event was the first turning point in how senior leaders saw me, leading to career growth and leadership opportunities. Being open and leading in challenging circumstances are some of the most important leadership lessons to prepare for. Your "why" starts with leading by example.

Lead yourself first, but always lead with a focus on the greater good. Why are you leading occupational safety?

DEFINING LEADERSHIP

In an article published in the Harvard Business Review titled "Managers and Leaders: Are They Different?" the author explores the differences between leadership and management. "It takes neither genius nor heroism to be a manager," he wrote, "but persistence, tough-mindedness, hard work, intelligence, analytical ability, and perhaps most important, tolerance and goodwill" (Zaleznik, 2004). These are admirable qualities, but they're not the only things you need to achieve sustainable safety and health performance in a complex and dynamic organization.

Leadership defines itself by what it excludes as much as what it encompasses. We often give a lot of leadership credit to successful leaders such as CEO Jack Welch, General Colin Powell, and President Lincoln because they were dynamic, intelligent, compelling, well-spoken, and had many other laudable qualities. Nevertheless, I also think about circumstances when leadership is thrust upon us. Todd Beamer and Thomas Burnett were passengers on United Airlines Flight 93 on September 11, 2001. In the back of their plane, a group of everyday citizens made phone calls home, only to learn they were part of a bigger terrorist plot, and they quickly assumed that their aircraft would become a weapon the terrorists would use to cause further carnage. After a brief discussion, the passengers fought back against their hijackers. Thomas Burnett Jr. told his wife over the phone, "I know we are all going to die. There are three of us who are going to do something about it. I love you, honey." Passenger Todd Beamer was heard saying over an open line, "Are you guys ready? Let's roll." They were bold and brave enough to lead, even in the face of great adversity.

Still, you do not need to be a hero to be effective. Look at Mark Zuckerburg, co-founder and CEO of the world's largest social media network. People often describe him as shy and aloof, caring more about coding and developing software at home than being a public figure. However, according to his former chief operating officer Sheryl Sandberg, that does not mean he cannot communicate. Zuckerberg's conversations with partners and staff members are powerful and meaningful, enhancing his business relationships. His approach to leadership is unique, and there is no denying his success in leading his businesses.

A leader inspires passion and motivation in those they work with. They have a vision and a path to realizing lofty goals. Your leadership approach as a safety practitioner is unique but requires boldness, bravery, and a desire to learn to reach your full potential. In addition, we should not forget that you must also be a capable manager with functional expertise. You hold the power to shift from simply knowing what to do to actively facilitating the robust growth of the safety process in your organization. You must aspire to be more than someone who simply manages safety and health.

LEADERSHIP ATTRIBUTES

A successful leader needs many leadership characteristics. Over time, leadership emerges through the complexities and challenges of the job. Achieving and sustaining success in your organization and career requires considering these crucial qualities.

Leaders have a Vision

To ensure safety success, a safety practitioner should have an unobstructed vision of the safety goals, be able to drive the process, and know how to demonstrate excellence. I will say more about this later in the book, but setting a vision is about the tone of what you are striving to become as an organization. As a safety practitioner and leader, your responsibility is to establish a captivating safety vision that elevates organizational energy by recognizing possibilities and effectively transmitting that energy to your workers to execute such a lofty expectation.

Leaders express Empathy

People are drawn to a warm and inviting safety practitioner who cares about their well-being. An empathetic leader seeks to understand the workers under their care and is sensitive to their feelings, thoughts, and actions. A leader who shows this trait values and respects their colleagues, actively engages with them, and builds relationships. When workers understand that your focus comes from a place of personal care for them, it fosters a relationship, allowing you to capture the hearts and minds of those you lead. It builds personal trust and inspires your team to follow you.

Leaders are Supportive

You will undoubtedly have workers working under your care with different perceptions, values, and capabilities. Because of these differences, some workers will be unwilling to connect with the safety process, which will require your leadership. This could be a pure competency issue. Workers who do not know what to do rarely value the work or perform it how you want them to. Developing a person's knowledge and skills is essential to prepare that person to meet your expectations thoroughly. It is also a behavioral problem. Expect some individuals to challenge success, disrupt collaboration, and disregard the organization's values, vision, and goals. For this group of people, you will need to be very intentional in influencing them to perform. Create activities that require participation and provide the necessary tools and resources to support them.

Leaders are Transparent

Transparency is an essential quality for a safety practitioner. Being open and honest with everyone, especially the workers you lead, is critical. A transparent leader sets clear expectations for everyone, including themselves, and shares their failures and successes. I should point out that being willing to admit mistakes and take responsibility is hard but necessary. A safety practitioner who practices full transparency, especially at the front line, builds trust and enhances performance and engagement among the team members. Transparency is a quality that can be difficult to achieve, but it is essential for fostering collaboration. Transparent leaders encourage feedback and are willing to listen to the opinions of others, which helps promote an interdependent culture and process innovation.

Leaders will Communicate

A pervasive part of your accountability as a safety practitioner is the ability to communicate. Communication is fundamental to building trust and vital to a successful safety and health process. Leaders are active listeners who do not just listen to answer a question. They diligently pay attention to information and feedback from their teams and incorporate it into their decision making. Workers feeling heard builds morale and increases trust in you and the organization. Being transparent and concise in communication fosters honesty and understanding. Communication done well creates cohesion and motivates the team to pursue success together.

Leaders take Command

Taking command is a leadership style that, over the years, has fallen further and further from favor within most organizations. An old military model gives rise to command leadership, which assumes that people require explicit instructions on what to do. Disappointing outcomes may follow if no one is giving precise directions. Although most of us dislike this leadership style, at times you will probably need to lead this way. A large chemical spill, a fire, a severe injury, or another impending crisis can suddenly thrust you into command, regardless of the incident management structure. As a safety practitioner, you can prepare for this by developing crisis scenarios that could occur in your organization and then mapping out how you would lead during such events. Leaders should employ effective command tactics such as setting rules, aligning people, making decisions, and communicating clearly.

Leaders are Competent

As I shared in the previous chapter, knowledge and the necessary skills are the basis for success. Competence alone cannot make a safety practitioner a leader, but incompetence can undoubtedly undo one. Competence does not mean that a leader knows how to do everything, but that a leader knows what to do and how to get it done. A competent leader will learn about their strengths and weaknesses and then work to develop themselves to fill the competency gaps. Aim for deep and broad safety, health, and organizational knowledge and continuously learn, even after reaching mastery. You must apply your talents and training to solve problems and effectively leverage the future growth of the safety process by becoming increasingly competent and skilled.

Leaders can Influence

I have saved this attribute for last because it is the culmination of many other leadership traits I have shared. Much of leadership is about influencing others to achieve a common goal and your vision for safety and success. You must have a clear purpose and communicate it effectively to the front line. A safety practitioner who wants to influence their team should be willing to embrace conflict, listen to feedback with empathy, show vulnerability, and adjust his or her approach as needed. As a leader, you should lead by example and demonstrate the desired behaviors yourself. Additionally, influencing requires adding soft skills such as emotional intelligence, establishing colleague relationships, and encouraging cross-organizational collaboration. Finally, you must put the team's interests above your own.

FIND A LEADERSHIP MENTOR

You can study plenty of online and print resources to improve your leadership skills. However, I encourage you to look for a mentor who understands where you want to go in your career and can help you get there. Even if you have no plan to progress from your current level, collaborating with a mentor can enhance your leadership capability and safety craft.

Here are some attributes of an effective mentor:

- Support: A mentor offers emotional support and encouragement as you navigate your current and future career paths.

- Knowledge: A mentor shares his or her knowledge and expertise with you, helping you develop new skills and gain valuable insights.
- Feedback: A mentor provides constructive feedback on your work, helping you identify areas for improvement and opportunities to grow professionally.
- Inspiration: A mentor inspires you to achieve your goals and pursue your passions, motivating you to succeed.
- Connection: A mentor helps build connections within your industry and introduces you to new people and opportunities.
- Development: A mentor can help you develop your leadership skills, build confidence, and prepare for new challenges. A mentor can guide and support you in navigating difficulties as you lead safety and health and provide the necessary tools and resources to succeed.

Now that you understand the type of person you should look for, you should know that not everyone is cut out to be a mentor. Looking for a mentor can be a daunting task, but there are several steps you can take to make the process easier. First, define your career goals and identify the mentor type that best fits you. Once you have a clear idea of what you want to achieve and what you hope to learn from a mentor, look for someone in your professional network with experience, knowledge, and wisdom who aligns with your career goals. Take a businesslike approach and be respectful of your mentor's time and expertise. Be open to critical feedback and stay committed to the process. Building a solid mentor relationship takes time and effort, but it can be an enriching experience that helps you grow personally and professionally.

Who comes to mind now when you think of the person who can best mentor you?

CLOSING

Throughout my career, people have often asked, "How many people does it take to lead safety and health in your organization?" I consistently give the same answer: "It is exactly the number of people who show up for work daily." This includes the management team, production and service workers, the maintenance department, and everyone who touches a portion of the organization. It takes everyone leading collectively in varying degrees to support the mission of broad safety ownership and an actual partnership at the front line.

Growth-minded leaders take opportunities to better themselves and others, which is necessary for success. Organizations are starving for effective and genuine leadership. Regardless of your organizational position as a safety and health practitioner, you are or should be a leader. You might have positional power and great authority because of your knowledge and experience on the job. Regardless of your position, do not underestimate your ability to influence the organization through effective leadership.

I will emphasize that many other leadership attributes exist for you to explore and evaluate. Every organization has diverse needs, so it is up to you to understand who you are and what you need to improve to be the best leader you can be. I did not include all of them. Are you brave and bold? Do you see where you want to go? Do people know you and trust you because you genuinely care for them? Can you take control when things happen, and are you competent to bring your organization forward? It is not merely your actions that define your most significant worth. Still, that, combined with thinking, aligning, developing, and inspiring, will lead you to success.

The safety practitioner, as a safety leader, exemplifies leadership in practice.

Chapter 4:

The Power of We

Your next step is simple. You are the first domino.

— GARY KELLER

I have spent much of my career working within safety management systems and collaborating with people at every level of the organization. There is often just one essential and consistent theme in almost all the work I do: "How do I engage the people that I am charged to protect, and how do I gain their partnership to solve problems, to learn, to implement programs, and, most critically, to actively care for one another?" Some see this concept as promoting organizational interdependence, but for you, the safety practitioner, it embodies the idea of servant leadership.

Effective leadership and teamwork require building solid relationships. Safety and health practitioners who prioritize relationships and cultivate trust and respect among team members have a higher chance of success. Strong relationships are essential to effective teamwork because they facilitate communication and collaboration. Influential leaders understand the value of forming connections and work to establish an atmosphere that promotes positive team interactions. These types of leaders also prioritize relationship building with external stakeholders, such as customers and partners, to ensure successful outcomes for the organization.

I cannot imagine a successful safety leader who does not have the qualities of a servant leader. Despite the need to be technically competent, it is the one essential skill that separates good safety and health professionals from the great ones.

In his essay "The Servant as Leader," from the 1970s, Robert K. Greenleaf introduced the Servant Leadership Theory (Greenleaf, 2007 Reprint). Servant leadership prioritizes serving others over the leader's interests. Servant leaders focus on empowering and supporting their team members rather than controlling or directing them. Their top priority is the well-being and development of their team members, and they work to create a positive and supportive environment that fosters growth and success. Servant leaders also prioritize listening to and understanding the needs of their team members, and they work to develop solutions that meet those needs.

Here are ten essential characteristics of a servant leader:

- Listening: Servant leaders listen to what their teams have to say. They give all members many opportunities to speak and then listen carefully to what the team is saying or not saying.
- Empathy: Servant leaders care about their teams on a personal level. They understand that when their team members feel happy and fulfilled in their personal lives, it contributes to success in their professional lives.
- Healing: Servant leaders understand the importance of fixing problems before moving on to new goals and projects.
- Awareness: Servant leaders are aware of what is happening around them. They are aware of the needs of their team members, the organization's goals, and industry trends.
- Persuasion: Servant leaders use persuasion instead of positional authority to influence others. They use logic and reasoning instead of their positional power to convince others.

- Conceptualization: Servant leaders have a sharp vision for the organization's future and can communicate it effectively to their team members.
- Foresight: Servant leaders understand the organization's past, present, and future. They use this knowledge to make informed decisions that benefit the organization overall.
- Stewardship: Servant leaders take responsibility for the well-being of their team members and the organization.
- Commitment: Servant leaders are committed to helping their team members grow personally and professionally.
- Focus: Servant leaders create a sense of community within their organization by encouraging collaboration, teamwork, and open communication among team members.

While some of these leadership attributes may sound familiar, it's crucial to note the stark differences between servant and traditional leadership. The key distinction lies in how servant leaders guide their teams to achieve results. This approach prioritizes the needs of others and involves serving and supporting those around you, rather than a top-down, directive leadership style.

THE LESSON BEGINS

With the idea of servant leadership as a backdrop, I learned about this more formalized approach to leading on the first day of my first corporate-level job in the late 1990s. I had just assumed the safety and health leadership role for one of the company's business portfolios. My boss, the business's senior leader, who would also become a great mentor and coach, sat me down and drew a triangle. It looked like this.

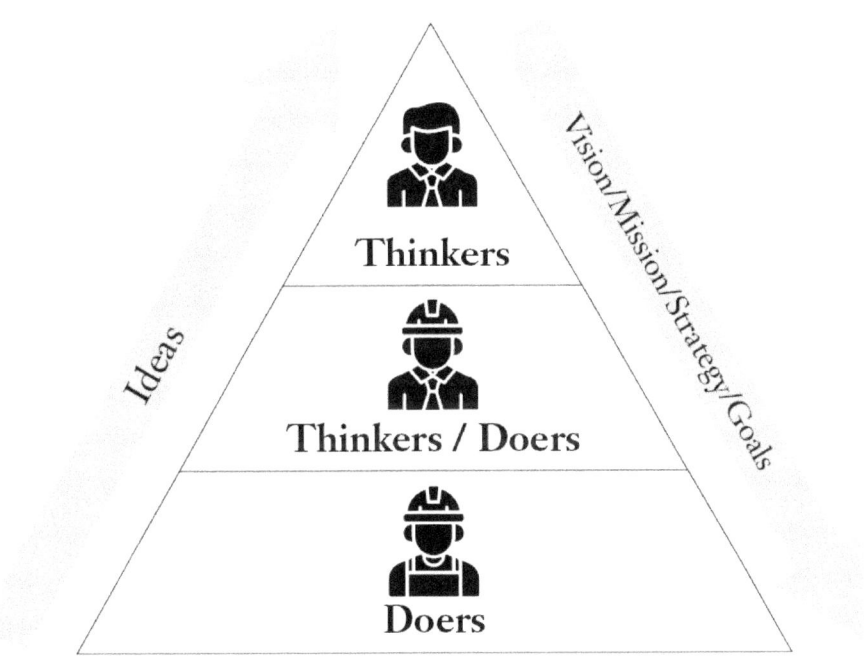

It was the standard triangle everyone uses to explain organizational structure. He drew dividing lines, splitting the triangle with the upper one-third reserved for what he labeled "thinkers," the middle one-third as "thinkers-doers," and at the bottom "doers." Off to the side, he wrote the words "vision and mission" and "strategy and goals." He explained that those things were in his and the other key leaders' hands, and the thinkers would send down objectives to the rest of the organization for action. I was assured at the time that I would be part of some of the "thinking" activities and would even have sub-organizational activities to support meeting our lofty strategy and goals. He then wrote the word "ideas" adjacent to the triangle and explained that I should ask the front-line workers for their ideas and send them back to him through the appropriate channels for consideration. It was a safe bet that doers were not a large part of the "thinking" process and did not appear to be any part of organizational strategy or objective setting.

He went on to draw several circles within the triangle, showing that he was at the top vertex of the triangle and was, in fact, the chief thinker and decision-maker. He was the person through whom all critical information would flow via the various formal channels and the other positional leaders below him. The more significant a decision, the higher it went to the thinkers. Then, findings and information would flow down formal channels until it reached its intended audience, usually the doers.

He then drew circles, indicating a few other leaders with whom I was familiar within the organization. Since I was a functional support and safety leader, I was considered a "thinker/doer" somewhere in the middle of the organizational hierarchy. My job was to develop a safety strategy and be tactical enough to execute the plan with those below me in the manufacturing facilities under my care. Yes, I was indeed a thinker and a doer.

Quite honestly, I was feeling good about the progress of our conversation. I finally was on a corporate business team where I could expand my reach and tell people, those doers below me, what to do. It was the *somewhat* typical command-and-control structure where authority and decision-making power were concentrated at the top of an organization, flowing down, and stopping at the appropriate level, where directives were conducted by subordinates. It was my first day in my new role, and I had just moved up the corporate chain of command.

FLIPPING THE LEADERSHIP TRIANGLE

Predictably, this would not be my leadership lesson for the day. As soon as he saw my head moving up and down in agreement, as we sometimes do to please our boss, he drew another triangle, this one inverted, much like the last, but with the dividing lines removed between senior leadership and the front line.

It looked like this.

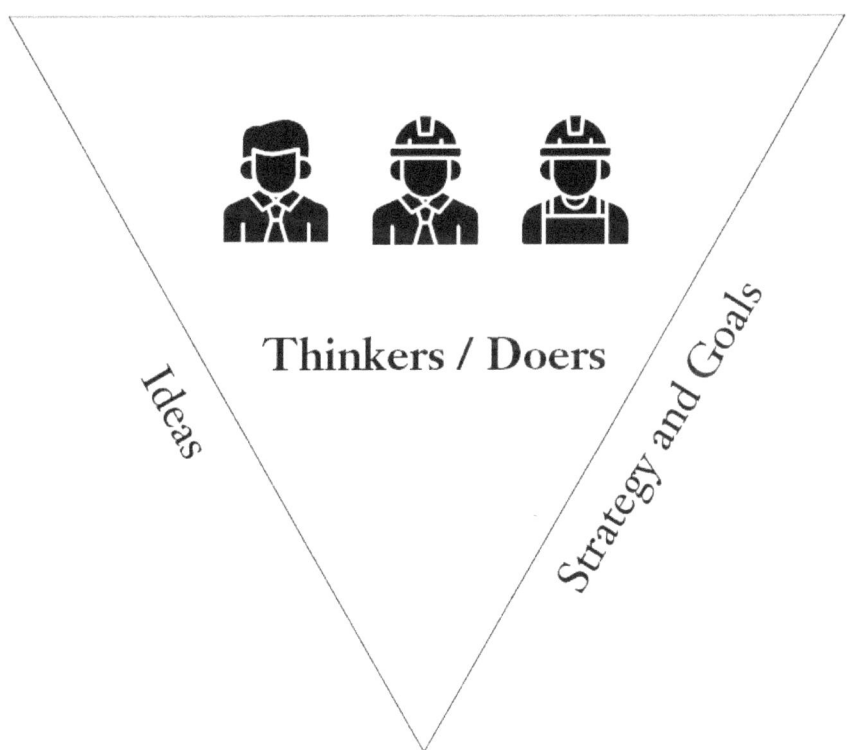

He then went on to draw circles indicating positions in the organizational structure. However, this time, he drew himself at the bottom, my circle above his, with other circles indicating the various executive positions continuing until the front-line workers were at the very top. He then wrote the same attributes we had previously discussed, but this time, they surrounded the triangle, and he explained that everyone shared those activities regardless of level or position.

Was there a punch line somewhere? It was my first day and my first big corporate job. I assumed I would hear and anticipated hearing some lofty explanation of why he had put himself at the bottom and why my circle was hovering above his. I certainly wanted to understand why he had placed the front-line workers at the top. At the time, I thought this was a way to explain some modern practices we would use to communicate to the front line that we cared, nudging them to see things our way. That was not the answer. He was teaching me an important lesson in leading organizations forward and what I've termed the power of "we."

INVERTED TRIANGLE LEADERSHIP

I understood later that this thinking was not necessarily a new concept or even how the company was changing its organizational structure, but simply how leadership expected me to perform in my job as a leader. Indeed, I was already leading this way for much of my work, but this was an excellent lesson in how I could extend my influence even further. He elaborated that his role was "to coach and mentor and remove the barriers" from my path so that I and everyone else who had a circle in his leadership triangle could succeed. Why? It was simple; he said, "The most important people in our manufacturing organization are the ones that make something." It was those workers on the front lines who manufactured a product or provided a service. He told me to work more like him. It is about the same message my grandmother gave me: to do my work as if she were working at the front line. I should note that my boss was incredibly good at decision-making, but it was clear that shared decision-making, shared work experience, and shared leadership were the places he and I would always start.

The idea of this leadership style is primarily conceptual when you study it, even though many organizations follow its design philosophy. This management approach empowers the front-line worker with higher decision-making authority and the freedom to act. Supervisors, managers, and other leaders take on the role of coaches and mentors, and, yes, they are primarily charged with removing barriers to forge pathways to success.

When this happens, accountability and decision-making are left at the proper level in the organization, thus increasing participation and partnerships between all groups and organizational levels. Based on my professional experience, I can attest that few workers ever came to work excited about the chance to make products such as bath tissue, feminine hygiene products, and paper towels. However, they were enthusiastic about the opportunity to be business partners. We could forge front-line partnerships if we led the way my boss asked me to lead.

A standard pushback I often hear when I mention this approach to others is, "My organization is not designed to support this direction." To this, I respond: Does that stop you from working this way as a safety practitioner? A huge lever in this leadership style is recognizing that everyone has a part in leading the organization, meaning the more you know, the more of yourself you are expected to give. From my boss's perspective, I was to go out and make mini versions of myself, giving away as much knowledge, wisdom, skill, and actual capability as I could muster to support my functional concentration. Since I led the safety and health function, my role was to develop an organization of safety and health partners.

ADAPTING TO LEAD DIFFERENTLY

So, does flipping the triangle, adapting to be more of a servant leader, and becoming a safety coach instead of the chief safety decision-maker excite you or make you feel threatened? It is a fair question because it requires you to work differently. Some people criticize this management style by saying it is only for organizations directly related to external customers. Is that true? During my career, I regarded my chief customers as the workers who were part of the journey to our desired success. I usually found them on the front lines. Granted, some organizations I worked for cared little about how I achieved success, but you can be sure they all wanted success. I have been successful in every facility and organization I have had a part in leading, really without failure. Every organization I was part of improved in its safety performance. The key to this success was my recognition that our chief customer was the person who made something or provided a service directly affecting the customer, just as my former boss and mentor had informed me.

Herb Kelleher, co-founder, and former CEO of Southwest Airlines, was asked once whether he prioritized shareholders or prioritized workers. He said, "Workers come first. If our workers are treated right, they treat the outside world right. The outside world uses the company's product again, and the shareholder is happy" (Kelleher, 2019).

With these ideas in mind, we can see that building a top-performing organization means taking on the responsibility to help people reach their full potential by creating a dynamic learning environment.

Organizational psychologist Adam Grant said in an article in Forbes magazine, "Servant leaders are not only more highly regarded than others by their workers, and they not only feel better about themselves at the end of the day but are more productive as well. They do not waste much time deciding to whom to give and in what order. They give to everyone in their organizations" (Forbes, 2013).

Leaders with this view believe that workers have both present and future value. They consider it their responsibility to nurture others toward achieving their full potential because they understand that it also delivers value and profit to the organization and safely returns them to their families. It is simple: leading this way fosters a sense of organizational interdependence.

CLOSING

I have learned through practice that flipping the organizational triangle has had a tremendous advantage in how I work as a leader. Does it mean I never take situational command or control? No. Again, in my role as a safety and health practitioner, there are times when that's what I need to do. Still, I have found that as the organization's maturity grows, partnerships grow alongside, and everyone understands they are integral to success, even when front-line workers give authority back to me when they are stumped. They recognize that I am the most senior subject matter expert and trust me. However, as organizational maturity grows, emergencies will become fewer, and even my decision-making rights will go to others because they have developed their capability and capacity to give back to the organization.

As for that boss to whom I reported, he was exactly as I described him. He had tremendous positional leadership power but demonstrated "we" daily. He often landed at a facility under his direct leadership and that I supported to do business reviews. He had a distinct and predictable pattern of going to the manufacturing floor first to see that we were implementing his ideas of worker inclusion and, more importantly, to ensure that we were supporting, training, and empowering the front line to be safe and to be a partner in the business. He was at the front line validating the work so he could review those results with senior facility staff in the conference room later.

During the following years that I worked for him, these business reviews expanded into the manufacturing production areas, the operations areas, where products were being made and services were being delivered. There we would find the front-line employees, using flipcharts and whiteboards telling the story of how their area of the plant was performing. Why? Well, they owned it. The good and the bad. They were our partners in the business and proud of it. Simple information transfer turned into conversations that were deeper, added context, and at times provided profound understanding.

Specific to my part in leading safety and health, I demonstrated the power of "we" as the front line took leadership of many aspects of safety and health management, allowing me to focus on even more forward-thinking safety plans.

Chapter 5

Coaching the Front Line, Your Peers, and Senior Leaders

*Coaching is unlocking a person's potential
to maximize their growth.*

— JOHN WHITMORE

My second role in safety and health was perhaps the most rewarding in terms of developing my skills. I joined Kimberly Clark Corporation in the early 1990s to design and lead safety and health for a new paper manufacturing facility being built in my hometown, Owensboro, Kentucky. When I joined, there was no plant, just a cornfield and construction crews. I was excited because I saw this as an opportunity to put my stamp on leading safety and health in the paper business in a brand-new facility with new people.

On my first day, I showed up for work early. Within the first hour, the senior leader of the organization asked to meet with me. This leader would eventually become the first plant manager for the new paper manufacturing plant upon its completion. Going to his office seemed like a scene from the movie *The Godfather*. I was sitting with a man who seemed quite odd, a guy with thoughts I could not keep up with at times, and a person who was sure of his opinions regardless of the topic. It did not seem like we were having a conversation at all, and I was being told what my role was to be in securing his idea of safety success.

He made one statement that floated in the air and hung there for what seemed forever. He said, "I want to build and run a paper mill where no one is ever hurt. Can you do that?" I was speechless. I sat, lost for words, hoping there was more that followed, but there was none. He sat stoically, waiting for my response. Understanding I had quit my last job for this one, I had only one answer to give: yes. From that day on, I never needed to question his value for safety. Returning people home safe and healthy was what I had better focus on. He was brilliant in many ways, and he told me everything I needed to know about my safety leadership role on my very first workday, with added clarity and the responsibility for helping deliver it.

I also remember my direct supervisor telling me at the beginning of my tenure and throughout my time working for him, "It's not success being the best at manufacturing high-quality paper products if we are hurting people in the process." These discussions seem small, but they all stuck with me.

I had my organization's values chiseled in my mind and the necessary runway to build a delivery process.

We were implementing a high-performance work organization, meaning we were indeed erasing lines between the top and bottom of the organization, treating everyone as equally as possible, and striving to develop people as business partners in the organization regardless of their position. Realistically, I had just left a similar-sized organization with several direct and other dotted-line staff members. I was to lead this new assignment with no safety staff but with a 500-member workforce with varying degrees of talent, skill, and motivation. It was up to me to determine how they would participate and partner with me. I needed to refine my coaching and mentoring skills to succeed in this organization.

CIRCLE OF SAFETY

Simon Sinek, a renowned author on leadership and organizational behavior, introduced the "circle of safety" several years ago. His idea revolves around fostering a work environment that is psychologically secure for workers. Sinek says that the need for safety and security, ingrained in us since the beginning of human civilization, is still pertinent in today's workplaces.

According to Sinek, the circle of safety is a culture in which employees' needs come before the interests of the business, where workers feel safe and supported by their manager and coworkers. It's an environment conducive to collaboration and innovation, one that prioritizes and coaches your workers' needs. This collective group forms the circle of safety.

This circle of safety is critical to collaboration and innovation. Sinek implies that supporting your subordinates means paying attention to them so you can monitor and fulfill their needs. By prioritizing your subordinates' needs, you establish an empathetic connection with them. You prove that you see them as people rather than mere assets to increase profits. Thus, your subordinates feel safe because they can trust you to support them and be invested in their success as well as your own. I cannot disagree.

As Sinek describes above, a circle of safety requires leaders to embrace new skills and mindsets to transition from a traditional leadership style to one that focuses more on coaching. Leaders must become adept listeners, empathetic supporters, and facilitators of personal and professional growth.

As we move forward, we will explore the essence of effective coaching for front-line workers, delving into the challenges these workers face, the pivotal role of leaders as coaches, the principles that underpin effective coaching, and the strategies and challenges involved in implementing such an approach. We will also look at coaching peers and coaching yourself, which, for most, is a significant task to perform.

UNDERSTANDING FRONT-LINE CHALLENGES

Common Challenges Front-Line Workers Face

Front-line workers navigate a complex landscape of challenges every day. They are the first to encounter customer complaints and the first to feel the pressure to meet production and sales targets and swiftly adapt to new products or services. For instance, a product change, a quality issue, or an order increase often means immense pressure to maintain stock levels, manage long queues, and deal with customer frustrations gracefully. As we witnessed during COVID-19, workers went from working in large crews as colleagues to working alone, separated by illness or health guidelines, dealing with the unknown almost overnight. The pandemic required new and rapid development of technical skills and the emotional resilience to manage stress and stay focused on the work at hand.

The Effect of These Challenges on Performance and Motivation

The constant pressure and stress front-line workers face can significantly affect their job performance and motivation. Increased stress levels can result in burnout, which includes emotional exhaustion, cynicism, and decreased productivity at work. This affects the workers' health and well-being, leading to lower productivity, higher absenteeism, and increased turnover rates.

Moreover, lacking support and recognition for these challenges can diminish job satisfaction and loyalty. Front-line workers who feel undervalued or unsupported are less likely to go the extra mile for the companies they serve or the products they support. This leads to a decline in service quality and customer satisfaction. The ripple effects of such challenges can undermine the very foundation of a business, highlighting the critical need for effective leadership and support systems to address and mitigate these issues.

THE ROLE OF THE SAFETY PRACTITIONER IN COACHING

Defining the Coaching Role of a Leader

Transitioning from traditional leadership roles to those of a coach is a significant shift in how the safety practitioner interacts with their teams. A safety practitioner, as a coach, not only directs but also facilitates worker growth and development. This role is less about providing answers and more about asking the right questions that encourage workers to explore solutions and learn from their experiences. It requires the safety practitioner to commit to the development of their people in a way that fosters growth and experimentation. You need to recognize and develop each worker's strengths and help workers set and achieve professional goals while guiding them through challenges and setbacks. Effective coaching by leaders can transform the workplace, creating a culture of continuous improvement, adaptability, and mutual trust.

Differences between Coaching and Traditional Management

The primary difference between coaching and traditional management lies in the approach to guiding and developing workers. Traditional management often focuses on task completion, process adherence, and achieving short-term results, such as production or service goals. It typically involves a top-down approach to decision-making and problem-solving, with leaders giving instructions and offering solutions for their teams to implement.

In contrast, coaching emphasizes empowering workers to develop their problem-solving and collaborative potential while encouraging them to take ownership of their work. It promotes a work environment in which workers feel valued and invested in the outcomes of their efforts. Considering these points, the safety practitioner must focus on long-term development by harnessing individual strengths and aspirations to achieve personal and organizational goals.

Adopting a coaching approach to leading safety can significantly enhance leadership effectiveness and organizational performance. Some of the key benefits are:

- Improved Worker Engagement: Coaching addresses workers' needs and aspirations, fostering a sense of belonging and value. Engaged workers are more motivated, productive, and committed to the organization's success.
- Enhanced Team Collaboration: Coaching encourages open communication and mutual support among team members, leading to a more cohesive and effective team.
- Increased Innovation and Creativity: Coaching fosters an environment where innovation and creativity flourish by empowering workers to explore solutions and take risks.
- Better Adaptability to Change: Coaching builds resilience and flexibility, enabling workers and organizations to navigate changes and challenges better.
- Higher Worker Retention: A coaching culture contributes to job satisfaction and loyalty, reducing turnover rates and the associated costs of recruiting and training new workers.

CORE PRINCIPLES OF EFFECTIVE COACHING

Active Listening and Empathy

At the heart of effective coaching lie active listening and empathy. Safety practitioners must be fully present in their interactions with front-line workers, listening attentively and empathetically to understand their perspectives, concerns, and aspirations. This involves hearing the words and interpreting non-verbal cues and emotions to understand. Active listening builds trust and respect, creating a safe space where workers feel seen, heard, and understood.

Empathy allows you, as the safety practitioner, to connect with front-line workers on a deeper level, acknowledging their feelings and experiences without judgment. This connection fosters a supportive environment conducive to open dialogue, personal growth, and meaningful learning experiences.

Goal Setting and Accountability

Effective coaching also involves setting clear, achievable goals that align with the organization's objectives. As a safety practitioner, you should strive to collaborate with workers and identify personal and professional goals, ensuring they are specific, measurable, achievable, relevant, and time-bound (SMART). I will share more about SMART in a later chapter, but this collaborative process empowers workers to take ownership of their goals and the steps required to achieve them.

Maintaining accountability is crucial in the coaching process. Leaders should establish regular check-ins to discuss progress, celebrate achievements, and address challenges. Ongoing support and guidance reinforce the importance of accountability and provide opportunities for continuous learning and adjustment.

Feedback and Constructive Criticism

Providing constructive feedback is a critical component of effective coaching. The safety practitioner should offer timely, specific feedback on behaviors and actions rather than personal attributes. Positive feedback reinforces desired behaviors and achievements, while constructive criticism offers valuable insights for improvement. Feedback should be delivered in a supportive and encouraging manner, fostering a culture of open communication and continuous development.

STRATEGIES FOR COACHING FRONT-LINE WORKERS

To coach front-line workers effectively, the safety practitioner should employ tailored strategies that address their unique challenges and opportunities. The following sections will explore strategies for personalizing coaching, encouraging self-reflection and self-improvement, and implementing continuous learning and development initiatives. These strategies will provide practical guidance for leaders looking to enhance their coaching skills and foster a supportive, high-performing team environment.

Tailoring Coaching to Individual Needs

A one-size-fits-all approach to coaching is ineffective in addressing the diverse needs of front-line workers. The safety practitioner must recognize and appreciate each team member's unique background, skills, learning styles, and aspirations.

Strategies:

- Conducting Individual Assessments: Support conversations to understand each worker's strengths, weaknesses, preferences, and goals.
- Setting Individualized Goals: Collaborate with workers to set personalized goals that are challenging yet achievable, aligning with both their career aspirations and the organization's objectives.
- Adapting Communication Styles: Modify your communication approach based on the individual's preferred style, whether directive, collaborative, or exploratory.
- Providing Customized Learning Opportunities: Offer learning and development resources that cater to the worker's skill gaps or career interests, such as workshops, online courses, and shadowing experiences.

Benefits:

- Enhanced Worker Performance: Effective coaching equips front-line workers with the skills, knowledge, and confidence needed to excel in their roles, leading to improved performance metrics and customer service outcomes.

- Increased Worker Engagement: Coaching fosters a more engaging work environment by showing workers that their development is valued, which increases their commitment and reduces turnover rates.
- Improved Problem-Solving Skills: Through coaching, front-line workers develop vital problem-solving abilities, enabling them to manage customer issues more effectively and independently.
- Higher Customer Satisfaction: Well-coached front-line workers are better equipped to meet customer needs, leading to enhanced customer experiences and loyalty.
- A Culture of Continuous Learning: Effective coaching encourages continuous personal and professional growth, ensuring the organization adapts and thrives in a changing market.

Encouraging Self-Reflection and Self-Improvement

Self-reflection is a powerful tool for personal and professional growth. Strategies:

- Asking Reflective Questions: Pose questions that prompt workers to reflect on their experiences, their decisions, and the outcomes of their actions. Questions such as "What did you learn from this experience?" and "How could this have been managed differently for a better outcome?" encourage deep thinking.
- Creating a Safe Environment for Sharing: Foster an atmosphere where workers feel safe sharing their reflections, challenges, and learnings without fear of judgment or retribution.
- Encouraging Journaling or Documentation: Suggest that workers keep a journal or log of their daily experiences, challenges faced, and lessons learned. This practice can enhance one's self-awareness and facilitate personal growth.

- Setting Aside Time for Reflection: Encourage workers to set aside regular time for self-reflection, whether at the end of a shift, the end of a week, or after completing a project. Promoting self-reflection and self-improvement helps workers take ownership of their learning and development, driving motivation and engagement.

Benefits:

- Enhanced Self-Awareness: Encouraging self-reflection helps individuals gain a deeper understanding of their strengths, weaknesses, and areas for growth, leading to more informed personal development plans.
- Increased Personal Accountability: Self-improvement initiatives foster a sense of responsibility in individuals for their own growth and progress, encouraging them to take active steps toward achieving their goals.
- Improved Adaptability: Individuals who regularly engage in self-reflection and self-improvement are better equipped to adapt to changes and challenges, enhancing their resilience and flexibility in personal and professional contexts.
- Higher Job Satisfaction: Workers who see clear pathways for self-improvement and are supported in their personal development efforts tend to have higher job satisfaction and motivation.
- Increased Innovation and Creativity: Self-reflection and continuous learning encourage creative thinking and innovation, as individuals are constantly exposed to innovative ideas and perspectives that can inspire novel solutions to problems.

IMPLEMENTING CONTINUOUS LEARNING AND DEVELOPMENT

A continuous learning and development culture is crucial for the growth of front-line workers and the organization.

Strategies:

- Offering Access to Learning Resources: Provide workers access to online courses, workshops, seminars, and conferences that align with their roles and career goals.
- Encouraging Cross-Functional Training: Workers should be allowed to gain experience in different business areas, enhancing their skills and understanding of the organization.
- Implementing Mentorship Programs: Pair less experienced workers with more seasoned colleagues for guidance, support, and knowledge sharing.
- Recognizing and Rewarding Learning Achievements: Acknowledge and celebrate when workers achieve learning milestones, such as completing a certification or successfully applying a new skill.

Benefits:

- Enhanced Skill Development: You can help front-line workers continuously develop their skills by offering access to diverse learning resources. This leads to a more competent workforce capable of adapting to new challenges and technologies, ultimately improving job performance and productivity.
- Improved Employee Engagement and Retention: Encouraging cross-functional training and implementing mentorship programs can significantly boost employee engagement. Workers feel valued and invested in their career growth, leading to higher job satisfaction and lower turnover rates.
- Increased Organizational Agility: Cross-functional training allows workers to understand different aspects of the business, making the organization more agile. Employees can step into different roles as needed, ensuring smooth operations and resilience during change or crisis.

- Strengthened Knowledge Sharing and Innovation: Mentorship programs and the recognition of learning achievements foster a culture of knowledge sharing. Experienced workers can pass on valuable insights, and celebrating learning milestones motivates employees to innovate and contribute new ideas, driving continuous improvement and creativity within the organization.

COACHING AMONG PEER LEADERS

In addition to coaching front-line workers, how safety practitioners coach their peers is equally essential to fostering a robust organizational culture. Peer coaching among leaders can enhance leadership skills across the board by fostering a culture of continuous improvement. When leaders share knowledge and provide mutual support to navigate challenges collectively, it can help strengthen the leadership of the entire organization.

The foundation of peer coaching lies in establishing a culture that values and prioritizes mutual growth. Leaders must:

- Cultivate Trust and Openness: Create an environment where leaders feel safe sharing challenges, seeking feedback, and offering honest, constructive feedback to each other.
- Encourage Vulnerability: Leaders should be encouraged to admit gaps in their knowledge or skills without fear of judgment, fostering a culture where learning from each other is the norm.
- Champion a Growth Mindset: Emphasize the belief that everyone can develop and refine leadership skills through effort, good strategies, and input from others.

Strategies:

- Have a Structured Approach: Peer coaching among leaders requires a structured yet flexible approach to ensure it is beneficial and constructive.

- Regular Feedback Sessions: Regularly scheduled sessions during which leaders can share experiences, challenges, and successes can facilitate meaningful exchanges of insights and advice.
- Goal-Setting and Accountability Partners: Leaders can partner as accountability partners to set professional development goals, share progress, and hold each other accountable.
- Skill-Sharing Workshops: Organize workshops where leaders can teach each other specific skills in which they excel, fostering skill development and cross-functional understanding.
- Reflective Practice Groups: Small groups of leaders can meet regularly to discuss their leadership practices, identify what has been effective, and explore areas for improvement.

Benefits:

- Enhanced Leadership Skills: Leaders can learn from each other's experiences and insights, improving leadership competencies across the team.
- Increased Collaboration and Unity: Regular peer coaching sessions can break down silos, fostering a more collaborative and united leadership team.
- Innovative Problem-Solving: Collaborating from diverse perspectives through peer coaching can lead to more creative and practical solutions to organizational challenges.
- Strengthened Organizational Culture: A culture that values continuous learning and mutual support among leaders sets a positive example for the entire organization, contributing to a more engaged and motivated workforce.

COACHING UP: STRATEGIES FOR INFLUENCING SENIOR LEADERS

Coaching up is the practice of providing feedback and guidance to more senior organizational leaders. It is a delicate process that requires tact, understanding, and strategic communication. This approach enables the safety practitioner to contribute to the growth and direction of the organization by influencing decision-making processes and organizational culture from below.

Strategies:

- Build a Foundation of Trust: Establish a relationship based on mutual respect and trust with senior leaders. Reliability, competence, and honesty are crucial to gaining their confidence and openness to your input.
- Understand Their Objectives: Gain a deep understanding of the senior leaders' goals and challenges. This insight will allow you to tailor your feedback and suggestions to align with their objectives, making your input more relevant and effective.
- Communicate Effectively: When presenting ideas or feedback to senior leaders, be clear, concise, and constructive. Focus on solutions and the potential positive effect on the organization's goals. Timing is also crucial, so choose moments when they are most receptive to feedback.
- Encourage a Culture of Openness: Advocate an organizational culture that values feedback from all levels. This can involve formal mechanisms for upward feedback or fostering an informal culture of open dialogue and continuous improvement.

Benefits:

- Enhanced Decision-Making: Input from various leaders can provide senior executives with diverse perspectives, leading to more informed and effective decision-making.
- Increased Organizational Agility: Organizations where feedback flows freely in all directions are more adaptable and responsive to changes in the external environment.
- Strengthened Leadership Development: Coaching up contributes to a culture of learning and development, benefiting

leaders at all levels by exposing them to innovative ideas and perspectives.

COACHING MICRO CULTURES

The reality is that everyone works in a different organizational culture. My favorite way to work is in organizations with decentralized cultures, where teams have more independence to make decisions and collaborate within the organization. Still, I have been equally successful in using the same methods I have discussed in every type of organization I have been part of, regardless of the organizational structure. If necessary, consider developing a microculture.

A microculture often refers to the culture of a small group of people with a specific value or commitment to a functional element in the organization, such as safety and health. It is also the distinctive culture that a group shares. A microculture has its own social microclimate, with values and norms of behavior differing from those of the general organizational culture. A microculture of safety and health can reside within the organizational hierarchy and influence the behavior of individuals within and outside the group. However, this is not the most straightforward path to success. There will be obstacles around every corner, and people will ask you why you are going in this direction. I briefly led one organization that did not value safety the way I did, nor did it adapt to what I knew worked well in leading safety and health. The organization was very compliance-oriented and not much else. Much of my work developing a culture of safety excellence involved developing a microculture outside the organizational norms of working. I started with one plant location and simply allowed its safety performance to tell their story. Although my success was slower than I desired, the culture grew over time in its ability to influence the rest of the organization in terms of safety. If you choose this working method, being an effective communicator, coach, capability builder, and skills developer is essential because you trust your small circle of partners to help achieve results. Microcultures offer many benefits, but ensuring they do not lead to division or exclusion within the larger organizational culture is crucial.

CLOSING

For front-line workers, effective coaching is about unlocking potential and fostering an environment in which learning, growth, and customer excellence are paramount. The safety practitioner is crucial in guiding these vital team members through challenges, setting clear goals, and providing the support necessary to achieving them.

Among peer leaders, coaching transforms into a collaborative effort to enhance leadership skills and strengthen team cohesion, which will help promote a culture of mutual growth and continuous improvement. The strategies outlined underscore the value of open communication, shared objectives, and constructive feedback, reinforcing the foundation for successful organizational leadership.

Coaching up or influencing senior leaders introduces a nuanced layer of communication and feedback that requires tact, understanding, and strategic alignment with organizational goals. It demonstrates the pivotal role of leaders at all levels in shaping a thriving organizational culture.

Integrating these coaching dimensions creates a comprehensive framework for leadership effectiveness that transcends traditional hierarchical boundaries. It fosters a culture of openness, learning, and adaptability, which is crucial in today's fast-paced and ever-changing business environment. An integrated coaching approach can enhance decision-making and organizational agility, strengthening leadership development across the board.

The art of coaching within an organization is a powerful catalyst for change. It drives individual growth and performance and shapes the fabric of organizational culture and success. By embracing the principles and strategies of effective coaching at all levels, leaders can forge a path of continuous improvement and innovation, creating a resilient and thriving organization.

Chapter 6:

Safety Communication

Communication works for those who work at it.

— JOHN POWELL

Effective communication in the workplace, especially at the front line, is essential for the safety practitioner. Our career is technical, complex, and challenging to explain to those with less knowledge. Effective communication is crucial for your success and is critical in both vertical and horizontal contexts for informed decision-making. Ensuring workers feel heard and valued enhances worker engagement and fosters motivation and commitment to their roles. Ensuring workers are aligned with the organization's mission and goals promotes a cohesive and effective workforce. The key is to excel in communication, which helps prevent incidents and promotes organizational interdependence. Motivating individuals and groups to unite around a shared vision and the mission of success to reach your safety objectives is paramount. How you communicate can only improve how you coach and mentor the organization going forward.

"The Dirty Dozen" is a concept by Gordon Dupont highlighting twelve common human-error conditions that can precede accidents or incidents (Memon, 2023). These twelve elements influence people to make mistakes. Communication is first on the list. Reflecting on having conducted hundreds of incident and accident investigations, the lack of communication or poor communication was often a significant causal factor, so mitigating this common problem has always been my top priority.

In my career, skilled safety practitioners have often struggled to communicate effectively due to complex messaging, a lack of active listening, or an unscrupulous desire to highlight their expertise. This alone impeded or sabotaged their careers, causing them to fall short of their potential. Communication is challenging, and sometimes, I have missed the message I wanted to communicate or failed to deliver a message with the transparency or authenticity it deserves. In this chapter, I will explain how to ensure you can communicate clearly.

Communication refers to the transmitter and the receiver, as well as the method of transmission. Unclear or inaccessible instructions can pose a challenge. The receiver could make assumptions about the meaning of these instructions, and the transmitter might assume the receiver has clearly understood the message, even if that is not the case. The prevailing belief is that people clearly understand verbal communication only about 30 percent of the time. This will only grow more challenging as younger workers enter the workforce. They grew up as digital natives with smart devices receiving and delivering much of their communications in small chunks. They understand communication differently from how older workers do.

People spend over three-quarters of their time in interpersonal situations at work, so it is critical to learn how to communicate clearly to different audiences.

COMMUNICATION STYLES

Fostering effective workplace communication requires an understanding of styles. A person's background, personality, and experiences will shape his or her communication style, so we do not all communicate in the same way. Communication styles can show up in different ways, including verbal and non-verbal cues, how direct or vague we are, and even how we write. Safety practitioners can focus on their communication styles by reflecting on themselves or seeking evaluation from coaches, mentors, or people they admire with excellent communication skills to enhance workplace communication.

Cultivating an understanding and appreciation of the diverse styles within your organization is crucial. Different preferences for sharing and receiving information among colleagues contribute to an environment in which everyone's voice has value. Still, if you are not delivering the communication in a way that is clear to the receiver, you are not likely to receive much from them, which is a danger to your safety process. Your role is to learn from your workers and to be flexible and agile in your communication styles. Understanding that workers are different and that you will need to know them through building personal relationships is pivotal in facilitating discussions and fostering an atmosphere of inclusivity that values the richness of diverse perspectives.

An example is when I implemented a new safety procedure to address a recurring issue with equipment malfunctions. I prepared detailed written documentation outlining the latest guidelines and distributed it to all employees. Additionally, I posted the changes on the safety information bulletin board and instructed the area supervisors to ensure that their workers swiftly adopted the new procedures.

However, as time passed, I observed inconsistent compliance with the new protocol. Upon investigation, many employees were unaware of the changes. One worker claimed he didn't receive the email due to his full inbox, while another admitted to seeing the email but not understanding the technical jargon. Furthermore, a group of night-shift workers disclosed that they rarely checked the safety information bulletin board because the information seldom changed. Lastly, many members of the plant's management team neglected to discuss the changes due to competing production priorities.

Realizing the seriousness of the communication breakdown and the urgent need to ensure full adoption of the safety procedures, I called an emergency meeting with our teams. I devised a multi-channel communication strategy to ensure everyone was informed about the critical updates. I introduced clear, easy-to-understand safety talks at the beginning of each shift, posted printed notices in high-traffic areas, and utilized the company's internal messaging kiosk for real-time updates. Additionally, I increased my presence in the manufacturing areas to ensure everyone understood the changes.

The new approach, which focused on clear, accessible, and varied communication methods, proved highly effective. Employees became more engaged and aware of the revised safety protocol, significantly reducing mistakes. This experience underscored the importance of such communication methods in effective safety leadership. Throughout my professional journey, I have tried to polish my skills in understanding an audience and blending communication styles to cultivate a productive work environment, even during less pleasant interactions.

In a previous chapter, I covered the leadership skills you need to better yourself. I presented most of them as inputs to help you effectively lead safety. Many of those qualities are related to how you will grow as a person and how you communicate with others.

Reflecting on these leadership attributes as a backdrop, we can now consider what you do with them. Think about using your knowledge to improve the work system and how you share and receive information with others. Undoubtedly, the work details of the safety practitioner are incredibly fluid, but here are five communication styles that can boost your adaptability and responsiveness to various situations your workforce may encounter.

- Authentic: Communication can be challenging, especially when dealing with front-line and senior leadership assignments. It is vital to preserve genuine expression. This style encourages safety practitioners to honestly communicate their thoughts, values, and emotions to foster trust and credibility and to form genuine connections with team members.
- Transformational: Communication also uses words to paint a picture that inspires creativity, innovation, and personal growth. Safety practitioners should encourage and motivate

their teams by fostering a shared sense of purpose and commitment. Transformational communication is a technique that expands on a shared vision. I will address the idea of safety vision in a later chapter.

- Empathetic: Perceptions at the front line become true regardless of whether you believe in them or not. Your role is to be empathetic by creating a supportive work environment, strengthening relationships, and showing that you value the team's and its members' well-being. The success of your actions relies on fostering empathetic relationships with your workers.

- Clear and Concise: We truly live in a work environment of complex regulations, rules, internal guidelines, and standards that govern much of our work as safety practitioners. Mastering a communication style that ensures clarity and facilitates efficient decision-making processes within the workforce is crucial to our success.

- Celebratory: This communication style is about keeping positive momentum in the workplace. We have consistently recognized and celebrated big wins and milestones. Still, as a safety practitioner, I have found that celebrating even minor victories is just as essential and accumulates toward ensuring the big wins. If you observe the workplace, the workforce, and how each team and individual contributes to success, you can usually find positive things to share. What is going well in your organization? Are you sharing it? By showing gratitude for the workforce's contributions, you can improve morale by reinforcing positive behaviors and strengthening your relationships.

Each item on the list is significant in facilitating communication. However, I would be remiss if I did not share two additional elements about how you receive communication, which are equally important.

- Bi-Directional: The art of conversation is often overlooked in our hectic, activity-filled workdays. The safety practitioner should practice active listening and be fully engaged in discussions, staying attentive and maintaining a genuine desire to understand another person's viewpoint, not just giving an answer, which is challenging to master for many of us who feel as though we know the answer. It takes time, but the other person must seek solutions through dialogue rather than having the safety practitioner provide them. Bi-directional communication not only shows respect for the members of your workforce but also contributes to improved decision-making and stronger relationships within the team. Read that previous sentence repeatedly until it becomes ingrained in your memory. We perfect the art of what we do best at the front line through conversation and relationship building.
- Feedback-centric: This communication style's primary goals are to establish a safe space where workers feel free to offer feedback, acknowledge and act upon constructive criticism, advance a continuous improvement culture, boost team morale, and cultivate an environment of openness and trust. It complements your approach to bidirectional communication.

LEARNING YOUR AUDIENCE

We often overlook the ways in which we perceive our personal and work environment through our five senses: seeing, hearing, touching, tasting, and smelling. Have you ever talked with someone and wondered whether he or she got your point? Of course you have. Every person is different, and learning from the information we send depends on that person and how he or she receives it according to their experiences.

I often explained information from bulleted slides and a well-written procedure during many years of teaching safety training classes. However, for some workers, I had to be very visual in my approach and show pictures of what I was talking about before they understood me. Other workers required a demonstration, like in fire extinguisher training. Once the worker laid their hands on the extinguisher, felt its weight, noticed how hard it was to pull the pin, and expelled its contents, things clicked because they learned through doing it in a safe environment before replicating that learning in an active work environment. Your communication style needs to pivot at times because people are different and lean toward how they like to receive communication from you. That said, prioritize the three primary senses: hearing, seeing, and touching. You can combine or use these styles individually to convey your message. Become savvy enough to know how to employ them.

BECOMING A STORYTELLER

People I've worked with frequently remind me of how I interacted with them during our time together. They tell me how our authentic and honest conversations made them feel and how I motivated them to act differently and participate actively in the work system. The reality is that I like painting pictures with my words. I am a storyteller, and I lead many of my communications with real-life stories in the hopes of changing how people see their work.

As safety practitioners, as mentioned, much of our work is technical, complex, and involves many rules and regulations. Of course, we also do a lot of exciting stuff, though it might not seem attractive to other people who don't work in safety. However, how we do it can make a difference.

I asked a friend one day why she enjoyed watching NASCAR. She was always in front of the TV if there was a race, from the green flag to the checkered flag. She answered me without hesitation that she loved to watch it for the red and yellow flags—in other words, to see the wrecks. This story demonstrates a fundamental truth: we are fascinated by disaster. What happens to our brains when we see destruction?

According to Dr. John Mayer, a clinical psychologist, the process triggers our survival instincts.

"A disaster enters our awareness—this can be from a live source such as driving and seeing a traffic accident or from watching a news report about a hurricane, a plane crash, or any disaster," he explains. "This data from our perceptual system stimulates the amygdala (the part of the brain responsible for emotions, survival tactics, and memory). The amygdala then signals the regions of the frontal cortex that engage in analyzing and interpreting data. Next, the brain evaluates whether this data—awareness of the disaster—threatens you. Thus, judgment gets involved. As a result, the 'fight or flight' response is evoked" (Page, 2017).

That said, I bet it is safe to say that you clearly remember some disastrous event in your personal life, as Mayer describes above.

We can use this cognitive process to tell impactful stories about safety. For example, I have sometimes noticed workers in my facilities not wearing the proper protection for specific tasks. Some workers believed their reasons were valid, but mostly, they did not see all of the risks associated with their work tasks. I could have reminded them about the rule of wearing protection or reprimanded them for not following it since it was a rule. However, I have often found it more effective when I give them an accurate and pertinent example of an injury or illness that could happen if they do not wear their protective equipment.

A story that comes to mind. For the longest time, I kept and widely showed the results of damage to a pair of safety glasses that a worker was wearing when parts of a grinding wheel shattered, hitting her in the face. The lenses were severely cracked, and the frames were badly scarred, but I am convinced her safety eyewear saved her vision that day, and after the event, she did, too. This personal example is a powerful reminder of the impact of safety measures. It's a shared responsibility, and this incident underscores that. For years after, all I needed to do was show those battered safety glasses as a poignant example to the workers under my care so they could fully understand the brevity of why I was asking them to do things they often did not fully have value to perform.

Since we have an evolved fascination with destruction and its relation to self-preservation, a story that evokes interest and even a mental pause can be very effective and powerful. Think about the people you like listening to. It could be a preacher, a teacher, a business leader, or, yes, a seasoned safety practitioner. You will find one thing they almost always have in common that piques your interest. They excel at capturing your attention and facilitating effective learning through storytelling. They paint a vivid picture you can see in your mind, all by their use of effectively connecting words.

Although storytelling is not the only way to communicate, it undoubtedly exerts a noteworthy influence on your safety process. Here are some tips for becoming a better storyteller.

- Relatability: Share stories that your audience can relate to. This could involve firsthand experiences, challenges, articles you have read, news clippings, or successes. Relatable stories help establish a connection and make your message more impactful.
- Clarity of Message: Create a story with a clear message. Whether it is a lesson learned, a point you want to emphasize, or a vision for the future, ensure that your story has a purpose that aligns with why you are communicating with the worker(s).
- Emotion: Engage emotions to make your communication memorable. People remember how a story made them feel more than the specific details. Incorporating emotional elements can create a connection and provoke a response.
- Authenticity: Be genuine and authentic in your storytelling. People eagerly respond to safety practitioners who share their true selves. Authenticity builds trust, and a trustworthy leader is more likely to inspire and influence others.

- Simplicity: Keep your stories simple and focused. Avoid unnecessary details that will dilute the critical message. People are more likely to remember a clear and concise narrative.
- Visualization: Help your audience visualize the story. Paint a vivid picture with your words to make the narrative more compelling. When people can see the story in their minds, it becomes memorable.
- Engagement: Encourage audience engagement by creating interactive storytelling experiences. This could involve asking questions, inviting discussion, or incorporating multimedia elements to enhance the narrative.
- Consistency: Use storytelling consistently as part of your communication strategy. Regularly sharing stories helps reinforce your message and build a narrative that aligns with your leadership style and vision.

No, I am not one of those safety practitioners who show blood-stained pictures of accidents, nor do I often craft stories to scare, but some of our work is to tie workers to the reality of outcomes that can actually occur without thoughtful control. Remember that compelling storytelling is an art that improves with practice. You can become a more influential communicator and leader by honing your storytelling skills.

CRITICAL FEEDBACK

Providing critical feedback to workers is essential for the safety practitioner and incentivizes individual and organizational growth, even if it is not always pleasant. Still, when done effectively, it contributes to the development of a motivated and skilled workforce. Effective feedback promotes open communication, trust, and collaboration, creating a positive work environment. When workers receive feedback focused on improvement and supported by guidance, they are more likely to feel valued, engaged, and committed to their professional development, even when the feedback is critical. Overall, consistent and constructive feedback contributes to the success of both individuals and the organization.

What works best is to ensure you use such communications confidentially and stay specific regarding the person's behavior or performance needs. It is crucial to refrain from statements that suggest a worker does not care about safety, as it is easy to fall into the trap of addressing his or her personality instead of their actions or behaviors. Although challenging, staying constructive and communicating how a worker can improve is a step toward success. Another technique is to frame your feedback as "I" statements instead of "you" statements so you do not appear accusatory. Using "I" statements creates a better chance of having a genuine conversation than delivering a lecture.

Of the thousands of people I have worked with, very few ever showed up to work to do wrong. As you can imagine, getting critical feedback from you stings when they believe they are doing their part. Figure 1 below shows an image explaining a method I learned long ago called the feedback sandwich approach. This communication strategy is sandwiching constructive criticism between two layers of positive feedback. It begins with an initial positive comment or acknowledgment of the worker's strengths and achievements. The critical feedback, the key component, follows this positive opening. It specifically and objectively targets areas in need of improvement. You then complete the sandwich with a closing layer of positive reinforcement, encouragement, or praise.

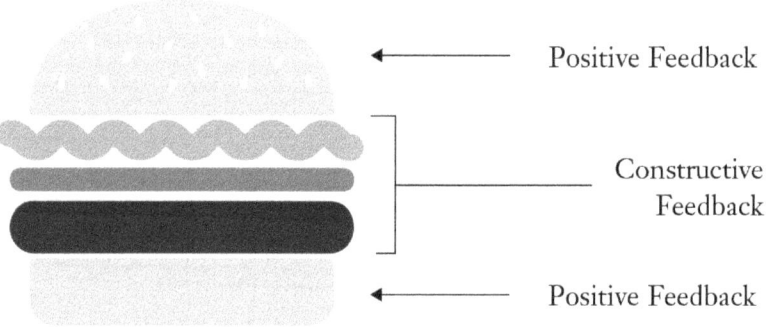

Positive Feedback

Constructive
Feedback

Positive Feedback

Figure 1

Here's an example of how I would manage critical communication with an employee not wearing their PPE.

Positive Feedback:
"I wanted to talk to you about something important. First, I want to say thanks and acknowledge how dedicated you've been to completing your work tasks. I know we have been behind in getting products to our customers, and your dedication to getting us back on schedule is amazing, especially since you have never been injured. Your commitment to efficiently getting things done is impressive and makes a big difference to the team and our success as a company."

Constructive Feedback:
"However, I noticed that you haven't been wearing your safety eyewear at times during your shift. I'm guessing it is because you are working fast and trying to complete your work tasks in a hot environment and battling fogging on your lenses. I know that wearing PPE can be a hassle at times, and be assured we are always looking for a way to limit PPE use, but for the job you are doing, it is still required and crucial for your safety. I would also remind you that we had two of your co-workers last month who were treated for eye injuries doing similar job tasks, and one of them had a significant injury that required a doctor's intervention. It's company policy to always wear PPE, and it's just to protect you from the potential hazards we have identified in the facility."

Positive Feedback:
"I know you care about doing a great job and contributing to a safe work environment, and I appreciate that. You are viewed as a leader here, and wearing your PPE consistently will set a great example for everyone else. Feel free to try different models of safety eyewear located in the medical office. The break room's safety eyewear cleaning station also has a non-fog spray. Let me know if you need anything or

have concerns about the PPE. Thank you for understanding, staying safe, and all your hard work!"

This method aims to balance the potentially challenging aspects of criticism with positive elements, making the feedback more palatable and encouraging a more receptive response from the recipient. Ensuring that the positive elements are genuine while meeting the overall objective and that the critical feedback remains clear and actionable is essential.

Remember, providing critical feedback aims to help workers grow and succeed. If done well, the receiver of your feedback understands that you have a critical point to express, but they also know that you recognize they are doing things well and that you are simply coaching them to be better. Approach the conversation confidentially and with empathy, and focus on creating a positive and supportive environment for improvement.

CLOSING

Being actively engaged, listening attentively to workers, valuing their input, and painting success with words and giving constructive feedback are all essential elements to communicating as a safety practitioner. Much of this is about building relationships through effective communication and conversations. You play a pivotal role in demonstrating a respectful interaction that helps you meet your performance targets. By modeling these communication techniques, you set the standard for how your workers communicate and you dictate how they see you as a safety leader.

Part II:
Laying the Safety Foundation

Chapter 7

The Path to the Safety Performance You Desire

Our only security is our ability to change.

— John Lilly

S o far, I have covered some basics of what you need to know about your capabilities, skills, communication, and safety leadership. They are all incremental but accumulative parts that are incredibly important for success in how you will support the work environment. Now, with an understanding of what is critical for personal growth, we need to think about the safety process and how it will develop under your leadership. You are developing yourself, and at the same time, you are developing your safety processes. You may feel like you are swimming upstream against the strong current of a preexisting organizational culture and a disparate management system, but trust me, how you choose to lead can influence it all.

There is no quick fix for building safety processes and a strong safety culture. Every organization is unique and dynamic, and each has its own personality. Customer satisfaction is crucial for safety success, and many of us have a broad and varied customer base. However, it is with the front-line workers that we truly experience the most significant benefit. There is no "one right way" to build process robustness. Instead, one must employ many elements that work best for them. The key to achieving great safety performance is having a process that promotes activities during which workers will partner with you to reach the desired targets, preventing losses and controlling variation.

Controlling process variation is not a new concept. It is the key to building highly effective programs that minimize variability and stabilize manufacturing and service processes. Successful organizations have adopted lean management and Six Sigma concepts to control process variation. When applying this thinking to building a desired safety process, the critical question is, "Can an organization leave so much variation within the work system that workers can make poor decisions while performing their work?" It makes sense that uncontrolled variability in the work system influences such behavior.

DEVIATION AND ERROR

In his book Human Error Reduction and Safety Management, one of the early safety pioneers, Dan Peterson writes, "Human error is involved in every accident, and there are many reasons behind this behavior." Peterson says, "When incidents occur, it results from system failure and human error" (Peterson, 1980). A worker's decision to perform a substandard act is directly linked to the work system where he or she resides.

Dr. Diane Vaughn's book *The Challenger Launch Decision* supports this idea as she explores the management and behavioral factors behind the Space Shuttle Challenger disaster. She writes that they launched the shuttle even though some equipment was malfunctioning. They ignored other apparent problems, which persistently pushed the limits of acceptable behavior. For many years, I kept a quote attributed to Diane Vaughn pinned to a bulletin board in front of my desk.

Here is the quote:

> *"The normalization of deviance is when small changes in behavior begin to occur, expanding the boundaries that allow additional deviations to become acceptable. When deviant events*

are tolerated, the potential for error grows, and events are overlooked, misinterpreted, or simply allowed without question."

(VAUGHAN, 1996)

Workers in your organization will become desensitized to deviant practices. This poses a continuous challenge if you want to avoid leading a safety management system that allows substandard behaviors. It is important to remember that the normalization of deviance occurs surreptitiously and sometimes over years before you experience a negative outcome.

The question is, what will you do about it?

THROUGH A QUALITY AND OPERATIONAL EFFECTIVENESS LENS

When considering this idea through the lens of quality and operational effectiveness, removing errors from a work system enhances overall operational efficiency and product or service quality. Organizations can streamline processes and use resources more effectively by identifying and correcting errors, which increases productivity, profitability, and customer delight while promoting positive behavior. It also promotes a culture of continuous improvement by encouraging feedback and learning from mistakes.

ERRORS CAN AFFECT BEHAVIORS.

Various government and independent research organizations continue to report that, depending on the industry, 70 percent to 90 percent of accidents result from unsafe behavior. Herbert Heinrich pioneered the domino theory of accident causation. He stated that "unsafe acts of persons" caused 88 percent of accidents and introduced what is widely known as Heinrich's accident triangle or pyramid. Heinrich proposed that in a group of, for example, 330 accidents, 100 would result in no injuries, 29 would result in minor injuries, and one would result in a significant injury (Marsden, 2017). Therefore, it would seem logical that if we fix the workers, we can improve the management system. We consider such an approach a single-point focus.

This thinking is substandard compared with how we understand safety today, because it drives a management system toward controlling the most unpredictable variable within the work system—the human variable. It should be noted, however, that Heinrich did his work almost 100 years ago. We can debate the numbers of his pyramid or the accident sequence found in his domino model of accident causation. However, there is little doubt that he brought to light that there is much work to do upstream of an event to prevent a negative outcome. Regardless of how many policies, guidelines, or behavior programs you have created, as a safety practitioner, I'm sure you have found it challenging to make the workforce consistently follow your program. Frank E. Bird, a researcher with the International Loss Control Institute, recognized this issue in the early 1970s when he introduced a revision of Heinrich's domino theory and established a model that added management system error to the sequence of causation.

You will only get enduring safety performance by concentrating on what workers are doing every day. Incident causes are seldom, if ever, linear, meaning there are an abundant number of causes that promote a negative output. Based on my experience, plenty of evidence shows that we must understand worker error as at-risk behavior within a management system that tolerates such variation.

Two models, Figure 1, and Figure 2, support this discussion above.

Heinrich Model			
Injuries are caused by accidents	Accidents are caused by unsafe acts and conditions	Unsafe acts and conditions are caused by the faults of persons	Faults of persons are caused by the social environment and ancestry

Source: Herbert William Heinrich

Figure 1: Heinrich Model

Bird Model			
Injuries are caused by accidents	For every accident there are immediate causes that are related to system errors	Operational or active errors are only symptoms of deeper underlying causes or latent errors related to system errors	The absence of a system of effective control permits the existence of the factors referred to as basic causes or latent errors

Source: Frank E. Bird

Figure 2: Bird Model

UNDERSTANDING CAUSATION

Before improving performance and achieving a desired safety culture, we must be clear: safety is an integral part of an extensive and often complicated work system with many components. It is essential to understand that deviance in one aspect of the system will often affect other system elements. To mitigate such errors, you need to establish control over the safety system. Two standard practices used in occupational safety are the hierarchy of controls and inherent safe design, and you should know both as fundamental to your role as a safety practitioner.

HIERARCHY OF CONTROLS

The hierarchy of controls, shown in Figure 3 below, is a popular system in many organizations that reduces or eliminates exposure to hazards. The control pyramid's hierarchy has five levels. The aim is to permanently eliminate the risk, which is the most effective control. If this is not practical, you look to minimize the risk by working through the other alternatives in the hierarchy.

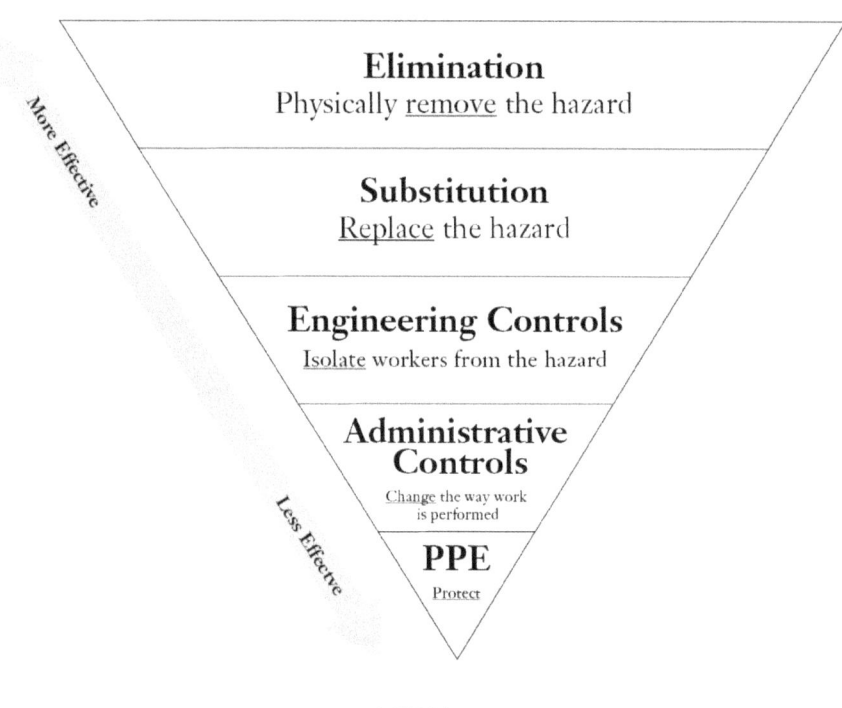

© NIOSH

Figure 3: Hierarchy of Controls Model

The hierarchy arrangement is from most effective to least effective methods:

- Elimination: physically removing the hazard or changing the work process.
- Substitution: replacing a hazardous material or process with a less hazardous one.
- Engineering controls: modifying equipment or the workspace to reduce the threats workers encounter.
- Administrative controls: changing work procedures such as written safety policies, rules, supervision, schedules, and training to reduce the duration, frequency, and severity of exposure.

- Personal protective equipment: requiring workers to wear and use PPE properly.

INHERENT SAFE DESIGN

Inherent safe design is an approach that complements the hierarchy of controls, especially in industries that require OSHA's Process Safety Management Standard (PSM) (1910.119). This approach to process risk management is vital in the chemical industry and other organizations, as it focuses on process safety rules and the feasible elimination of hazards. It contrasts with the approach of simply relying on safety systems and procedures to manage risk, much in line with some elements found in the hierarchy of controls. However, regardless of the PSM requirements for your organization, it can provide valuable lessons for your safety program.

Inherent safe design uses four guiding principles:

- Minimize: reducing the amount of hazardous material present at any time.
- Substitute: replacing one material with a less hazardous one.
- Moderate: reducing the strength of an effect.
- Simplify: eliminating problems by design rather than adding additional equipment or features to deal with them.

Two further principles are important:

- Error tolerance: designing equipment and processes to withstand faults or deviations from design.
- Isolation: locating or transporting equipment to produce less danger.

An important lesson for the safety practitioner is that inherent safe design embraces the idea of "removing risks at the design stage," meaning reducing the likelihood and consequences of the adverse effects that extend throughout a process lifecycle—from cradle to grave.

The hierarchy of controls and inherent safe design have tangible lessons you should consider. Another model that comes to mind is the Swiss cheese model, as it opens a dialogue to gain better control of the safety system and exposes discussion to areas such as human factors, conditions found in the work environment, worker knowledge and skills, behaviors, and management commitment and accountability.

SWISS CHEESE MODEL

As shown in Figure 4 below, the Swiss cheese model is a framework for analyzing how sequences of small, often seemingly insignificant failures can lead to significant adverse outcomes. James Reason, a British psychologist and expert in human error and risk management, developed the concept. The model visually portrays an organization's defense systems as multiple layers of Swiss cheese stacked side by side. The critical aspect of the model is that while each layer (or slice of cheese) has weaknesses, the layers' alignment is usually such that at least one layer will catch a hazard (an error or series of errors).

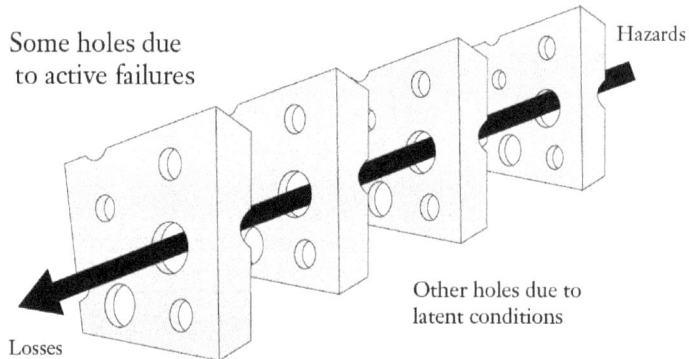

Successive layers of defenses, barriers and safeguards

Source: Reason J, Carthey J, deLeval M. Diagnosing "vulnerable system syndrome":
An essential prerequisite to effective risk management. Qual Health Care, 2001

Figure 4: Swiss Cheese Model

Here is what I have learned from the Swiss cheese model:

- Latent Errors: These are underlying system issues or latent conditions that create the conditions for active failures to occur. Latent failures may include inadequate training, insufficient staffing, flawed organizational policies, and equipment design issues. These latent failures exist long before an accident happens and may remain dormant.
- Armed Errors: These are errors within the system that are primed to occur but have not yet done so. These errors are often a result of latent errors but are facilitated to strike because of management decisions, organization pressures, inadequate training, or maintenance, to name a few.
- Active Errors: These are the immediate and often human errors or actions that can lead to adverse events. Active failures are the last layer of defense before an accident occurs. They include actions such as a worker reaching into a machine turned off but not isolated from its energy, a pilot misinterpreting a control input, or a nurse administering the wrong medication.

The key idea is that losses occur when the holes in these multiple layers of defense align, allowing an active failure to pass through the system's defenses. When this alignment happens, it can result in an adverse event. Although the Swiss cheese model is a theoretical framework, the basis for using it for safety is practical and valuable. The key concept for you as a practitioner is to reflect on all the errors living in your safety system now. Also, consider what variability outside the safety system, such as operation and maintenance systems, could negatively affect your desired success.

What are the layers (the cheese slices) in your system?

The Swiss cheese model matters for several reasons:

- It helps us understand the factors contributing to safety and accidents in complex systems. It underscores a fundamental truth: accidents are rarely the result of a single error.
- By identifying the weaknesses and vulnerabilities in each layer of your defenses, you can proactively assess and mitigate risks. You can strengthen defenses by plugging holes and improving safety measures.
- It emphasizes the role of human factors in safety and the importance of addressing latent, armed, and active errors.
- It promotes a culture of continuous improvement that reflects on errors. It underscores that errors are an inherent part of the work system, and that you can use them to understand and enhance prevention systems and develop a better safety culture.

CASE STUDY

Several years ago, I investigated a workplace incident in which a worker died while using equipment that was not isolated from its energy sources. The worker was crushed by the equipment while performing unplanned maintenance. I was at the dinner table with my family celebrating a holiday when I received a call from the most senior leader in that business sector informing me that the corporate jet was coming to pick me up. Several hours later, I was five hundred miles from home with the one task no safety practitioner ever wants: a fatality investigation. When I entered the plant where the death took place, one of the safety coordinators stopped me and said something that I will never forget. He said, "I have been concerned about three people at our plant because I thought they were bad risk-takers. We are now down to two." I was shocked, anguished, bothered, and angry, but over several days, I began to understand that there was much truth in what he said to me.

As I reviewed this unfortunate event and analyzed the scene and equipment involved, my reaction was, why? The worker was trained, hazards were apparent, and the energy-isolation procedure was complete. Although everything appeared fine initially, further investigation revealed a work system with uncontrolled variability, leading to inevitable human error. The worker was emulating the behaviors of a work system that supported such risk-taking. My investigation of the fatality revealed latent errors dating back years before the incident. The machine had design flaws and inadequate guarding. The training and procedure writing was long and complicated, and it did not have a measurable component of success. Both the preventive and reactive maintenance plans were insufficient, and the management system lacked good discipline and control. The organization allowed too many variables (latent error) to live in the work system, creating a potential for catastrophic loss when the worker accepted the deviant errors as the norm (armed error) and the worker erred (active error), which cost him his life.

MANAGEMENT SYSTEM ELEMENTS AND ACTIONS

I will delve into management systems in a later chapter. Still, it is critical to understand that there are elements within a safety management system that are error-prone and may cause you to lose ground. You need to start by controlling system variability and reducing loss considering the models I have shared. However, as a safety practitioner, you should also consider how the process acts and moves, which is the transformational part of reaching your desired performance and cultural growth.

In Figure 5 below are four elements I have personally adopted in my safety practice, and I will explore them more explicitly in the book's third part. Before we get there, however, it is essential to begin thinking about how you will start the safety planning process. These elements include the work environment, the people performing work, the organizational culture including worker behaviors, and how leaders lead and support it all. Under each element are dominant actions that, at least for me, have been important as I planned control efforts. Each has been a critical starting point and a necessary test in all my safety plans throughout the years.

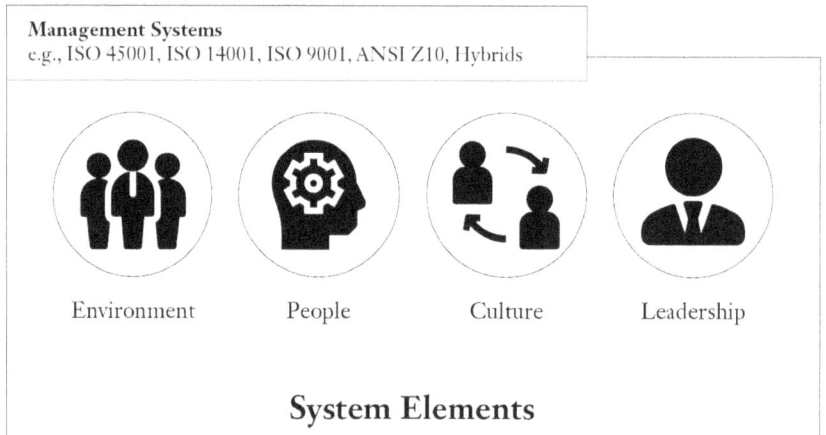

Management Systems
e.g., ISO 45001, ISO 14001, ISO 9001, ANSI Z10, Hybrids

Environment   People   Culture   Leadership

System Elements

Figure 5

As I think back over my career, I see that many of the elements in the above figure have appeared in various incident investigations. Many of these elements intervene between the design of a system and the production or service process, resulting in conditions that make errors more likely to occur.

Harkening back to my previous discussion about other management systems such as operations and quality, we can also see that these elements can work against your safety process. Here is an example. In my years as a safety practitioner at two large manufacturing facilities, one of the first observations to emerge during trend analysis of past incidents was that few workers were injured when equipment ran true to its design. However, when operators were forced to intervene, the outcome was only as good as the worker's ability to avert potential incidents. I identified "process upset" (controlling, engineering, designing, and purchasing) as significant variables over which I needed better control to stem future incidents. I actively pursued getting equipment manufacturers, engineers, and process specialists involved to increase the reliability and efficiency of the equipment, and I supported it all with better work instructions. I based my motivation on the belief that when workers worked outside of the defined control of the established work process, they often drew reasonable but flawed conclusions that sometimes led to a negative outcome.

You must therefore address the critical questions of how much variation to allow in the work system and what you need to control. As a starting point, consider these approaches:

- Review data from past incidents, near-miss reports, planned inspections, and maintenance logs. Benchmark similar industries to determine the latent errors that have allowed losses to enter the system(s) in the past. Each incident is independent in this scenario, but standard errors are most identifiable.

- Recognize the errors that need resolution and determine the severity of the threat to the system and the likelihood of their reoccurrence.

- Identify where the error lives within the safety system to diagnose more significant systemic issues. This includes the safety system's physical aspects, people, behavior, and leadership factors.

- Understanding the "mess" or the uncontrolled aspects of the work system will paint a different picture, showing where control is necessary.

- Determine probable solutions and consider the consequences of outcomes related to each proposed alternative.

- Determine what level of control you need and determine the severity and likelihood before and after control.

- Promote solutions to your shareholders and gain their endorsement. Act to close gaps and reduce variability in the safety management system. Monitor for compliance, and revise if needed to ensure success.

Again, from my time as a facility safety practitioner, I noticed a sharp increase in hand lacerations occurring in a facility's paper converting department. Trend analysis over twelve months revealed that workers using utility razor knives were to blame for 72 percent of all injuries at the facility at that time. A further study showed that workers used utility razor knives for over one hundred different tasks, carried them personally as part of their work equipment, wore no hand protection, and had little training to operate a razor knife safely. Additionally, there were no established policies or guidelines to govern the use of razor knives. Because of these results, the facility completely changed how it used its utility razor knives. We eliminated 98 percent of the tasks that needed utility razor knives by adopting new, better-designed tools, changing how tasks were planned, and removing some tasks altogether. We also implemented new safety rules and training, made hand protection mandatory, and switched to a safer knife design for the remaining few tasks requiring a knife. We sought to understand the latent errors residing in the system and determined the desired level of control and the probable errors that threatened such control. In this case, we were looking to limit the number of active errors that could occur and the tasks that armed them, which resulted in the desired performance and heavily mitigated hand injuries from the work site.

CLOSING

Managing workers' behavior to achieve desired expectations recognizes that most of the variability in system performance comes from the responses of workers, regardless of how well you have designed the system. Human error is almost always a potential cause of accidents, but it is not the only one. The work system and its design and life cycle have an effect on the workers' safe performance and their relationship to the environment. The most important lesson I can share with you, and one that you need to learn as a safety practitioner, is this one: By removing that variability (errors) that allows workers to make poor—and occasionally catastrophic—decisions, you can overcome resistance and gain momentum for safety success. It is important to understand that it is unlikely, if not impossible, that you will remove all variability from a work system. However, you should still take action to eliminate as much as possible.

This is also the point in your development and understanding at which you will begin to consider a path that your safety process will follow. I firmly believe that there is not one magic path. You must focus on the errors in your work system and the workers who are interfacing with them. A question I often ask myself is this: what is driving the undesired behaviors in the workforce? As I mentioned earlier and in the preface of this book, consider the benefits of combining Safety I and Safety II approaches to build a more robust framework for enhancing safety. Safety I focuses on minimizing adverse outcomes by identifying and eliminating hazards and potential risks, providing a solid foundation for addressing issues in the work environment and, it is hoped, before a loss occurs. Safety II complements this quite well by emphasizing the importance of seeking to understand without blame, seeking to understand the context of what is driving undesired behaviors, and gaining better control through a series of defenses that foster successful operations and encourage adaptability and resilience of the work process. This dual approach allows organizations to mitigate incident potential and proactively learn from everyday performance, promoting continuous improvement and a solid safety culture. Numerous opportunities exist to bolster risk reduction and ensure safety success.

What are the holes in your cheese, and what will you do about them?

Chapter 8

Safety Vision and Mission

If you do not know where you are going, any road will get you there.

— Lewis Caroll

Vision, mission, and understanding your safety purpose are essential elements of any great organizational culture. Every thriving culture that genuinely cares about its workers aspires to keep them safe. I am sure you have heard the phrase "Go slow to go fast." What that means for the safety practitioner is that you need to understand how to extend safety and build long lasting partnerships at the front line. You need to slow down to set the natural momentum for this work. So often, we start with the "how" of our roles as safety practitioners. Instead, consider the "why" of safety excellence and your role in helping make it happen.

Does your organization value safety? What makes safety the chief value among every other significant value in your organization?

Over the years, I have lost count of how many times I have asked senior leaders and safety practitioners to share with me and discuss their company's safety vision and mission. I am often met with puzzled expressions or just a restatement of the high-level corporate vision, with varying degrees of how it applies to safety. To get the leadership endorsement you need requires cultivating relationships, trust, and honesty. This is the beginning of your robust safety management system journey, even if it means taking a step back from your day-to-day activities. Knowing where you want to go, knowing the actions you will pursue to get there, and working with the front line to understand and endorse a shared vision and mission are essential. It means you will profoundly affect how everyone performs safely from that point forward, and it will be the anchor that will securely hold you in place when challenges arise.

Several years ago, I took over safety and health for a large organization, and one of my first activities was working with other safety practitioners to develop a new corporate safety vision. I was unsure whether I aspired to be part of the discussion after I failed to move the group past what I felt was a long, uphill battle with corporate speeches filled with short-sighted vision statements. It was not aspirational, and I wasn't inspired by it. The statement read: "As a company, we are to promote and support occupational safety and manage our safety and health program in a manner that seeks to eliminate occupational injuries and illnesses." Ugh. If our safety vision were to stop terrible things from happening to good people, why didn't we say so? We wrote a statement saying we wanted to seek things out, manage stuff, and hopefully eliminate bad things. I did not feel we committed much other than what we felt comfortable obtaining. If I was not inspired, how would the workforce be inspired?

In improving safety in the workplace, the first question to ask yourself is: What is our laser-focused vision for safety success? During Ronald Reagan's presidency, political commentator Richard Brookhiser famously described Reaganism as something that could fit on the back of a business card. Regan's vision and his mission merged into four words. "Defeat communism; lower taxes." I am sure being president was more complicated than that, but his aspirational vision and mission during his presidency were clear.

SAFETY VISION

Let us first define what we mean by "vision." In the simplest terms, it is a statement about where the organization is going. It is what the future looks like if you accomplish all your goals and activities. A vision statement is a long-term, ideological state of the future that does not yet exist. It is an inspiring rallying cry that invites everyone to contribute and become a part of it.

Here are a few companies you may be familiar with that have successful vision statements:

- Disney: "To be one of the world's leading producers and providers of entertainment and information."
- Amazon: "To be Earth's most customer-centric company."
- Google: "To provide access to the world's information in one click."

My familiarity with Amazon, thanks to the weekly arrival of packages at my doorstep, is influencing my opinion, but its vision statement is exceptional. I can find products I want and purchase them quickly, and it delivers them on time every time (with very few exceptions). If I am not satisfied, I can return my purchase with few questions asked and get a refund often before my purchase reaches their return center. Amazon focuses on customer delight, and I have been a committed customer for years.

There is a high probability that you are currently employed by an organization with an established corporate or business vision. Look at your organization's corporate vision as your starting point to understand it before you craft a laser-focused safety vision for your part of the organization.

This exercise should force you to ask this question: How does doing safety exceptionally well help deliver the organization's corporate vision?

I would also like to emphasize that it is your job to assist in leading, not to do all the work. Creating the organization's safety vision is a leadership exercise that belongs to those with at least three years of experience in leading but depends on cross-functional input to ensure widespread adoption. Those who value safety, such as senior-level leaders, mid-level managers, and select front-line workers, are necessary for crafting vision. Until we have honest conversations across the organization, debate our differences, agree, and endorse our shared vision, the work is only an aspiration you share with leadership.

As context, at Kimberly Clark, I collaborated with leaders who constantly challenged me to understand the "why" in everything I did or planned to do, and I am asking you to consider the same.

Why is worker safety critical to the success of our organization? Why do we even need safety vision?

I can answer this. The number of people who go home safely every day is the standard by which you measure everything. Yes, we do many other things, but our chief role is actively controlling the work environment and process to prevent or thoroughly mitigate injury and illness to an acceptable level. As I mentioned earlier, my job as a safety leader was to lead a process where injuries did not happen. That is our challenge, which means we need to be able to look into the future to identify what we want our safety culture to become.

When beginning this work, here are the key characteristics of a vision statement:

- Future-Oriented: A safety vision statement focuses on the future, describing the desired state or position that the organization aims to achieve over the long term. Think three to five years in the future.
- Inspiring and Motivational: A safety vision inspires and motivates your workers, customers, investors, and other stakeholders. A compelling vision statement should evoke enthusiasm and a sense of purpose.
- Clear and Concise: A safety vision statement is laser-focused and to the point. It will communicate the essence of the organization's vision, making it easy for people to understand and remember it.

- Aligned with Corporate Vision and Value Statements: The safety vision should reflect and support the organization's corporate vision and values.
- Ambitious Yet Attainable: The safety vision should be ambitious, forward-thinking, realistic, and attainable. It sets a challenging but achievable direction for the organization.
- Focused on Purpose: The safety vision statement goes beyond specific business objectives and addresses the purpose and effect of safety on the organization.
- Timeless: A well-crafted safety vision statement stays relevant over time, even as the organization grows and adapts to changes.

Reflecting again on my time at Kimberly-Clark, here is the first safety vision statement we created:

"To be the world's safest paper manufacturing facility."

That is short, concise, aspiring, effortlessly memorable, and laser-focused on where we were heading as an organization. When we created our safety vision, we were far from being the world's safest paper manufacturing facility. Still, we all woke up every day convinced we could deliver the vision. Our statement may look like many you have seen. However, the benefit of this work for me was watching the process unfold and taking part with senior-level leaders, mid-level managers, and workers from the front line in crafting a vision that captured the attention of our workforce. The challenge is that you cannot simply leave this at the safety vision stage. You must press forward to the next step by understanding your safety mission.

SAFETY MISSION

A company's safety mission statement is like a roadmap that directs its actions toward its vision. It is more like an actionable vision statement.

Mission statements help you define your immediate goals and maintain your focus on the plan.

Here are the mission statements of the organizations I mentioned earlier.

- Disney: "To entertain, inform, and inspire people around the globe through the power of unparalleled storytelling, reflecting the iconic brands, creative minds, and innovative technologies that make ours the world's premier entertainment company."
- Amazon: "To be Earth's most customer-centric company, where customers can find and discover anything they want to buy online."
- Google: "To organize the world's information and make it universally accessible and helpful."

Once more, contemplating Amazon's brief mission statement reveals much about their approach to realizing their vision. The company's mission is to make a wide range of products available for purchase and to use technology to put those products in front of customers in a way that makes them happy. I am always astonished that I can jump online, find anything I want, and even some things I did not know I wanted until I saw them, and have them on my doorstep a day after ordering.

Here was our safety mission statement at the Kimberly-Clark facility I was part of:

> *"Every day, we will be the world's safest paper manufacturing facility because of our capabilities, skills, and capacity."*

Our mission was to achieve our safety vision, and that would require a broad range of capabilities and skills in areas such as safety, quality, maintenance, and production. We were helping develop the best people by building their knowledge and skills to support our business. We wanted performance and were looking for everyone to give back part of themselves every day to help us improve and build robust processes. We were encouraging everyone to partner and own the work completely.

An important note to consider. I often tell those whom I mentor this: "Safety isn't safety. It is system effectiveness." In this context, the capabilities that best deliver safety success are deep and require knowledge and skills that support safety. You should be fully vested in how capable the workforce is in many other parts of your business, as they all have their risks and influence safety positively or negatively. Have you ever had a maintenance issue, a quality issue, or a production downtime issue that jeopardized the safety of your workers? I have no doubt you have.

Here is a story that comes to mind. A worker was injured at one of my facilities when he reached to grab a product from a solid surface conveyor system and caught two of his fingers in a drive belt. His fingers were struck when they dropped below the conveyor surface, resulting in a serious injury.

During my investigation, I found that maintenance had falsified their required equipment inspections and incorrectly marked the conveyor system as safe just hours before the incident. Pressure to increase production led to a situation where the maintenance team was reluctant to shut down the conveyor for repair. Essentially, the organization knowingly operated the equipment under hazardous conditions until an incident occurred.

After the incident, I discovered that maintenance, production, and even the safety team failed to protect the injured worker's safety. This incident underscores the need for collective responsibility in our safety processes. Your mission should capture everyone who touches the safety process. Here are some essential qualities of a mission statement:

- Identifies the Target Audience: It specifies the target audience or beneficiaries of the organization's products, services, or activities.

- Outlines Core Values: Mission statements include the core values and principles that guide the organization's behavior and decision-making.
- Conveys Scope: The mission statement shows the organization's operations, including the products, services, or solutions it provides.
- Inspires and Motivates: Like a vision statement, a well-crafted mission statement inspires and motivates workers, stakeholders, and customers by providing a sense of purpose.
- Puts Forward Specific Actions: While concise, a mission statement should be specific and actionable, giving a clear sense of the organization's primary activities.
- Guides Decision-Making: The mission statement guides decision-making within the organization, helping align actions with the overall purpose.

CRAFTING THE SAFETY VISION AND MISSION

- Look for natural safety champions in your organization and assemble a "vision and mission team." Take the time to create a team of dedicated colleagues from all levels of the organization who share your passion for and dedication to safety.
- Seek multiple perspectives. Assess your organization from top to bottom and inside out. Ask workers what motivates and inspires their commitment to safety and whether the current safety vision aligns with their perspectives. Gather external feedback, and do not be discouraged if comments from the manufacturing floor do not align with comments from the front office.
- Review your organization's safety performance and objectives before crafting the safety vision and mission.
- Once the safety vision and mission statement are complete, try a draft version with workers, other safety practitioners, and colleagues outside your organization. Remember, if the statement

does not inspire, it will not work. By sharing drafts, you will work toward gathering support for your vision and mission.

- Since your laser-focused safety vision and mission statement are values-based, endorsement from others is crucial. The stamp of approval signifies the collective agreement to help you realize the vision. Many grand visions have failed because of poor endorsement practices. If the vision is done right, however, you can move past a workforce of safety participants to a workforce of safety partners who help sponsor and actualize the vision.

- Finally, communicate the safety vision and mission broadly throughout the organization. Post it in areas where people can see it and include it in relevant worker content. Consider beginning team meetings by periodically restating your safety vision and mission. The key is to be creative and to ensure that your safety vision is always top of mind in your organization.

YOUR PERSONAL SAFETY MISSION

Here is another question: Have you considered your personal mission as a safety practitioner and leader? What does it reveal about you? We have discussed organizational vision and mission, but it is vital to understand your leadership role in making them happen. I am an ardent fan of John Maxwell, an author, speaker, and pastor who has spent over forty years authoring best-selling books on leadership. My bookshelves are filled with his books, and I read, reread, and reflect on his straightforward but essential values-based instructions.

We should develop an organizational safety vision and mission because they are valuable to organizational success. However, it is equally essential for you to work on your personal mission to support your work.

John Maxwell mentioned his own personal mission in an article he posted several years ago. He called them his twelve simple words that serve as a daily reminder (Maxwell, 2016).

"Every day, I add value to leaders who multiply value to others."

Then, he described his "Rule of Five" as the method he actively used to pursue his mission statement.

- Every day, I value people.
- Every day, I think of ways to add value to people.
- Every day, I look for ways to add value to people.
- Every day, I do things that add value to people.
- Every day, I encourage others to add value to people.

This sounds remarkably similar to how I described how I like to work in the book's second chapter. I prefer to function as a servant leader. Understanding John Maxwell's mission became a cut-and-paste activity because it describes how I choose to live out my purpose at work and in my personal life. I have learned to prioritize serving others over my interests, which can be difficult, especially as a safety practitioner. I have learned to focus on building, training, enabling, supporting, and establishing relationships with people rather than controlling or directing them.

Having said that, I am imperfect, and I sometimes catch myself not always upholding my personal mission. Still, I have learned to add value and extend leadership opportunities, especially at the front line. Working this way is a pivotal part of the safety success I want to bring to my organization.

What is your mission, and how will you contribute to the success of your organization?

CLOSING

Yogi Berra said, "You've got to be very careful if you don't know where you are going because you might not get there" (Berra, n.d.). It took me a while to unravel his thoughts, but Yogi may have hit it out of the proverbial ballpark with that statement. Over the years, I have watched many safety practitioners work from a "to-do" list, correcting failures rather than embracing and leading safety in their organizations. While there may be valid justifications for operating in this manner, depending solely on correction after the fact will never get you where you want to go. Your organization needs clarity, or it will suffer along a path that wanders between reactive and dependent parts of your cultural journey.

Safety begins with an aspirational and inspirational look at the future. It continues with a safety mission and how the company will pursue its vision. Without either, safety success will likely be limited. Our role is to be technically proficient and to inspire, energize, and motivate others to achieve success and add value.

If I visit your organization, could you describe your safety vision and mission succinctly? Would I recognize your values for safety and the roadmap that will get you there? Have you landed on your personal mission?

In the next chapter, I will discuss safety purpose as the clear expression of safety in your organization, as well as the principles and behaviors that support every safety action. From now on, we will go deeper into the organization, where feedback and endorsement loops from the front line have the greatest effect.

Chapter 9

Safety Purpose, Principles, Policies, and Rules

*Policies are many, principles are few, policies
will change, principles never do.*

— JOHN MAXWELL

You might be thinking by now that much of the work I am writing about, especially the organizational stuff, is someone else's work. Yes, it could be the work of the senior leadership team in your organization, but you should not give away helping lead and being part of this work. Much of your success is how you extend your reach to the front-line workers. That means you are creating an organizational environment in which purpose, principles, and concise rules create a self-managing work culture. Your workforce needs to understand clearly what they need to do to be safe, and you have to inspire them to own that work.

Safety can be like bowling. I have never been great at bowling. Rolling a heavy ball down a 60-foot-long, 42-inch-wide wooden lane to the exact spot I want to hit is daunting. Sometimes, I get lucky and roll a strike, but you will likely find me in the gutter. Bowling can be very frustrating if you know you will likely wind up in the gutter. I have also noticed that when small children are bowling, the bowling alley operator will often install bumpers that fill the gutters. When the children roll the ball poorly, it will hit a bumper and self-correct until it strikes a pin. The difference between happiness and great sadness is a well-placed bumper. Leading and managing safety sometimes feels like bowling without the bumpers, but it does not have to be that way.

Rules are quite common in the work of the safety practitioner; much of your work probably involves developing policies and rules based on mandatory regulations. For many, it is the natural fallback plan to control safety risks in the work environment.

My time leading my first paper manufacturing facility taught me quite a lot about how to think about policy and rule development, why they exist, and the large gray area surrounding the work that policies or rules did not govern. In an earlier chapter, I shared a story about the expectations of the plant manager who led that operation. If you remember, he told me, "I want to run a paper mill where no one is ever hurt. Can you do that?" Then he said he did not want me to write many safety policies or rules for the organization. His premise was that if we developed people correctly and made them more capable of doing their jobs, they did not need rules. Yes, it was another one of those episodes that created this uncomfortable and awkward moment between us. My first thought was that I did not know how to meet regulatory requirements or mitigate risk without rules, so that could not happen. My second thought was that his challenge was worthy of consideration because I had already been part of writing overly complex and comprehensive rules in the past. I am sure you have too. Once we write them, we have to police them, which seems endless, and that alone is a sign that we need to improve how we look at such work. A lengthy list of comprehensive rules feels like our role, but it is not. For most workers, rules can be a hindrance. Complex rules lead to confusion, non-compliance, and a lack of effectiveness. They are also administrative controls and closer to the bottom of the hierarchy of controls, meaning they possibly won't guarantee better safety performance. Our job is to lead with a safety purpose based on principles. Once you can do that, you can consider policy and rulemaking for the areas of control that make sense or are necessary because of regulations or internal standards. Even then, you need to write and communicate them simply, clearly, and concisely.

You might be a fantastic bowler, never land in the gutter, and be a skilled safety practitioner. Still, you are leading a workforce that does not have your expertise or experience, and they also have an abundance of other operational responsibilities in their job, so they need the bumpers. A safety purpose supported by principles and simple rules are the bumpers that keep your workers going down the right lane. If an errant ball rolls in the wrong direction, the process nudges it back to the correct path.

SAFETY PURPOSE

Both vision and mission are essential for creating tangible results. The piece that will tie this all together is getting clear on leading with purpose and defining how it shows up daily.

In this context, "purpose" is the sense and feeling of resolve or determination. In my experience, the best way to find an organization's purpose is to ask questions. Why are you doing the work you are doing?" "What significant problems are you solving, or what work are you championing?" "If you don't do it, what are the consequences? Who loses?" And finally, "Why do you show up for this company and not the one down the street?"

Digging into an organization's morals, ethics, and beliefs can help deliver a purpose worth working for. If you cannot define it at its core, you have work to do. Most morale problems fester here because of an ill-defined or, worse yet, nonexistent purpose. When a solid human brand leads people to a conversation that says, without hesitation, "I love my job, I love what I do, I love the value we bring to our customers, I love my company, and I love the people I work for and with," their purpose is usually at the center.

Vision is the picture. The mission is the road map to get there. Purpose is the feeling everyone has when you are accomplishing what you set out to do. The organization's purpose is what you have in place that drives the values you appreciate and, in turn, creates an evolving human-centric culture. This idea of purpose and associated behaviors creates the feeling we want, not only when we have accomplished the big goals and achieved the desired outcomes, but also in the work process.

It will always be about how we want to feel. The people on the front line will always be at the core of those feelings. A purpose statement seems overly simple and, to some, unnecessary. Still, it serves as a clear expression of the reasons for safety in the organization you lead. A well-documented purpose will lead to abundant conversations about how to face your safety challenges. It will articulate the fundamental goals and harken to your vision statement in a way that guides the actions and decisions of people, from the senior leaders' offices to the front line.

Again, it's your work to help lead, not to do all the work, meaning that developing the organization's purpose for safety is a shared responsibility. Yes, I had a senior leadership team driving exceedingly lofty expectations for a robust safety purpose in my organization. They had firm ideas about what our safety purpose should be. Still, until we could have honest conversations across the organization, debate our differences, reach an agreement, and endorse our shared purpose, the work was simply words on paper.

This brings me to the next point. Your feedback loop should focus on understanding workers, where much of your safety risk is, and where success matters most. Your work comes to life on the front lines. The front-line worker will tell you things that supervisors and senior leaders cannot, and they will also share what they are willing to do and are not willing to do. I want to be clear: Do not exclude anyone in your organization from this work. However, recognize that the front line is probably where most of your losses will occur, so front-line feedback is extremely valuable.

Again, from my time at Kimberly Clark, much of my work started with understanding, communicating, and ensuring we lived our shared safety purpose.

Here was the first purpose statement from my time there.

> *"To create a work environment, culture, and an absolute belief in every one of us that we can and will achieve and manage a 100% injury-free workplace."*

We followed our purpose statement with statements of intention on how we would meet our safety purpose.

We would perform our work in a way that:

- Established responsibility for a safe workplace at the individual and team level.
- Focused on eliminating an environment that promotes injury rather than just meeting regulatory requirements.
- Established team and individual accountability to confront and eliminate unsafe behaviors and conditions.

Here are some ways you can successfully begin work for your organization's safety purpose.

- Understand the opportunity: Focus on an opportunity that improves the work system or solves a problem. What do you most desire to solve in safety, and can you describe it in one or two sentences?
- Leverage the power of the team: As mentioned, this group exercise requires conversation, debate, and endorsement. A safety purpose is the intended desire or the reason "we" exist to achieve something, not simply your personal desire.

- Agree on the solution: What is the chief outcome of reaching your safety purpose? Can you clearly describe the actions you will take to pursue the opportunity?
- Promote the benefits: What will happen when we meet our purpose? This element becomes your go-to concise (elevator) speech on what success looks like in your organization and what the positive outcomes will be. Trust me; you will repeatedly use your safety purpose statement and make it part of whom your team will become, so you need to be able to remember it and replay it often.

Now, go back to the safety purpose and intention statements above. In a few concise sentences, you know exactly what the purpose was for my organization. You can see that our overall goal was to ensure people returned home safe and healthy every day. I didn't write it. It came from a team of people from across the facility, from the front line to the senior leader's office, agreeing on success outcomes and helping workers understand why we were asking them to be their personal best.

Your safety purpose does not have a charted plan but must clearly and concisely communicate an overall path toward success. What is the purpose of safety for your organization?

SAFETY PRINCIPLES

Safety principles are the next granular level of expressing safety value. They are the overarching behaviors that support the organization's safety purpose. They are the foundation from which most other work begins. Everything of value starts with a test against your safety purpose and principles. If you get them right and include workers in the process of forming them, they help workers make decisions independently.

Why do I want you to do this work? Because it fosters partnership and interdependence throughout the organization, especially at the front line, where it matters most.

We can perform safely because we can agree on our principles. It also goes back to the challenge that we cannot write policies and rules for every situation a worker will face. There will be moments when workers must decide outside of a written rule, and safety principles help guide such decision-making. Remember, this work is not yours. It is your work to help lead the group exercise that requires conversation, debate, and endorsement from the senior leader's office out to the front line. Your safety purpose is the reason "we" exist as an organization, and safety principles are how "we" will meet those desires.

During my time in the paper manufacturing facility, the work was to support our safety purpose with safety principles that ensured we would exhibit the right behaviors and make the correct decisions. Through simple tenets, we gave decision rights to everyone, authorized every worker to make the best safety decision without question, erased titles and authority when it came to safety, and slowed down or stopped the work operation if we were unsure it was safe. As a side note, one of the significant things about a paper manufacturing facility is that it rarely shuts down unless there is a considerable amount of planning. Unless there is a breakdown or unplanned outage, paper manufacturing is a 24/7/365 operation. At our organization, from the front line to the senior leader's office, we said production operations would never be as important as keeping our workers safe. That happens when you align on safety vision, mission, purpose, and principles. Our principles governed everything we did. There were only three, but they covered almost everything we faced daily. Here were our safety principles:

- *Any person can and must confront unsafe behaviors and conditions. No one is authorized to disregard such a warning.*
- *No one is expected to perform any function or accept any direction that they believe is unsafe to themselves or others or creates an unsafe situation, regardless of who directs such an action.*

- *Anyone who feels that a process is unsafe will shut down that process and work with appropriate team members to create a safe situation.*

I caution you that copying and applying these safety principles above to your organization would be a mistake. Although they would cure many ills, the most significant benefit is the conversation and debate about the safety principles that will matter most to your organization. Without comprehensive agreement and endorsement, principles are insignificant to the workers who must embrace and apply them.

Here are some strategies to help you get started on this exercise:

- Understand the organization: Know your safety vision, your mission, and the core purposes that drive your organization.
- Involve critical stakeholders: Engage key stakeholders, especially front-line workers, supervisors, and senior leaders. Gather input and perspectives to understand the organization's values comprehensively.
- Define core values: Identify the fundamental values essential for your organization's safety. Ensure that these values reflect the beliefs and priorities of the organization, and assess them against your safety vision and purpose.
- Articulate clear statements: Express each principle clearly and concisely. Use language that all members of the organization can easily understand. Make sure each principle is specific and actionable.
- Prioritize principles: Keep principles to the critical few, and prioritize them based on their importance and relevance to the organization's vision, mission, and purpose.
- Consider organizational culture: Consider the organization's existing culture. Principles should resonate with and contribute to the current culture, or you can use them to shift it in the desired direction.

- Communicate effectively: Communicate the safety principles to all organization members through internal communications, training sessions, or other appropriate channels.
- Integrate your principles of decision-making: Guide behavior and actions at all levels by integrating these principles into daily decision-making processes.
- Review and update: Periodically review and, if necessary, update the safety principles to ensure they remain relevant and aligned with the organization's evolving needs and goals.

Safety principles shouldn't be exhaustive, and their application may vary depending on the industry, context, and specific risks involved. They should be memorable. In our facility, I could ask anyone about our safety principles, and they could easily recite them without much effort at all. I firmly believe that sound safety principles provide a solid foundation for developing and promoting a comprehensive approach to safety.

POLICY AND RULE MAKING

Policies and rules can help shape the culture and influence behavior in the organization by providing clarity and consistency to workers in their day-to-day activities. They offer a roadmap for navigating the complexities of the workplace, ensuring that workers understand regulatory compliance and risk management. By setting clear expectations, policies and rules become a cornerstone of accountability, fostering a sense of responsibility among workers for their actions. Clear and straightforward guidelines ensure that every organization member, regardless of background or experience, can easily understand and adhere to established protocols.

At Kimberly Clark, leadership challenged me to limit the number of policies and rules and to simplify the ones that remained. This was the right approach. Let's face it: safety policies and regulations are fragile, usually because they are too complex to understand or because workers do not realize the purpose of specific rules. Yes, it is challenging to remove or simplify regulations and policies. However, doing so facilitates better understanding and stronger compliance, as workers are more likely to remember and follow the rules if there are fewer of them. Moreover, simplicity reduces the likelihood of errors in interpretation and application, streamlining operations and saving time and resources. Simple regulations and policies adapt to changes in the business environment and quickly become part of the organizational culture. The value of simplicity lies in its ability to foster clarity, accessibility, and efficiency, contributing to the overall success and cohesiveness of the organization.

Here are some strategies for creating effective policies and rules:

- Challenge existing policies and rules: Policies and rules grow over time, but you should also review them to see whether they're obsolete. Review regulations to understand whether you still need them, and remove those no longer needed.
- Solicit feedback: Seek feedback from the workers or individuals for whom you created the safety policies and rules. Ask for input on clarity and practicality and use this feedback to make improvements.
- Prioritize critical policies and rules: Identify the most critical safety policies and rules that address high-risk activities or potential hazards. Review past losses, adverse event reporting, and regulations, and focus on those that have the most significant effect on overall safety.
- Consolidate and combine policies and rules: Look for opportunities to consolidate or combine policies and rules that cover associated topics. This can help reduce redundancy and make such directives more digestible.
- Simplify policy and rule language: Your rules affect many front-line workers, so simplify the language. Avoid technical

jargon and use straightforward terms that everyone quickly understands.

- Incorporate policies and rules in routine safety training: Provide training sessions to explain and clarify complex policies and rules. Use real-world examples to illustrate how the policies and regulations apply in specific situations. Your workers face many daily obstacles and responsibilities, and written documentation is often not a priority. Using creative training approaches will help.
- Provide visual aids: Use visual aids such as infographics, diagrams, and flowcharts to supplement written policies and rules. Visual representations can enhance understanding and serve as quick references.
- Create a summary or quick guide: Develop references that distill the most critical safety policies and rules. This can serve as a handy reference or job aid.

Remember, the goal is not to have an overwhelming number of policies or rules but to establish a practical and effective set of guidelines that contributes administratively to a safe environment. Keeping safety policies and regulations simple, clear, and focused on critical priorities is vital to supporting the front line and ensuring your organization meets regulatory compliance. They assist in good decision-making to remain safe in the work environment.

CLOSING

Understanding your safety purpose and the principles you embrace as a team is the launch pad for much of your work going forward. The safety policies and rules you develop are pivotal in supporting the foundation for compliance and risk mitigation. In the previous chapter, I shared how your safety vision and mission started this journey. That, combined with what I have shared in this chapter encapsulates the core of what you can become as an organization and how your workers will conduct themselves. Now, let us move on to putting these thoughts into action.

Chapter 10:

Safety Management System Led Strategy

A vision without a strategy remains an illusion.

— Jim Rohn

Now that you know where you want to go and the behaviors you need to support to get there, you need to think about how you will accomplish the lofty safety vision, mission, and purpose while embracing the principles that support them. To do that, you need a strategy for your safety system. You have discovered by now that I ask many questions. I encourage you to do the same and to become more curious. When figuring out how an organization conducts or needs to pursue its work, I often ask these questions:

1. Can you describe your safety management system and the supportive strategy?
2. What losses or challenges are you trying to eliminate or reduce, and are you involving front-line workers in developing your strategy and plans to do that?
3. Will leadership's organizational strategy help you achieve your safety success?

Developing a strategy that considers a robust and integrated safety management system (SMS) as a major driver for much of this work is essential. Safety practitioners often prioritize regulatory compliance as their organization's strategy. Our fundamental duty is to protect the health and safety of workers, but how we do that is complicated. Compliance is necessary, but it's not the goal. A well-defined safety strategy exceeds regulatory compliance and supports operational continuity. A safe workplace helps reduce financial costs associated with accidents, injuries, process losses, and legal proceedings, which supports financial stability. Workers feel safe and secure, which leads to job satisfaction, resulting in increased productivity and better quality. It also supports a strong brand image and trust among workers, customers, and the community. All of this is critical to measuring safety success.

An effective SMS is the key to reaching your safety objectives. You must have a method to proactively identify the risks that could prevent you from reaching your vision and milestone performance targets. A well-designed management system helps establish objectives and promotes continuous improvement and performance measures. It enhances communication and coordination across the organization, which fosters a collaborative environment. Moreover, it promotes adaptability to changing circumstances and proactive responses to challenges. Engaging stakeholders, including workers, customers, and investors, becomes more seamless, fostering a sense of shared purpose. It facilitates a culture of continuous learning and innovation by integrating feedback, analysis, and lessons learned into the strategic planning process while helping you navigate complexities. By now, you've seen that I follow a similar path and rarely develop or implement plans without input from the front-line worker. Safety strategies affect front-line workers more than they do any other group, so we need to get them on board. We need them and everyone else in the organization to help create and endorse the safety strategy. Let's look at the path for this work.

MANAGEMENT SYSTEM INTEGRATION

When you do a good job of managing safety and health, there is almost always a positive bump in the performance of the rest of the organization. Integrating safety into the business management system improves quality, increases production, aligns maintenance expenses with the plan, and improves worker morale, among other benefits like returning a financial benefit to the company. The organization's safety strategy should parallel how you develop strategies for the distinct parts of your business. However, if you are new to using the safety management system to support strategy planning, or if you are new to using management systems in your organization, you have work to do. A successful safety strategy is not another item on your to-do list. The success of safety efforts decreases as they become more separate from day-to-day functions. Programs and processes that do not mesh into the fabric of daily activities are seldom successful, or they become unsustainable. Integrating safety, quality, maintenance, and operational management systems is vital for many reasons. Simply put, your management system has multiple dependencies, and a change to one part of the management system commonly affects the other parts.

These key factors sum up the effect of integrating management systems:

- It enables an integrated approach to organizational management.
- It leads to increased efficiency and streamlines processes.
- It helps identify, assess, and manage risks across safety, quality, maintenance, and operations management, enabling a better understanding of system-wide risks.
- It can save costs by eliminating duplicate efforts, reducing waste, and optimizing resource allocation.
- It promotes better communication and collaboration among different departments and teams, meaning it reaches the front line.

- It aids in maintaining consistent compliance with safety, quality, maintenance, and operational standards, thus reducing the risk of regulatory violations.
- It ensures that products or services meet or exceed customer expectations.
- It supports continuous improvement to learn from experiences in different areas, implement corrective and preventive actions, and drive ongoing improvements.
- It enhances organizational resilience by enabling effective responses to changes in the business environment, market conditions, or regulatory requirements.
- It optimizes organizational performance. The integrated approach enhances the organization's success and sustainability in a dynamic and competitive business environment.

A well-defined management system built on a recognized framework is necessary to identify strengths and areas for improvement. It should ensure the precise definition and alignment of organizational objectives and goals with the overall strategy. Choosing a management system is incredibly important, especially given the importance of integration.

Here are a few more points to think about.

- Engaging stakeholders is crucial for organizational success. A management system enables communication with stakeholders, including front-line workers, at every level. Their perspectives and concerns are critical when you plan and execute the organizational strategy.
- An effective management system fosters a culture of ongoing learning and innovation. You must gather feedback and analyze performance metrics to incorporate them into strategic planning for evolution and growth.

SAFETY MANAGEMENT SYSTEMS

Regarding safety management systems, ISO 45001 and ANSI Z10 are invaluable for the systematic approaches they provide. Both standards emphasize the importance of worker participation and inclusion, advocate worker partnerships, and promote safety at the front line.

ISO 45001

ISO 45001:2018 Occupational Health and Safety Management Systems: Requirements with Guidance for Use is an international standard for managing occupational health and safety. The International Organization for Standardization (ISO) developed it to assist organizations in establishing and maintaining efficient occupational health and safety management systems following specific elements as shown below in Figure 1.

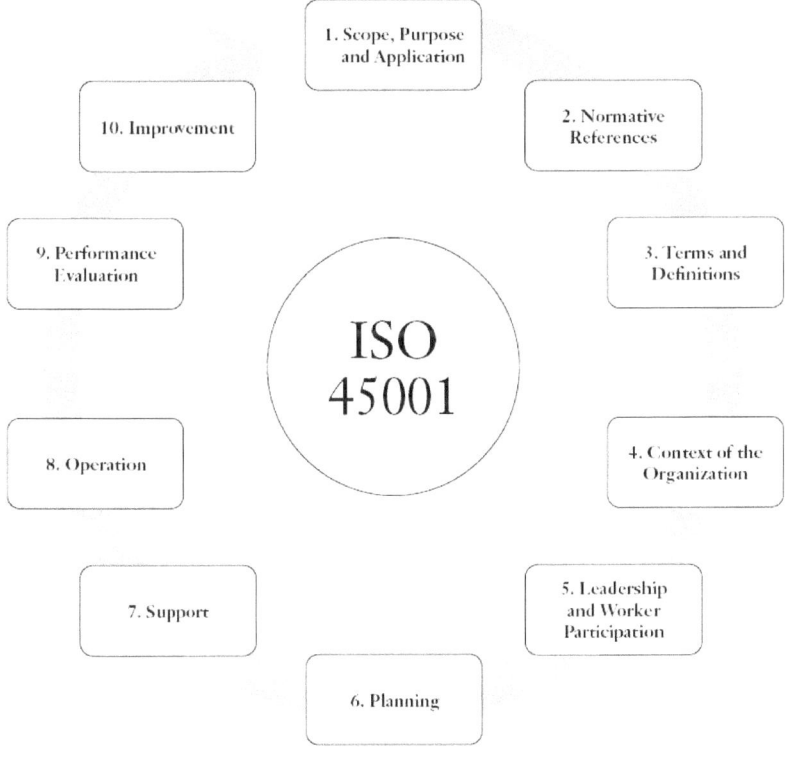

Figure 1: ISO 45001

ISO 45001 replaced OHSAS 18001 and follows the High-Level Structure (HLS) used by other ISO management system standards. This alignment has facilitated the integration of multiple management systems for organizations.

ANSI Z10

ANSI developed ANSI/ASSP Z10-2019: Occupational Health and Safety Management for occupational health and safety management systems. It covers various occupational health and safety aspects, including policy development, planning, implementation, evaluation, corrective actions, and other elements, as shown below in Figure 2.

Figure 2: ANSI Z10

ISO 45001 and ANSI/ASSP Z10-2019 offer solid frameworks for OH&S management systems.

Let's explore the critical similarities between ISO 45001 and ANSI Z10. Both standards:

- Endorse a systematic approach to managing occupational health and safety,
- Emphasize the importance of leadership commitment to occupational health and safety,
- Recognize the importance of involving workers in developing and implementing the occupational health and safety management system,
- Emphasize the need for active worker participation and communication to improve the system's effectiveness,
- Promote a culture of continuous improvement,
- Encourage organizations to monitor and evaluate their OH&S performance, and
- Emphasize the need to systematically identify hazards, assess risks, and implement controls to mitigate or eliminate those risks.

While there are similarities, it is essential to note that there are also differences between the two standards. Chart 1 below includes these differences in terminology, specific requirements, and structure. Organizations looking to implement an occupational health and safety management system should carefully review both standards to determine which aligns better with their needs and regulatory environment.

COMPARISON OF ANSI Z10 AND ISO 45001 OCCUPATIONAL HEALTH AND SAFETY MANAGEMENT SYSTEM STANDARDS		
ANSI Z10	**OR**	**ISO 45001**
• Comprehensive, system-based standard.	PRIMARY FOCUS	• A global standard for OSH management systems.
• Designed to align with ISO 45001 for organizations desiring conformance with both standards. • Considered the gold standard of OHSMS in the United States.	UNIQUE CHARACTERISTICS	• Can help create a global foundation of worker safety standards and inspections that can be used by all global supply chains covering contractors and subcontractors in every country that supply products, into these supply chains.
• Not being currently used by certification bodies.	CERTIFICATION	• Developed with the goal of certification along the lines of other management systems standards such as ISO 9001 and ISO 14001.
• Easier to understand and implement, based on United States business practices, legal system, and union/management relations.	EASE OF USE	• With 64 countries involved, consideration was given to a wide array of cultures, business practices and legal systems.
• Only available in English.	LANGUAGE	• Written in International English. Language compromises were necessary to accommodate translation and practices in countries around the world. This standard is available in many languages.
• Provides flexibility in tailoring its requirements to an organization's.	FLEXIBILITY AND SCALABILITY	• Does have some flexibility but is more specific in some sections.
• Includes an occupational health section with a strong emphasis on health.	OCCUPATIONAL HEALTH	• Not as focused on occupational health as the Z10 Standard.
• Emphasis on worker participation.	WORKER PARTICIPATION	• Emphasis on worker participation.
• A guidance and implementation manual is available.	IMPLEMENTATION AND SUPPORT	• A guidance and implementation manual is available.

Chart 1

Here are a few crucial variations between ISO 45001 and ANSI Z10.

- The ISO, a global organization, developed ISO 45001 as an international standard. Organizations around the world have adopted it and recognize its value. The American National Standards Institute (ANSI) and the American Society of Safety Professionals (ASSP) developed ANSI/ASSP Z10-2019 as an

American standard. Although influential in the United States, it is not as globally recognized as ISO 45001.

- ISO 45001 uses the HLS, which is common to other ISO management system standards, such as ISO 9001 and ISO 14001. This makes it easier to integrate with other ISO management systems. The ISO HLS has a different structure and format from those of ANSI Z10.

- The terminology in ISO 45001 is different from that in ANSI Z10. The variation in terms and definitions between the two standards can influence how organizations interpret and implement certain concepts.

- Following ISO 45001, organizations must establish procedures to ensure awareness of and adherence to applicable legal and occupational health and safety requirements. ANSI Z10 prioritizes legal compliance but does not explicitly mandate a process for evaluating and ensuring compliance with legal and regulatory requirements.

- Risk assessment is essential to both standards, but the specific requirements and approaches vary.

- ISO 45001 includes requirements for internal audits to assess the effectiveness of the OH&S management system, and certification bodies can accredit this system through system auditing. Meanwhile, ANSI Z10 does not have specific audit requirements.

- Both standards highlight the importance of worker participation in occupational health and safety, but the specific requirements and expectations for worker involvement differ.

As a safety practitioner, you should carefully review each standard's requirements, considering their organizational context, your regulatory environment, and the strategic goals you want to establish. This will help you determine which framework is more suitable for your needs. Some organizations may align with one format, while others may integrate elements from both standards to develop a comprehensive occupational health and safety management system.

An important consideration is that a management system is an internal framework to manage processes and activities effectively. At the same time, regulatory compliance involves meeting external laws, regulations, and standards requirements. A well-implemented management system can help you achieve and demonstrate regulatory compliance by providing a structured approach to meeting internal and external obligations. Still, a management system framework does not usually replace the need to satisfy regulatory standards and requirements.

As I have demonstrated above, there is a high degree of overlap between ISO 45001 and ANSI Z10, and there are even hybrid management system approaches you may consider. However, the basic principles behind effective safety management—process improvement, worker participation and training, risk assessment, and control—have not changed. Regardless of the selected framework, success depends upon management support, worker involvement, a willingness to analyze hazards, and a willingness to make changes when necessary.

THE ROLE OF THE FRONT LINE

Including front-line workers in developing and implementing safety strategies is crucial for the success and sustainability of the safety process. Since they are directly engaged in day-to-day operations, front-line workers possess invaluable insights into their work's practical aspects, challenges, and improvement areas. The management team might not be aware of the value of this distinctive perspective, but accessing it can give you realistic and implementable strategies. It is vital that your strategy pushes your organization to reach more, but not to the point at which your safety strategy seems impossible to achieve. Moreover, and most importantly, this inclusive approach encourages a sense of partnership and motivates front-line workers to actively contribute to the organization's safety vision. Their participation creates a shared responsibility for the strategy's success, as they recognize the connection between their contributions and the organization's progress toward its goals. Including the front line in developing strategy improves decision-making quality and fosters a collaborative and empowered workforce, creating a foundation for a resilient and adaptive organization. It is a cultural lever. Workers must feel that their input is valuable, which is essential for a collaborative safety culture to thrive.

Here are a few strategic points to consider when working on a safety strategy with front-line workers:

- Connect the front line with your organizational commitment to safety. Demonstrate your investments in technology, training, and protocols that protect them. Use real-life examples and case studies to engage front-line workers and show them how the SMS prevents accidents and mitigates risks. Also, explain the organization's prevention plans for adverse events.

- Provide management system training. Training front-line workers on the importance of the SMS is critical to fostering an organization's safety culture. Start by laying the groundwork with fundamental concepts, outlining the SMS's objectives, and emphasizing its direct impact on their well-being.

- Recognize expertise where you find it. Acknowledge that front-line workers possess valuable knowledge about the practical aspects of their work. Recognize their expertise in identifying potential risks in the work environment and developing effective safety measures to include in safety strategy planning.

- Form safety committees and safety project teams. Representatives from various departments and levels, including front-line workers, hold regular meetings to discuss safety issues, review incidents, and brainstorm solutions.

- Conduct regular safety inspections and audits. Incorporate using front-line workers to identify hazards and practices for improvement. As a safety practitioner, you want to begin teaching risk assessment methods to your front-line workers to increase their understanding of safety risks and the development of specific control strategies.

- Establish a system for front-line workers to provide feedback on safety protocols, equipment, and procedures. Foster a culture that encourages communication, in which everyone feels comfortable sharing their thoughts and concerns.
- Promote open communication channels. Open communication is the cornerstone of any successful safety strategy. It facilitates the free flow of information, allowing for the identification of management system gaps and the development of an adequate safety strategy to fill those gaps. Workers who feel that information is shared transparently are more likely to participate actively.

LIVING IN ENDORSEMENT

Everything you do as a safety practitioner should be based on the broad endorsement of the activities you want to implement. When you endorse a person, idea, product, or initiative, you give it your formal or official backing. It would be best if you had the front line's endorsement, alignment, and agreement for much of the work you have planned to do.

Endorsement carries weight and credibility, as it signifies the organization's collective decision or stance. It does not mean, however, that everyone agrees with everything. I have endorsed plenty of activities while not agreeing with everything they include. Yes, it can sometimes be challenging, but it is not uncommon. Gaining endorsement from the front line means you are open, transparent, and ready to discuss their reservations about your planned activity. This type of communication often leads to a more acceptable compromise or adjustment to the idea. Debates and honest conversations are healthy aspects of effective organizational decision-making.

Here are some ideas to consider:

- Sometimes, it might be necessary to endorse a collective idea to foster team unity, collaboration, and professionalism. Can you inspire the front line to see an idea's value and overcome their skepticism?
- At times, there are long-term implications for an idea. Although workers may disagree with it in the short term, can you communicate it effectively, looking outward to your safety vision or as part of a larger strategy?
- Allow constructive feedback to improve the idea. This shows that you are engaged in the process and value their opinions to contribute positively. Are you open to hearing feedback?
- Clearly define your plan's purpose, goals, and expected outcomes.
- Identify and build positive relationships with critical stakeholders who influence decision-making.
- Craft a persuasive message tailored to resonate with the values of your workers and address any potential concerns.
- Provide supporting evidence, data, and examples to strengthen the feasibility and success of your proposal.
- Seek feedback from colleagues or mentors before formally presenting your plan, and be open to adapting based on the input you receive.
- Follow up with stakeholders to address any remaining questions, and express gratitude for their time and consideration.

CLOSING

Integrating ISO 45001 or ANSI Z10 offers organizations a solid framework to develop a successful safety strategy. By considering an integrated approach that considers the strengths of these standards, your organization can create a plan that promotes leadership commitment, encourages worker participation, manages risks effectively, continuously strives for improvement, and delivers a seamless management system and strategy. By engaging front-line workers in the creation and execution of a safety management system-led strategy, you access their valuable knowledge and foster a more robust dedication to safety within the organization. The use of this collaborative approach can result in a caring, protective work culture that is both more effective and more sustainable. Front-line workers are vital. Their close involvement in day-to-day operations makes them crucial contributors to safety and setting strategies that prioritize the well-being of all employees. By empowering front-line workers to take ownership of safety protocols and procedures, organizations can benefit from their unique perspectives and experiences. This collaborative effort enhances safety measures and cultivates a sense of accountability and responsibility among all team members. Ultimately, the inclusion of front-line workers in safety management strategies helps create a workplace environment that is proactive, innovative, and focused on continuous improvement.

Chapter 11:

Organizational and Personal Safety Objectives

Setting goals is the first step in turning the invisible into the visible.

— TONY ROBBINS

So far, I have prepared you to lead and urged you to think about what success looks like as you plan and develop your safety process using a robust safety management framework. This will help you reach your organization's safety vision and mission. However, this will happen only if you are pursuing the right objectives, which I believe is crucial for achieving success in safety. Setting clear and specific goals provides direction and focus for your safety initiatives. By defining your objectives and aligning them with your organization's safety vision, purpose, and mission, you can ensure your efforts are purposeful and effective. Remember, success in safety management is not just about meeting compliance standards; it is about creating a culture of safety that protects and values every individual in your organization. The organization performs best when everyone is on board and committed to upholding safety standards and practices. By fostering a culture where safety is a chief value, you can create a workplace that is compliant with regulations and promotes all employees' well-being and productivity.

I cannot overstate the importance of safety objectives, especially considering the profound effect of workplace accidents on individuals and organizations. Success does not happen by chance, and I don't believe it will happen by simply doing work to meet safety regulations. For over a decade in the United States, we have seen a plateau in eliminating fatalities in the workplace. According to the Bureau of Legal Statistics, in 2022, 5,486 deaths were reported in the workplace, showing no improvement and an actual 5.7-percent increase from the 5,190 fatalities reported in 2021. A worker died every ninety-six minutes in the United States from a work-related injury in 2022, which is the most recent reporting year as I write this. In Great Britain, in 2022–2023, 135 workers died from injuries at their workplace, more than in the previous year. In reviewing fatalities throughout Great Britain over the past decade, there has been marginal improvement, but not enough that we can be satisfied that suitable controls are in place to eliminate workplace death. According to workplace fatality reporting in the European Union, they have experienced improvement. Still, progress is slowing, and they have yet to gain their desired level of control.

I have reviewed many other governmental reports that show similar challenges. Still, regardless of geographic location, as safety practitioners, we cannot be satisfied knowing that workers are still losing their lives at work. It is simply improbable that pursuing a program built simply to satisfy compliance requirements will ever eliminate fatalities or even serious injuries or illnesses. The human toll, encompassing injuries, suffering, and, tragically, loss of life, highlights the critical need for us to take a proactive approach. We need a robust safety management system that supports the work and high-value safety objectives to fill the management system gaps.

THE ROLE OF SAFETY OBJECTIVES

Safety objectives serve as linchpins in a robust safety management strategy. They are forward-thinking, specific goals you develop by systematically identifying potential at-risk conditions, documenting concerning human factors and system gaps, and establishing proactive approaches to mitigate such risks and reduce losses to an acceptable level. Safety objectives provide a structured approach to assessing, analyzing, and monitoring risks to build controls, ensuring that the organization is not merely reactive but anticipatory in creating a safe working environment.

LINKING TO ORGANIZATIONAL GOALS

You should align and integrate safety objectives with the broader organizational goals to be most effective. Your safety vision, mission, and purpose should reflect such broader considerations. This is not always possible, but if you can, do it. Working this way involves aligning safety objectives with key business objectives, including production targets, maintenance, and quality objectives, financial milestones, and market or service expansion. I talked about management system integration in the previous chapter, and the list of the other business objectives could be lengthy. Still, it would be best to understand that safety objectives must be a prominent part of your organization's overall business objectives.

When safety becomes an integral part of organizational priorities, it not only safeguards workers but also contributes to the overall success and sustainability of the business, which again supports worker partnership and helps lead the overall business successfully. However, be cautious and ensure that your safety objectives fill priority gaps in the safety management system.

Integrating strategy and prioritizing goals is essential and requires data-based conversations. Pursuing every safety objective, I wanted during a calendar year was always an improbable venture. Still, I successfully integrated the mission-critical ones to eliminate or mitigate risks and support the safety management system.

Remember that safety is interwoven with many other parts of the overall business management system, meaning change in one part usually affects others. Look at how the strategies and work objectives of other functions in your organization affect safety. For example, a preventive maintenance program could aim to mitigate downtime. It would likely not be a safety objective, but it could have a massive positive effect on safety performance. Effective preventive maintenance means a worker can plan the job, take the necessary precautions, and perform in a more controlled environment. Conversely, a worker interfacing with a broken machine or in an upset condition changes the control landscape, and the work is rife with unknown variables that could threaten worker safety.

ENSURING CONSISTENCY WITH VISION AND MISSION

Safety objectives gain significance when they resonate with the organization's vision and mission. Consistency with the overarching safety purpose, the values, and the principles you have agreed upon is critical if you want broad participation in meeting safety goals. On more than one occasion, front-line partners challenged me on the objectives I wanted to pursue because they did not think these goals would get us closer to our safety vision. Granted, some safety objectives are simply about compliance, but even then, I should have discussed such objectives and goals broadly. Organizational alignment means we are endorsing a set of objectives we can stand behind because they reflect a commitment to creating a workplace that prioritizes safety and embodies the broader aspirations and principles upon which we have agreed.

SETTING SAFETY OBJECTIVES

A workplace safety objective is a specific, measurable, and time-bound goal that an individual or a team within an organization aims to achieve. These objectives provide a roadmap for workers, guiding their efforts and helping them prioritize tasks and activities. Setting organizational safety objectives involves a strategic process that begins with thoroughly assessing risk in your work environment, auditing and inspecting findings, recording losses and near-misses, and identifying gaps in the safety management system.

You should have a quantifiable method for understanding the gaps in your management system and the risks such gaps impose if left untreated. Collaboration with stakeholders, including front-line workers and contrasted levels of management, is essential to gather diverse perspectives on safety priorities. Of course, you always have to consider legal and regulatory compliance, but as I have said, there is so much more than compliance.

Here are some important points for you to consider:

- Audit your safety management system to identify gaps or areas that represent the most significant challenge keeping you from reaching the organization's safety vision.
- Identify workplace risks by reviewing safety inspections, audits, work-related medical costs, and process losses to identify safety concerns within the organization. Prioritize safety risks based, at a minimum, on their severity and likelihood of adversely affecting the organization.
- Ensure safety objectives align with legal and regulatory requirements. Stay updated on relevant safety standards and compliance obligations.
- Involve critical stakeholders and gather input to understand various perspectives on safety priorities.

OBJECTIVE-SETTING FRAMEWORKS

SMART

SMART Goals is one of the most popular and reputable goal-setting frameworks. SMART is an acronym for specific, measurable, achievable, relevant, and time bound. Peter Drucker created SMART as part of his Management by Objectives framework, with the purpose of using it to help the organization set practical goals. Unlike other frameworks that cover strategy creation, organizational hierarchy, and performance management, SMART is a simple structure that describes how to create and measure progress toward goals.

Here are explanations of the five key aspects of a SMART goal:

- Specific: Objectives should have a clear and specific outcome. Define the goal and the actions you need to take to achieve the goal. Be precise about what needs to be performed. Answer the five "W" questions: What? Why? Who? Where? When?
- Measurable: To track progress, you need a quantifiable objective. Define the data you will employ to measure the goal and set a method for collecting it. Everyone must agree on the best measures for showing progress.
- Achievable: Objectives should be realistic and attainable. Consider resources, skills needed, and time constraints. Setting lofty goals is good, but they have to be realistic. If the goal is not doable, you lose enthusiasm quickly, so taking small, accumulative steps may be a good approach. Goals should stretch individuals or teams without being impossible to achieve.
- Relevant: Objectives should align with the vision, mission, and purpose of safety success in your organization. They should also align with your broader business objectives and be meaningful for the organization. Objectives that are not meaningful will not drive the enthusiasm required to deliver the objective.
- Time-bound: Objectives should have a deadline. They should include milestone dates to show progress toward your final goal. Objectives without a deadline do not do much. How can you identify success or failure? This is why SMART goals set a final date. Keeping objectives time-bound allows you to tweak and tune throughout the goal to ensure your goals are achieved.

SMART goals keep things simple and use brief statements followed by a detailed explanation of each aspect in the SMART acronym. Chart 1 below is an example and details a SMART objective for an organization that wants to improve its confined-space-entry training program.

SMART	Examples
Specific What are you trying to improve?	Describe your goal precisely so there is no confusion about what needs to be accomplished. Try answering the "W's" (who, what, where, when, and why). Example: Confined Space Entry is a critical skill required to work in our organization. As a result of last year's accumulative worker test and skills scores being lower than 70% across the organization for Confined Space Safety and Skills Training, the training program will be revamped to ensure we improve worker capability and skills development to at least 85% before the end of the year.
Measurable How will you measure progress?	Ensure that you include measures to judge your progress towards achieving the goal. The goal must be written so that you can measure your progress towards it and, most importantly, so that you know you have completed it. Example: Because of the recent changes to Confined Space Training, workers will be better prepared for such work. 100% of all workers will attend and complete the latest training course, 100% will follow a skills development exercise, and 100% will take the required tests with an accumulative test and skills assessment score at or above 85%.
Achievable Do you have the skills, motivation and resources?	Be cautious to construct an achievable goal. Do not set it too high if you are concerned failure will likely happen or it will be viewed as demoralizing. Example: A 15% improvement in test and skills scores is incremental but will show timely progress for the year and improve safety performance. The workforce will widely accept this goal because of the near misses experienced last year, more valuable content changes, and the addition of the new skills development labs. Planning discussions with workers shows motivation to accept and improve on this goal.
Relevant Why are you setting this goal and how is it aligned with overall objectives?	Meaningful goals align with the overall safety or business objectives and are necessary to improve. Example: The goal is being set because of the complexity of the confined space entry program, the increased number of near-miss events reported last year, and lower test scores that indicate knowledge and skills needs. It is also a compliance issue that should be addressed.
Time Bound What is the deadline, and is it realistic?	Determine the date, time, and milestones for your goal. Example: The organization will have a new accumulative baseline training and skills development score at or above 85% by the last day of the fiscal year. Scores from the training program will be monitored monthly to ensure milestones are met and the goal is progressing as planned.

Chart 1

Objectives and Key Results

The Objectives and Key Results (OKR) is another framework I want you to consider. The OKR framework differs from SMART because you can use it for more ambitious or "moonshot" goals.

Ambitious goals are so important that Google's "Ten things we know to be true" mentions them directly: "We set ourselves goals we know we cannot reach yet because we know that by stretching to meet them, we can get further than we expected" (Klau, 2012). OKRs are goals that are about stretching your organization toward something big. Organizations that embrace OKRs usually attempt to reach only 60–70 percent of their stretch goal because they are naturally lofty.

Besides being aspirational, OKRs bring relevance and set up resource teams to start achieving big, challenging goals. Goal setting with this framework will make you rethink how you can reach peak performance.

Objectives need to be clear and inspire everyone to rally around them. The golden rule of writing objectives is that any reasonable person should be able to understand the objective's aim and motivation immediately. When looking at examples of objective and critical results, imagine ways to make the statements less generic and more inspiring.

Here is how to think about them:

- Objectives are the overarching, qualitative goals you aim to achieve. They are inspirational and provide direction. Objectives should be ambitious, motivating, and easy to understand.
- Key results using the characteristics of SMART indicate progress toward achieving the objectives. Each objective typically has two to five key results. Key results should be quantifiable and relate to the goal they support.

Now, use this formula and turn it into an objective:

We will *(objective)*, as measured by these *(key results.)*

Remember the safety vision I shared in an earlier chapter?

"To be the world's safest paper manufacturing facility."

Granted, I did not know we were developing OKRs in the 1990s, but as an organization, we knew what success looked like, and that drove our pursuit of developing our OKRs to reach our shared safety vision. The four areas below always existed in our minds while developing our moonshot goals.

We will be the world's safest paper manufacturing facility as measured by:

1. Improving our physical environment
2. Improving our teams' safety capability and capacity
3. Moving to an interdependent work culture
4. Ensuring a leadership team that proves its commitment and accountability

If you go down this path, keep your OKR to three to five significant objectives. In my time leading using the framework, I could personally never get my organizations under the four stated above. As you remember, I have commonly used the same ideas for success for every organization I have led, so they were often these four. When we audited our work system, looked at our losses and management system gaps, and assessed it against our safety vision, we usually had four ambitious goals in the areas of concern expressed above to reach what I believed safety success could be. It is a safe bet that most of the above are transferable to your organization.

Some organizations value combining SMART and OKR frameworks to leverage each framework's strengths. For example, you might use OKRs at a higher level for setting ambitious, strategic objectives and then use SMART goals to break them down into specific, actionable steps at a more granular level. This combination balances aspirational, long-term objectives with your required detailed, measurable actions.

Figure 1 below shows how I combine the two frameworks:

Figure 1

The choice to use one or a combination depends on the organization's culture, the nature of the organization's goals, and your preferred approach to goal-setting and performance management. Both frameworks are valuable tools for organizations striving to improve focus, improve alignment, and achieve objectives.

FRONT-LINE SAFETY OBJECTIVES

Yet another layer of objectives you should consider is personal safety objectives for the front line. Personal objectives are common for many in management but less common for front-line workers. I have had personal objectives throughout my career, but I often wondered why not everyone did. When I ask friends who work the front lines at their workplaces whether they have personal objectives, the answer is usually "no" or just "I will not get hurt," which falls far short of all that I want from a relationship with the front line. Personal safety objectives are actionable statements for individual growth to better oneself and to benefit others. Personal safety objectives are focused on internal or external outcomes. They provide a tangible result that improves the organization and promotes inner growth, elevating workers and leading the organization forward. I have often said that working in safety is "a little work for all of us, or much work for a few."

Again, from my time working in manufacturing facilities, every worker, from the most senior leader to the person manufacturing products, had two or three specific safety objectives to meet during a particular period. I didn't always fully apply this idea to front-line workers when they were unfamiliar with it. However, I quickly embraced it as a lever that moved the organization forward, improved the competence and capacity of the workforce, helped gain better control of the physical environment, drove an interdependent work culture, and kept leaders accountable. We were asking for and getting skin in the game from the front line. You will need to judge when to employ personal objectives in your organization.

Doing this well had tremendous benefits for me because it did not allow outliers to wiggle away from staying accountable or owning a part of the safety process.

Safety practitioners often challenge me by saying that developing 800 to 1,000 safety objectives for 400 to 500 workers is impossible. My reaction is that you do not own their personal objectives; you are there to guide and mentor the front-line workers to develop their high-value objectives. Also, various groups can have many of the same objectives. For example, a personal objective for a front-line worker might be to join the industrial fire brigade. To do this work, you would need a large group of interested workers who could meet the regulatory requirements, such as OSHA CFR 1910.256, the Fire Brigade Standard. This could become a personal objective for many in your organization interested in developing a team of emergency responders. This may be an individual development objective for many workers on the front line. With this thinking in mind, I am convinced that significant objectives in the hands of the front-line leverages culture and gets you closer to your organization's safety vision.

I would also challenge you to think more deeply. I had over five hundred workers in three facilities where I was the site safety leader, and in two of those facilities, workers had safety objectives and they performed better. Granted, some would claim that I made up work for them to do, which may be accurate looking back, but they were also genuine objectives that supported the robustness of our safety management process. Every conversation I had with a front-line worker about personal safety objectives was about something I knew we had to get better at doing. I had skin in the game to do our work together, and that allowed every worker to collectively celebrate safety success.

Here are some examples of how I counseled front-line workers to develop personal objectives.

- Would you consider developing your knowledge and skills to be the expert for energy isolation on your work crew?
- I have noticed that you are great at public communication. Would you consider a personal development goal to become a safety trainer for the organization?
- Considering that you are a seasoned machine operator, how about a personal development goal to lead safety inspections for your area and help design the inspection program?
- I have noticed you are interested in safety practices and leadership. Would you consider it a personal development goal to attend safety classes to become a crew safety leader I can count on?

This list could be pages long. Think about your entire work environment and the gaps you have found in the management system, the work conditions, and any other areas you need to improve. Consider your organization's safety vision, mission, purpose, values, and principles. Remember your bodacious safety objective? I can promise that you will have plenty of safety objectives for every worker to consider and adopt as their own if you think about the work that needs to be performed.

Aligning objectives with organizational safety goals is crucial on a personal level. Self-assessment helps identify areas for improvement, and personal objectives should address specific safety-related skills or behaviors. Regular feedback and evaluations assist in refining personal safety goals, while adaptability and a commitment to continuous learning ensure relevance in a changing safety landscape. The constructive collaboration between organizational and personal objectives supports a robust safety culture within the workplace.

CLOSING

Safety objectives play a pivotal role in addressing the objective-setting roadmap for organizations to not only meet compliance requirements but also genuinely nurture a workplace where the well-being of individuals is at the forefront of operational priorities.

A strong safety culture is the foundation of a successful organization. Implementing safety objectives sends a clear message to workers that their well-being is a top priority. Personal development objectives improve individual contributions to safety. Effective collaboration and communication with colleagues on safety matters are integral to fostering a safety partnership. This commitment fosters trust, loyalty, and a sense of high confidence.

It becomes part of the organizational DNA and improves morale, productivity, and overall performance.

Part III:
Leveraging the Front Line for Transformational Safety Change

Chapter 12:

Transformational Safety Change

*If your ship cannot navigate without you at
the helm, your leadership is failing.*

— John F. Kennedy

U p to this point, I have focused on the foundations of leading safety and expanding your reach across the organization. Now, I want to look at how to generate the momentum to move the safety process forward. Over my career, I have found that leading safety is not a "fill in the blank" exercise. Instead, we have to leverage the safety system to move forward. I have performed numerous corporate safety and health program audits over the years. I have reviewed many facilities' safety plans and their objectives. They often fell flat because their ambitious plans stayed in the hands of a safety and health team or within the ranks of the management team, and in every case, I found a lackluster connection to the front line.

Driving a safety management system forward is foreign to some safety practitioners. Some practitioners look through long lists of system elements and select the ones that address a problem or a gap between current and desired performance. At times, I have done that myself. However, it's more than that. The management system should be a living, breathing process that reaches the front line. It requires a dynamic approach through worker partnership that recognizes the necessity of change and recognizes that continuous improvement is a normal part of work. As discussed in earlier chapters, positive safety change occurs along a roadway filled with stops along your journey. It includes things like physical environment protections, worker development, culture, and management leadership accountability. Everything becomes a data point to consider. It's about making better decisions and experiencing how the system can thrive by doing more than just sustaining the safety management system and compliance with regulations.

The guarantee of safety success does not come from simply having the right capabilities and a sound foundation built on a solid safety management system. You also need to know how to move the safety process forward.

LEVERAGING THE WORK SYSTEM TO MOVE

I use the word "leverage" frequently. The people I've worked with over the years might tell you I use it so much it nauseates them. I use many action words because they are dynamic and denote specific activities that are essential for the work I want to do. For example, when I say I want to "leverage" something, it gets varied responses from most people, such as "Why, What, When, Where, and Who?" Action words convey a distinct action that opens the conversation between the front line and the senior leadership team about why we are heading in a specific direction, what is required for success, when we will start, where success will occur, and who will be part of it. It's simple, right? It requires us to discuss our work versus telling what the work will be, and that's good.

Can we leverage an entire work system to affect our work positively? Of course, but it requires a lot of different actions to make it happen. I am always searching for a way to increase the momentum by getting other people to join me for much of the work, which also helps remove as much variability and potential for error as possible. Several years ago, I stood before a group of young safety practitioners who had just finished their university requirements for their occupational safety and health degree. After my presentation, I opened the floor for questions. A young woman stood up and asked me this question.

"What do you believe is the most important thing you do as a safety practitioner?"

Without hesitation, I said.

> *"A vital, and possibly the most important job for safety practitioners is to force the behaviors of workers to make correct decisions by removing variables from their work that drive them to make the wrong decisions."*

Every now and then, I wish to take back hastily spoken words, particularly when the word "force" stands out so prominently. Yes, "force" is an action word. It denotes the act of making someone or something do a particular thing by using physical strength, power, or another form of pressure. I am confident that even though I said it over ten years ago, my company's HR department would have raised their eyebrows and enrolled me in sensitivity training had they known. Some situations warrant a kinder, gentler Scott Gaddis.

However, this is precisely what I think about my work, and it has informed much of the material in this book. I want to force change at the front line so that every decision is sound. I want to keep every worker safe and healthy so they can go home every single day. I wish it were as easy as saying it.

Various dictionaries define the word "force" as:

- The powerful ability to influence.
- To move against resistance or inertia.
- To move, open, or make clear a change in direction.
- The influence on a body that causes it to accelerate.
- To gain momentum to seek balance.

These are good summaries that capture what I ask you to consider. I want you to influence the organization through a robust and inclusive management approach driven by a safety vision, mission, purpose and a robust management system. I want you to shape your organization with highly effective communications and conversations built on deeply rooted principles.

Furthermore, to clarify, there is a kinder, gentler Scott Gaddis. Not long after using "force" to describe my work, I changed it to "leverage" to denote what I really wanted to do. I wanted to accelerate my safety process by enlarging my safety team and sharing ownership of the work with the front line. I wanted to leverage the work I thought was essential through establishing partnerships, and I want you to consider doing the same.

BARRIERS TO SAFETY CHANGE

Implementing safety change, or any change for that matter, within any organization can be a formidable task because of a myriad of factors. A significant challenge arises from the inherent resistance to change among workers, who perceive change as threatening their established routines and stability. We are all resistant to change. I would not say I necessarily like change, and I have found that the older I get, the more I like things to stay the same. However, everyone, especially the front-line workers, is pivotal for the work you want to do, and their resistance to change could challenge moving the safety process forward.

Here is how safety change often fails:

- Management excludes front-line workers from the safety decision-making processes.
- Management believes they have all the information needed.
- Organizations keep hierarchical structures in place with authority lodged at the top.
- Management sees consulting the front line as a barrier to urgent decision making.

- Management thinks front-line workers lack the expertise to add value.
- Organizations have an established culture of decision-making being centralized in management.
- Management is risk-averse and maintains high-leverage decision rights to stem consequences.
- Effective communication channels that value conversations with the front line are lacking.

These are the challenges you will face in gaining momentum for the work you must do as a safety practitioner. Factually, without a compelling change initiative through communication and inclusion, as I discussed in Part I, and a captivating narrative that lifts the safety roadmap, as I discussed in Part II, workers will feel disoriented. They will resist because they are left to wonder what their part is in safety success. Safety has never been a bottom-up initiative. Instead, it is a top-down value that should spread throughout the organization. It begins with leadership. Their support is crucial, and the absence of a committed leadership team can cast doubt on the legitimacy of the reason for change. Have you ever tried to lead safety with poor safety commitment from the rest of the management team? I bet you have heard "Safety is not my job; it is your job" from those around you, which is untrue. Safety is everyone's job; doing it differently is like pushing rope, meaning your process will wander everywhere but where you want it to go. Leaders must be involved even as we drive toward a culture that fosters interdependence.

NAVIGATING SAFETY CHANGE

Let's face it: today's work environment is evolving quickly. I often consult and guide my current organization and other safety colleagues because many of them, even seasoned safety practitioners, swim against a current of significant changes. My work often involves providing counsel for adopting technology-supported management systems.

Still, there is little doubt that you face plenty of rapid changes that threaten your safety performance success. A hybrid adaptation of Dr. John Kotter's 8-Step Change Management Plan, in Figure 1 below, is one well-known framework I have relied on for a long time. This framework provides a systematic yet straightforward approach to navigating the complexities of change and ensuring a smooth transition to what I believe in managing safety change.

Eight Steps of Change

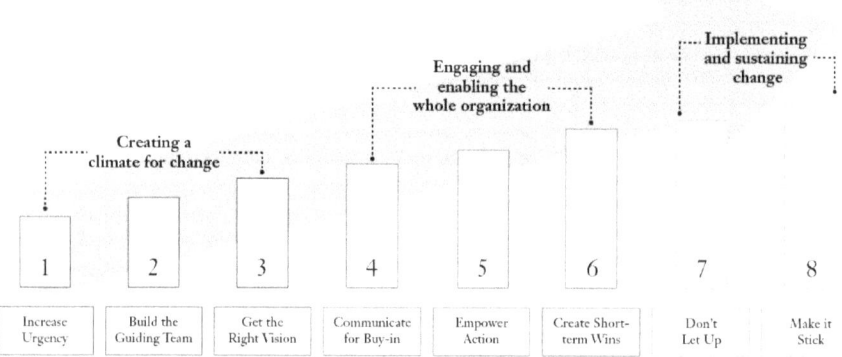

Source: Kotters, John P. and Cohen, Dan S. The Heart of Change. Boston: Harvard Business School Press

Figure 1

Let's look at each step of this transformative process.

Increase Urgency

The first step involves creating a compelling reason for change. As a safety practitioner, you perceive it as a pressing issue and recognize the importance of communicating the urgency of the change. This step requires you to articulate the risks associated with not doing anything versus the opportunities and challenges related to the change.

Build the Guiding Team

To ignite change, you must partner with influential and committed workers viewed as leaders. It would be best to draw these partners from various organizational levels and functions, from the senior leaders' office to the front-line workers, where they serve as a directional force to align efforts and maintain momentum throughout the change process. Their collective influence can help overcome resistance and foster collaboration.

Get the Right Vision

A clear and compelling safety vision serves as the roadmap for change. You have already studied the importance of creating a vision and the strategy to achieve it. As we have discussed, a vision should inspire workers and provide direction, while your strategy and objectives outline the concrete steps required to bring the vision to fruition.

Communicate for Buy-in

Effective communication is crucial, especially when you ask for change. Safety practitioners and other leaders must consistently and transparently communicate the vision and strategy to all stakeholders. This helps dispel uncertainties, align everyone toward a common goal, and build trust within the organization.

Empower Action

Change requires the collective effort of the entire organization. Leaders should facilitate workers by removing obstacles, encouraging innovation, and providing resources and training. In other words, you are urging the front line to get involved with you. This step fosters a sense of ownership and worker engagement, driving the change forward from within. This is a critical step toward achieving a partnership with the front line.

Create Short-Term Wins

Celebrating quick and visible victories is essential for maintaining momentum and leveraging progress. These early victories prove that your team can achieve your goals and benefit the organization. Recognizing and rewarding the efforts of individuals and teams enhances confidence and enthusiasm for the most significant transformation. As discussed, you will deliver strategies for reaching your safety vision probably in small chunks. They are cumulative, so think about success as the steps toward the ultimate safety goal.

Don't Let Up

After achieving initial successes, it's important to build on them and embed the changes into the organizational culture. This step involves reinforcing new behaviors, processes, and structures while addressing lingering issues. You and the other leaders should leverage your momentum to implement additional changes and improvements.

Make It Stick

The ultimate step is ensuring that the changes become a permanent part of the organization's DNA. This involves embedding the new behaviors and practices into the organizational culture, aligning systems and processes, and fostering a continuous learning mindset. When the changes are anchored in the culture, the organization becomes more adaptable and resilient in the face of future challenges.

SETTING SAFETY CHANGE MANAGEMENT OBJECTIVES

Now, thinking about safety in the vein of how I have explained change management and leveraging the safety system, here are some areas that need your attention so you can achieve even faster change:

Strategies:

- Select a change management process that aligns with your organization's needs and goals. I have shared one framework here, but others may better suit your organization.
- Articulate your desired vision, mission, and purpose, but break it down within reasonable and achievable timelines. Use

your goals and objectives-setting process to show this work. Remember, goals should be SMART.

- Engage front-line workers in transparent communication about the need for safety change, including discussing the safety management system and how best to leverage it to reach the safety vision. Communicate the goals, benefits, and expected outcomes with clarity. Ensure there is two-way communication to address concerns and gather valuable input.

- Encourage front-line workers to identify potential safety risks in their daily activities. Involve them in the risk assessment process through auditing, inspecting, hazard reporting, and concern reporting. Their learned knowledge provides critical insights that inform the change management strategy.

- Provide comprehensive training programs for front-line workers to ensure they are well-equipped with the skills and knowledge they need to be active participants in the safety process. This can include hands-on training, workshops, and regular updates to keep everyone informed.

- Foster a sense of ownership and authorization among front-line workers by giving them decision rights. Allow them to contribute ideas, propose solutions, and take responsibility for implementing safety measures. This boosts morale and ensures front-line workers embrace the changes.

- Establish clear and accessible communication channels for reporting safety concerns or suggesting improvements. These can include digital platforms, regular safety meetings, and open-door policies. Ensure efficient mechanisms for addressing and communicating resolutions promptly.

- Instill a culture of continuous improvement by encouraging front-line workers to provide feedback on the effectiveness of safety measures. Establish regular feedback mechanisms to gather insights that drive ongoing improvements.

- Develop a robust monitoring system to track the effectiveness of safety changes. Regularly evaluate key performance indicators related to safety, seeking input from front-line workers closest to the work. Use this approach to make data-driven decisions and adjustments as needed.
- Ensure that leaders engage, demonstrate a firm commitment to safety, and provide the resources and support to implement additional safety measures.
- Document the entire change management process, including successes and challenges. This documentation can be a learning tool for future initiatives. Share your insights with the organization to facilitate a broader culture of safety awareness.
- Acknowledge and celebrate front-line workers for their work on safety initiatives. Recognize individuals or teams for their commitment to safety, fostering a positive environment that encourages others to participate actively in the change management process.

You are now on your way to building a partnering organization and an interdependent team.

SAFETY MANAGEMENT SYSTEM ELEMENTS

In Chapter 7, I touched on four elements that have caused me sincere concern as a safety practitioner: the work environment, the people performing work, organizational culture including workers' behaviors, and how leaders lead. These elements have had me scratching my head many times as I've tried to stay ahead of their loss potential. Each of these elements represents a threat to your safety process. I am utterly convinced that what hampers safety change for many organizations is that the safety system lacks control over certain control elements, which causes the system to get stuck, or, as I like to think about it, it becomes difficult to move it in a positive direction in a way that improves performance as quickly as you desire. Some reasons for this are condition-based, but many are baked within the human elements that slow your performance. The more human elements are what many of us are constantly struggling to control. Human factors address what we ask people to do (the work and its characteristics), who is doing it (the worker and his or her related competence), and where they are working (the organization and its attributes, such as leadership and culture).

All of this reminds me of the periods in my career when environmental programs were among my responsibilities. In those roles, I found that once I got an environmental system in place and working, it stayed true to its design. My overall theory was that much of my work in the environmental space had fewer interactions with people, thus producing much fewer human factors to control. Naturally, this is not an absolute truth, as there are multiple worker touchpoints concerning the environmental aspect of the practice. However, at least in my practice, I usually had fewer touchpoints than those in safety and health. Regardless of the system, elements in the work environment influence human behavior and threaten success.

SYSTEM LEVERS

In Figure 2 below, I have represented four elements that have long been part of my management system framework. As I have said, the value of recognized safety management systems like ISO 45001 and ANSI Z10 lies in their ability to methodically provide a comprehensive framework for the organization to manage risk. Each framework establishes standards and guidelines for forming, implementing, maintaining, and improving an effective safety management system. As we have discussed, adopting a robust management system shows your commitment to ensuring a safe and healthy work environment for your workers and stakeholders. Further, even if you have a hybrid management system, you should assess it for issues against a recognized management system.

Regardless, a management system should help identify and evaluate potential hazards, implement preventive measures, and monitor performance through regular evaluations.

However, there remains work to be done. How do you make the process move? I have relied on four elements that I often refer to as levers.

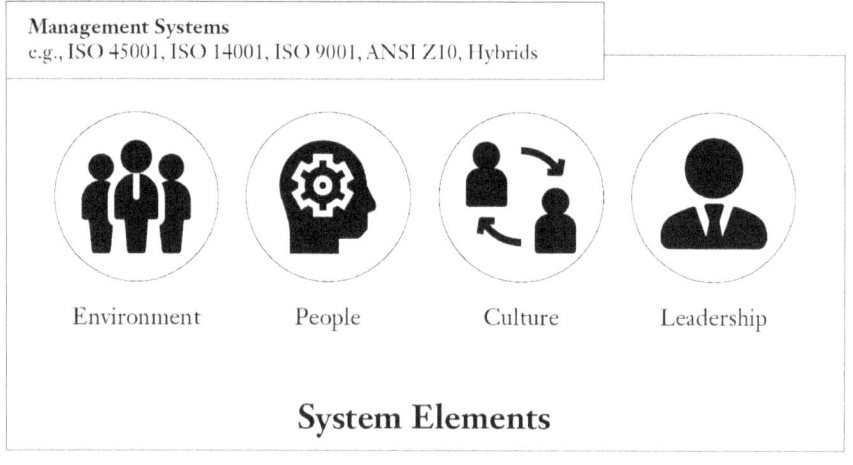

Figure 2

With this in mind, you can see the areas where your front-line workers and the management team are an integral part of the safety process, and their actions, decisions, and performance will significantly affect overall safety performance. It is more than simply asking the workers to change their behaviors and work safely. Below, in Chart 1, are the four elements again that I discussed previously. This time, however, I've emphasized how each has an action that is prone to error.

Environment	People	Culture	Leadership
Assessing	Understanding	Partnering	Guiding
Controlling	Performing	Involving	Monitoring
Developing	Supporting	Mentoring	Expecting
Inspecting	Elevating	Coaching	Engaging
Designing	Hiring	Embracing	Communicating
Engineering	Motivating	Ensuring	Adapting
Purchasing	Thriving	Disciplining	Innovating
Preparing	Reasoning	Recognizing	Celebrating

Chart 1

USE YOUR WORDS

As you can see, I have used action words to support the four strategic elements. Each action can propel a safety management system forward, ensuring its evolution and effectiveness in safeguarding the workplace. By helping everyone in the organization understand and adapt, we establish a foundation for a safety culture that is both resilient and responsive, capable of adjusting to emerging threats and changes in the work environment. Engaging workers through mentoring and coaching emphasizes the importance of safety training and building a knowledgeable workforce adept at recognizing and mitigating risks. Partnering across diverse levels of the organization and involving everyone in safety initiatives fosters a collective responsibility for maintaining a safe work environment.

This collaborative approach ensures that you integrate safety practices into daily operations, making safety a shared value rather than a top-down directive. Elevating safety standards and disciplining processes to ensure adherence to these standards is crucial for maintaining an elevated level of safety performance. Consistent communication, support for teamwork, and recognizing individuals or teams for their contributions to safety can boost morale and reinforce the importance of safety in the organizational culture. By designing and engineering specific safety strategies that incorporate these action words as core principles, the safety management system becomes more than a set of guidelines—it evolves into a dynamic framework that actively engages everyone in the organization. This comprehensive approach enhances the immediate safety environment and prepares the organization to efficiently address future safety challenges, driving the safety management system toward sustained success.

Using action words to describe work is a powerful technique for several reasons:

- Clarity and Precision: Action words clearly and concisely describe what you want to do. They precisely convey your actions, making your contributions and responsibilities more understandable to the audience, whether for a corrective actions report, a safety project plan, or any professional documentation.
- Impact and Effectiveness: These verbs highlight your desire for achievement and the impact of your work on the safety process. By using robust and dynamic action words, you can show the results and effects of your actions, emphasizing how you will contribute to your team, project, or organization.
- Engagement: Action words can make your statements more engaging and livelier. They draw the front-line worker in and help keep their attention, making your narrative or descriptions more compelling.
- Openness: Action words expand workers' attention to make them more aware of the environment in which they are performing their work.
- Expansive: Action words expand the horizon that promotes an additional focus of work that will be discovered as process

maturity grows and as additional gaps are found in the management system.

FLIPPING YOUR ACTION WORDS INTO SAFETY LEVERS

Consider these elements and their support actions as levers that can intervene between the design of the safety system and the actual work your front-line workers are doing. In the simplest terms, consider finding the risk areas in your work system and grouping them within the four elements I have listed above. Now, go down each column and identify the exposures for the examples I have added to each element (can you see them?). How do you perceive the hazard's risk on the work system (do you understand it?), and finally, can you tolerate the risk, or do you need to do something about it (do you accept it, eliminate it, or mitigate it?)? They are dynamic and denote specific actions, making them practical for describing activities, responsibilities, achievements, and roles in various contexts. Each of these verbs conveys a distinct action that can help illustrate the required contributions, knowledge, and skills and the impact each could bring to your safety success.

When introducing these elements and actions, I am often asked whether some elements or actions hold greater importance than others or are all equal. How you weigh and prioritize what you will work on depends on your system gaps and risk tolerance for each element. For instance, when taking on a new facility, I always weigh much of my initial work on first gaining better control of the physical work environment and working within the people element to build capability and skills so that workers become better contributors to the safety process.

I caution that this work is specific to your organization, and understanding where risks lie in your work system is imperative in selecting the proper actions within each element. Undoubtedly, your work will encompass all the system's elements and even more, showing a clear need for improved control and much conversation that expands your action words. Expect your action word list to grow under each element as your understanding of the management system and your safety process grows in maturity.

CLOSING

Organizations can construct a resilient safety process by focusing on the change management concepts and ideas I have shared and, more importantly, engaging everyone in the safety change management process. By understanding the barriers to success, following a robust change management framework, and partnering with the front line, you can navigate change and create a culture that embraces continuous improvement in an era where adaptability is critical to success. Mastering the art of change management is a strategic imperative for you as you drive forward to reach your safety vision and thrive in a dynamic and growing business landscape.

These approaches enhance workplace safety and promote collaboration, worker engagement, and shared value through a high and engaged commitment to creating a secure and healthy work environment. You also need to understand the required system elements and actions you need to undertake for better control. For some people, the work will be particular to a specific element. The work will bridge several elements for others, giving you better success and momentum to reach your safety goals. As someone who has experienced the challenges firsthand, I understand the need to minimize variability in the safety process. In the following four chapters, I will share my experiences and explain how I collaborated with front-line workers to improve the four elements and key actions mentioned in this chapter. Although I will not capture every idea, I will discuss the ones I think were tremendously beneficial to effective partnerships at the front line and for bridging everyone's wants and needs.

Chapter 13:

The Environment Element

Great things in business are never done by one person; a team of people does them.

— STEVE JOBS

I have always viewed the physical work environment as foundational. As safety practitioners, it is one of the things that demands our time and possibly where many will focus most. This initial investment in safeguarding the physical aspects of the workplace is crucial, serving as the springboard for more nuanced work, particularly related to human factors. Addressing the complexities of creating a secure, healthy, and productive environment for those on the front lines is no small task. It involves a wide array of considerations, all vital for ensuring the well-being of workers. As I have highlighted, safety and health regulations and a robust safety management system form the cornerstone of our efforts in this area. Both offer a structured approach to complying with regulations and actively fostering a culture prioritizing safety at every level. The effectiveness of these systems, and indeed, our success in protecting the physical workspace, relies on a series of critical actions.

In this chapter, I zoom in on eight specific actions instrumental in enhancing workplace safety. Through a dive into the core of securing a safe work environment, I am peeling back the layers to reveal the essential strategies for robust protection and improvement and the benefits of such work. The actions I focus on are as follows:

- Inspecting
- Assessing
- Controlling
- Developing
- Designing
- Engineering
- Purchasing
- Preparing

Each is pivotal, and together, they form the backbone of effective safety management in the physical realm. Although I will not cover every facet or action related to workplace safety here, the areas I explore have profoundly shaped my approach to better safety controls. I hope that by sharing these insights, I will inspire you to think more deeply about these actions and how you can enhance them in your organization. My goal is to provide a holistic view of the strategies and benefits of improving safety in the physical work environment. This is where I began my journey of integrating actions that supported a cohesive and powerful safety network of change.

With that, let's put our toes in the water.

INSPECTING

Safety inspections are systematic, regular workplace assessments to identify potential hazards, ensure compliance with safety regulations and evaluate the effectiveness of existing health and safety protocols. These inspections are a cornerstone of an effective occupational health and safety management system, preemptively addressing issues before they result in accidents or injuries. By thoroughly examining equipment, processes, and the environment, safety inspections help organizations maintain high workplace safety standards, fostering a culture of continuous improvement and vigilance. This proactive approach not only protects workers but also contributes to operational efficiency and regulatory compliance, making it an indispensable practice for businesses aiming to prioritize the well-being of their workforce.

Strategies:

- Develop a Comprehensive Checklist: Tailor safety inspection checklists to specific areas, processes, and equipment within the workplace, ensuring that you systematically assess all potential hazards. Regularly update these checklists to reflect changes in operations, new equipment, or revised regulations.
- Train and Empower Workers: Invest in training for workers and safety officers to enhance their ability to identify hazards and understand safety standards. Encourage a culture that openly reports and addresses safety concerns.
- Leverage Technology: Use technology, such as mobile apps and management software, to streamline the inspection process, facilitate real-time reporting, and track corrective actions. This can also help analyze the data over time to identify trends and areas for improvement.
- Schedule Regular and Surprise Inspections: Conduct planned and surprise inspections to maintain safety standards. Regular inspections help identify long-term trends, while surprise inspections focus on everyday practices.
- Involve External Auditors: Periodically involve external safety auditors to conduct inspections. External auditors can provide an unbiased view of safety practices and may identify hazards or areas of non-compliance that internal inspectors have overlooked.

Benefits:

- Prevention of Workplace Accidents and Injuries: Safety inspections significantly reduce the risk of accidents and injuries by proactively identifying and mitigating hazards, ensuring a safer work environment.

- Enhanced Compliance with Safety Regulations: Regular inspections help organizations stay abreast of and comply with relevant safety regulations, reducing the risk of legal penalties and fines.
- Improved Worker Morale and Productivity: A safe work environment boosts worker morale, as workers feel valued and protected. This can lead to increased productivity and job satisfaction.
- Cost Savings: Safety inspections can lead to significant cost savings by preventing accidents and ensuring regulatory compliance. These savings come from reduced medical expenses, legal fees, insurance premiums, downtime, and equipment damage costs.
- Reputation Management: A strong workplace safety record enhances an organization's reputation among clients, suppliers, and potential workers. It demonstrates a commitment to worker well-being and corporate responsibility, making the company more attractive to work for and do business with.

ASSESSING

Risk assessment is the bedrock of any effective safety management system, and I will spend ample time explaining it here because it is imperative. Risk assessment weaves through most of our work as practitioners and bridges all the other components in this chapter. It involves a systematic process of identifying potential hazards that could harm workers or disrupt business operations. Once they are determined, the next step is assessing the severity and likelihood of these hazards, for which you need a good understanding of the work environment and its activities.

The process typically begins with a comprehensive workplace inspection to identify potential sources of harm, ranging from physical hazards such as machinery and chemicals to human components such as ergonomic and psychosocial risks. Engaging the front-line workers in this process provides valuable insights, as the front-line is often most familiar with the nuances of its work areas. More importantly, risk assessment teaches a skill. One of the most pivotal levers in my toolbox, if not the chief lever, is integrating risk assessment skills organizationally, especially at the front line. There are several methodologies, but it is in your best interest to always consider the people with whom you want to use your tools. In this case, you want to employ a risk assessment process that is simple to use because you want to embed it at the front line.

Strategies:

- Hazard Identification: Systematically identify physical and human hazards in the workplace through inspections, worker feedback, and reviewing accident reports.
- Risk Analysis and Evaluation: Assess the likelihood and severity of harm from identified hazards, considering existing control measures. This step prioritizes risks based on potential consequences and guides allocating resources.
- Control Measures Implementation: Based on the risk analysis, develop and implement appropriate control measures to mitigate identified risks, following the hierarchy of controls from elimination and substitution to engineering controls, administrative actions, and personal protective equipment.
- Training and Communication: Educate workers on the identified risks and preventive measures through regular training sessions and effective communication strategies. Empower workers to report hazards and understand their partnering role in maintaining a safe work environment.
- Monitoring and Review: Regularly monitor the effectiveness of control measures and review the risk assessment process to identify new hazards or changes in the workplace.

Benefits:

- Enhanced Worker Safety and Health: Organizations can significantly reduce workplace injuries and illnesses by identifying and controlling hazards, promoting a safer work environment.
- Compliance with Legal Requirements: Safety risk assessment helps organizations meet legal and regulatory obligations, reducing the risk of legal penalties and fines associated with non-compliance.
- Improved Organizational Reputation: Demonstrating a commitment to safety enhances the organization's reputation among clients, investors, and potential workers, contributing to business growth and stability.
- Operational Efficiency: Organizations can achieve higher productivity and operational efficiency by minimizing disruptions from accidents and process downtime.
- Cost Reduction: Effective risk management leads to lower costs related to absenteeism, insurance premiums, and compensation claims, contributing to the organization's financial health.

CONTROLLING

After identifying and prioritizing the risks you have in the work system, implementing hazard controls is the next step in improving workplace safety. This process involves selecting and applying the most appropriate measures to mitigate the identified risks, aiming to eliminate hazards or reduce their effect on workers and the workplace. Safety hazard control is essential to workplace safety management, focusing on implementing measures to eliminate or mitigate risks associated with identified hazards. This proactive approach is crucial for maintaining a safe working environment, preventing accidents and health issues, and ensuring that operations comply with safety standards and regulations. Safety hazard control involves a systematic process that starts with identifying hazards, is followed by risk assessment, and culminates in applying effective controls. These controls range from engineering solutions and administrative policies to personal protective equipment and training. By prioritizing safety through hazard control, organizations can protect their most valuable asset—their workers—while safeguarding their operational integrity and reputation.

Strategies:

- Implement the Hierarchy of Controls: Apply the hierarchy of controls, a framework for prioritizing workplace hazard reduction. Start with elimination and substitution, followed by engineering controls, administrative actions, and PPE as a last resort.
- Engage in Continuous Risk Assessment: Conduct ongoing risk assessments to identify new hazards and reevaluate existing risks, ensuring that control measures remain effective. Update risk assessments in response to changes in the workplace or processes.
- Invest in Safety Training and Awareness Programs: Develop comprehensive training and awareness programs for all workers, focusing on hazard recognition and the importance of safety controls.
- Use Technology and Safety Data Analysis: Leverage advanced technologies and data analysis tools to monitor workplace conditions, track the effectiveness of control measures, and predict potential hazards for proactive management.
- Encourage Worker Participation and Feedback: Promote an open-door policy for reporting hazards and safety concerns. Include workers in safety committees or meetings to discuss safety controls and improvements, enhancing ownership and compliance.

Benefits:

- Reduction in Workplace Injuries and Illnesses: Implementing adequate hazard controls significantly reduces the risk of workplace injuries and illnesses, protecting workers' health and well-being.
- Compliance with Legal and Regulatory Standards: Effective hazard control ensures that organizations comply with relevant safety legislation, avoiding fines and legal penalties associated with non-compliance.
- Enhanced Operational Efficiency: By minimizing disruptions caused by accidents and associated downtime, hazard controls contribute to smoother operations and increased productivity.
- Cost Savings: Effective control of safety hazards leads to lower costs related to workers' compensation claims, insurance premiums, and legal fees, positively affecting the organization's bottom line.
- Improved Organizational Reputation: A strong workplace safety record enhances an organization's reputation among clients, partners, and current and prospective workers, contributing to business success and growth.

DEVELOPING

Supporting a robust safety management system requires developing and implementing safety policies and procedures that work principles cannot always govern. As I have said, you should vet every policy and procedure decision to ensure it's necessary. Policies and safety procedures outline the organization's commitment to safety, the responsibilities of both management and front-line workers, and the specific guidelines for managing risks that confront the organization.

Strategies:

- Regulatory compliance: Adhere to laws, regulations, and guidelines relevant to workplace health and safety.

- Scope and Objectives: Clearly define the purpose of the safety policies, the scope of their application, and the objectives they aim to achieve. Detail the safety responsibilities of individuals at all levels of the organization, from top management to front-line workers.
- Risk Management Procedures: Incorporate the findings from the risk assessment process and outline the procedures for ongoing hazard identification, risk assessment, and control.
- Training and Communication: Develop the training requirements for workers, ensuring they know how to perform their roles safely and know emergency procedures.
- Monitoring and Review: Establish procedures for regularly reviewing and updating safety policies and procedures to reflect changes in the workplace, emerging risks, or the outcomes of incident investigations.

Benefits:

- Consistency in Safety Practices: Providing a clear framework for safety, policies, and procedures ensures that every applied practice is consistent across the organization.
- Enhanced Compliance: Clear policies and procedures help organizations comply with legal and regulatory requirements, reducing the risk of penalties or legal issues.
- Improved Safety Culture: Well-defined safety guidelines contribute to a culture of safety in which workers understand their roles and responsibilities in maintaining a safe workplace.
- Effective Risk Management: Incorporating risk assessment and control strategies into safety procedures ensures that a thorough understanding of workplace hazards informs safety practices.

- Enhanced Operational Efficiency: Minimizing disruptions from missed policy and procedure development can contribute to safer operations and increased productivity.

DESIGNING

Safe work design is a proactive approach to enhancing workplace safety and health by integrating safety considerations into the design, planning, and execution of work processes and environments. This approach identifies and mitigates risks at the source, ensuring that organizations design jobs, workstations, equipment, and workflows with worker safety and health as core considerations. By incorporating safety principles from the outset, organizations can create more efficient, ergonomic, and compliant workspaces that protect workers and improve overall operational performance. Safe work design is essential for fostering a culture of safety, minimizing the potential for accidents and injuries, and enhancing the well-being of workers. It represents a shift from reacting to safety incidents to preventing them through thoughtful and strategic planning.

Strategies:

- Early Integration of Safety Principles: Incorporate safety, job and task flow, and ergonomics principles at the earliest stages of design and planning for new processes, workplaces, and equipment, considering safety from the start rather than an afterthought.
- Cross-functional collaboration: Facilitate collaboration among engineers, ergonomists, safety practitioners, operations, and front-line workers to ensure a comprehensive approach to safe work design, leveraging diverse expertise to identify and mitigate potential hazards effectively.
- Worker Involvement: Engage workers in the design and planning process. They offer valuable insights into the practical

aspects of their work and potential safety concerns, ensuring that solutions are practical and effective.

- Continuous Improvement and Risk Management: Adopt a continuous improvement mindset, regularly reviewing and updating work designs based on feedback, incident data, and changes in operations or regulations to manage risks proactively.
- Use of Technology and Data Analysis: Leverage technology and data analytics to simulate work environments, assess risks, and evaluate the effectiveness of design interventions. This allows for data-driven decisions in the safe design of workspaces and processes.

Benefits:

- Increased Worker Safety and Health: By prioritizing safety in design, organizations can significantly reduce the risk of workplace injuries and illnesses, promoting a healthier and more productive workforce.
- Improved Operational Efficiency: Safe work design often leads to more efficient workflows and processes, as it emphasizes eliminating waste and optimizing human and equipment interactions, contributing to higher productivity and lower costs.
- Increased Compliance with Regulations: Designing work processes and environments with safety in mind helps ensure compliance with occupational health and safety regulations, reducing the risk of legal penalties and fines.
- Reduced Costs Associated with Workplace Injuries: Effective, safe work design can lead to substantial cost savings by minimizing the direct and indirect costs associated with workplace accidents, such as medical expenses, compensation claims, and downtime.
- Improved Worker Satisfaction and Retention: A safe and well-designed work environment enhances worker satisfaction,

morale, and engagement, increasing retention rates and attracting top talent.

ENGINEERING

Engineering controls involve the application of engineering principles to design out hazards or to place barriers between the workers and the hazards. Unlike administrative controls or PPE, which rely on human behavior and compliance, engineering controls aim to make changes at the source of the hazard. This approach is often more effective because it can eliminate the hazard or mitigate exposure without relying on worker intervention.

Strategies:

- Substitution of Materials and Processes: Replace hazardous materials or processes with less hazardous ones. For instance, using water-based paints instead of solvent-based paints reduces the fire risk and health hazards from volatile organic compounds.
- Isolation of Hazards: Physically separate the hazard from workers through enclosing processes (e.g., soundproof enclosures for noisy equipment) or remote-control operations to keep workers away from high-risk areas.
- Ventilation Systems: Use local exhaust ventilation to capture and remove airborne contaminants at the source before they can disperse into the workplace environment.
- Safety Engineered Machinery: Design machinery and equipment with built-in safety features, such as guards, emergency stop buttons, and safety interlocks, to prevent accidents.
- Ergonomic Design: Workstations, tools, and equipment should be designed to fit the user, reducing the risk of musculoskeletal injuries. This includes adjustable chairs, workstations at the correct height, and tools designed to minimize strain.

Benefits:

- Long-Term Solutions: Engineering controls provide sustainable solutions to workplace hazards, often eliminating or significantly reducing the risk for as long as the control remains in place.
- Cost-Effective: Although the initial investment may be higher, engineering controls can be more cost-effective overall by reducing the need for ongoing expenses related to PPE, training, and injury management.
- Improved Productivity: By designing safer work environments and processes, engineering controls can also improve efficiency and productivity, as workers are less likely to interface with equipment and can work in a controlled environment.
- Operational Efficiency: Organizations can achieve higher productivity and operational efficiency by minimizing disruptions with effective engineering practices.
- Cost Reduction: Effective engineering control leads to lower costs due to work or process flow interruptions.

PURCHASING

Purchasing decisions have a direct and significant effect on workplace safety. The selection of equipment, materials, and services can introduce new hazards or mitigate existing ones. Consequently, incorporating safety considerations into purchasing decisions prevents workplace injuries and illnesses.

Strategies:

- Incorporate Safety Criteria: Develop and implement safety criteria for procuring goods and services. This includes evaluating the safety features of equipment, the hazardous properties of materials, and the safety records of vendors and contractors.

- Supplier and Product Evaluation: Thoroughly evaluate suppliers and their products for compliance with safety standards and regulations. This may involve assessing product safety data sheets, reviewing manufacturer safety records, and considering equipment ergonomics.
- Engage Stakeholders: Involve safety practitioners and end users, including front-line workers, in purchasing. Their insights can identify potential safety issues and ensure new equipment does not introduce hazards or usability issues.
- Prioritize Quality and Reliability: Choose products and equipment known for their quality and reliability. High-quality items are less likely to fail and cause safety incidents.
- Consider Lifecycle Costs: Evaluate the total cost of ownership, including maintenance, operating costs, and disposal. Products with lower lifecycle costs may also pose fewer safety risks over time.

Benefits:

- Reduced Workplace Hazards: Organizations can reduce worker hazards by selecting safer equipment and materials.
- Compliance with Safety Regulations: Purchasing decisions prioritizing safety and health to ensure compliance with relevant regulations, reducing legal and financial risks.
- Enhanced Safety Culture: Demonstrating a commitment to safety through purchasing decisions reinforces a culture of safety within the organization, highlighting the value you place on worker well-being.
- Improved Productivity: Purchasing the right equipment and materials can improve efficiency and productivity, as workers are less likely to experience work inefficiency or risk of injury.
- Cost Savings: Although safer options may sometimes have a higher up-front cost, they can provide significant savings by

reducing accidents and injuries and by increasing the longevity of the equipment.

PREPARING

Emergency preparedness involves planning for unexpected events that can pose significant risks to health and safety and business operations. These include natural disasters, fires, chemical spills, medical emergencies, and other critical incidents. Preparing for these scenarios ensures an organization can respond effectively, reducing potential harm and facilitating a quicker return to normal operations.

Strategies:

- Risk Assessment: Use the initial risk assessment process to identify potential emergency scenarios specific to the workplace. This assessment should consider the likelihood of diverse types of emergencies and their potential effects.
- Plan Development: Develop a detailed emergency response plan for each identified scenario. These plans should outline the steps to protect workers and assets before, during, and after an emergency. Key components include evacuation procedures, communication plans, emergency roles and responsibilities, and the availability of resources such as emergency supplies and equipment.
- Inclusion of Special Needs: Ensure that plans consider the needs of all workers, including those with disabilities or specific requirements. This may involve developing specific evacuation procedures or designating individuals to assist in emergencies.
- Worker Training: Conduct regular training sessions to ensure all workers know the emergency plans and understand their roles and responsibilities. Training should be tailored to the specific needs of different organizational areas and roles. Regular drills are essential for practicing emergency response procedures and help familiarize workers with evacuation

routes and procedures, communication, and the use of emergency equipment.

- After-Action Reviews: Following drills or actual emergency events, conduct after-action reviews to evaluate the effectiveness of the response. Gather feedback from participants and identify areas for improvement. Regularly review and update emergency plans to reflect changes in the workplace, lessons learned from drills and actual events, and any changes in external conditions or regulations.

Benefits:

- Enhanced Safety: Comprehensive emergency preparedness directly contributes to the safety and security of workers during critical incidents.
- Reduced Impact: Effective response and recovery procedures can significantly reduce an emergency's impact on operations and financial stability.
- Regulatory Compliance: Specific emergency preparedness measures are legally required in many areas.
- Improved Worker Satisfaction and Retention: A safe and well-prepared work environment with emergency plans enhances worker satisfaction, morale, and engagement, increasing retention rates and attracting top talent.
- Strengthened Reputation: Demonstrating a commitment to safety through effective emergency preparedness can enhance an organization's reputation with workers, customers, and the community.

CLOSING

This exploration has provided strategic insights and practical measures to strengthen your commitment to safety and well-being, aligning with the principles of a robust safety management system. The involvement of front-line workers in all these actions is essential for creating a safe, efficient, and inclusive work environment. By leveraging the insights, experiences, and expertise of those on the front lines, your organization can develop even more effective safety strategies that protect workers, enhance productivity, and foster a culture of safety that permeates every level of the organization in the physical work environment.

Chapter 14:

The People Element

Knowledge must become capability.

— Carl Von Clausewitz

When navigating workplace safety, the "people element" emerges as a constant presence and a source of significant variability. The front-line worker, invariably at the heart of operations, embodies the organization's most significant potential for change. Reflecting on moments when I doubted my safety strategies—because I did not see the expected results—I recognized a common theme: the unpredictability of human behavior. I once humorously lamented to a senior leader that my job would be much simpler without people, a sentiment that, although amusing now, underscored a crucial realization. The front line was critical to my success, and as I have said, leaving too much variability in work processes often leads to inconsistent performance.

Front-line workers play a critical role in successfully managing the complexity of daily tasks and hazards. Their active engagement in safety practices is indispensable for weaving safety competence into the very essence of an organization. This chapter delves into eight key actions:

- Understanding
- Performing
- Supporting

- Elevating
- Hiring
- Motivating
- Striving
- Reasoning

My approach, which draws from my experiences in safety leadership, aims to share the actions I frequently encountered and how I used front-line partnerships to develop the actions for better control rather than cataloging every possible action. Our journey through the people element aims to highlight the invaluable role of front-line workers by building their knowledge and skills to perform and developing their capacity to give it all back to the organization using their unique perspectives to improve safety. This exploration will not cover every conceivable action, but I hope to highlight those I often encountered and the strategies I employed for better competence. Engaging with the front line effectively mitigates hazards and strengthens the links that further forge a collaborative safety culture. We move to a place where safety becomes a shared duty through learning and giving back, building partnerships where the organization benefits immensely from each worker's active involvement and contributions.

Now that you've dipped your toes into the water in the previous chapter, let's move further from shore.

UNDERSTANDING

Knowledge and understanding of the work to be done are pivotal to the success of any safety program. In my experience across various organizations, dedicating time to enhance the workforce's knowledge invariably led to superior organizational performance. This highlights the critical importance of cultivating a well-informed workforce that understands the complexities of the work environment and the necessary precautions for a safe operation. Moreover, it emphasizes the need for an ongoing education and adaptation process, ensuring that every worker, from newcomers to experienced personnel, stays abreast of the latest safety standards, procedures, and potential risks.

Strategies:

- Comprehensive Training Programs: Deploy continuous training efforts specifically designed for the distinct needs of various roles within the organization to guarantee their relevance and efficacy.
- Knowledge-Sharing platforms: Promote a culture that encourages knowledge exchange through forums, regular safety briefings, and peer mentoring schemes, which support collective advancement in safety comprehension.
- Dynamic Training Programs: Offer training initiatives that evolve in tandem with the changing landscape of safety, maintaining their applicability and benefit for every role within the organization.
- Technology and Tools: Allocate resources to technologies and tools that simplify the learning process and minimize classroom time, including digital training management systems, micro-learning platforms, and two-way communication tools.
- Cross-Functional Safety Workshops: Conduct workshops that bring together workers from different departments to share safety practices and learn from each other's experiences, fostering a more unified approach to workplace safety.

Benefits:

- Higher Retention of Safety Practices: Dynamic and engaging training methods, supported by technology, improve worker retention of safety information and practices.
- Informed Decision-Making: A workforce knowledgeable about safety can make well-informed decisions when faced with potential hazards, markedly decreasing the risk of accidents.

- Enabled Workers: Workers who are well-versed in safety protocols and the rationale behind them are more inclined to assume responsibility for their actions and the safety of their surroundings.
- Increased Safety Innovation: With a continuous learning environment, workers are more likely to suggest innovative solutions to safety challenges, enhancing the overall safety process.
- Strengthened Team Cohesion: Cross-functional safety workshops and knowledge-sharing initiatives promote teamwork and a unified commitment to safety across the organization.

PERFORMING

Moving beyond basic knowledge, cultivating specific safety skills, and performing work safely is paramount to ensuring front-line workers can practically apply their understanding of safety principles to everyday tasks. Bridging the gap between theoretical knowledge and practical application involves enhancing tangible safety skills. Consequently, skill development equips front-line workers with the tools to comprehend and execute the required actions efficiently and safely. Such development initiatives should be dynamic, adapting to the shifting landscape of workplace hazards and integrating innovations in technology and procedures.

Strategies

- Hands-on Training: Offer hands-on training sessions that allow workers to practice learned safety measures in realistic settings, reinforcing their ability to respond effectively to real-life situations.
- Skill-Based Training: Conduct training emphasizing technical skills and safety procedures, ensuring workers are adept at their tasks and know how to perform them safely. These programs use simulation-based training and practical workshops

to bridge the gap between theory and practice, boosting skill mastery.

- Cross-training: Promote cross-training to expand workers' skill sets and understanding of various roles and associated safety risks. This strategy enhances workplace flexibility and fosters a comprehensive appreciation of safety across different job functions.
- Mentorship Programs: Establish mentorship arrangements in which experienced workers guide novices. This allows for the direct transfer of essential skills and safety insights and cultivates a solid internal safety culture.
- Feedback Loops: Implement structured feedback mechanisms so workers can share insights and experiences from applying safety practices. This feedback can help refine skills training programs to meet workforce needs.

Benefits:

- Practical Competence: Front-line workers understand their safety responsibilities and excel in performing them, significantly improving operational safety.
- Increased Worker Confidence: Front-line workers gain confidence in managing their own and others' safety, leading to a more proactive and empowered workforce.
- Resilience Against Safety Incidents: A workforce that is well-trained, adaptable, and confident in safety practices is more resilient against incidents, capable of responding effectively to emergencies and minimizing their consequences.
- Adaptability to Change: A versatile workforce proficient in navigating new challenges is invaluable in an ever-evolving business landscape. Skill development equips workers to adapt to novel technologies, approaches, and business structures, keeping the organization agile and robust.

- Futureproofing the Workforce: Continuously refreshing and expanding the workforce's skill set ensures that workers stay relevant and competitive, ready to meet the demands of future industry evolutions and technological breakthroughs.

SUPPORTING

Enabling and supporting front-line workers to give back what they know by contributing their safety knowledge and work insights is a tremendous lever for building partnerships with the front line. However, it requires thoughtful capacity planning. To leverage partnerships at the front line, you should consider creating an environment where sharing safety knowledge and skills is encouraged and expected. This involves allocating time for safety meetings, debriefs, and training sessions within the regular work schedule and encouraging the front line to participate and lead. Capacity planning in the context of safety ensures that workers have the time and resources to learn and lead by sharing how they apply safety practices and contributing essential insights and experiences to improving organizational safety.

Strategies:

- Time Allocation: Allocate time within work schedules specifically to allow front-line workers to lead or facilitate safety training, meetings, and knowledge exchange sessions. By partnering with you in leading safety, the front line will be encouraged to connect more deeply.
- Tailored Work Assignments: Customize work assignments based on individual workers' strengths, skills, and capacity to give back.
- Technology and Tools: Invest in technology to streamline tasks and reduce manual workloads. Automating repetitive tasks, for example, will free up worker capacity for more valuable and rewarding work, enhancing productivity and authentic engagement.

- Worker Autonomy: Grant front-line workers greater autonomy in managing their workload and schedules. Autonomy can enable workers to optimize their capacity by allowing them to work in a way that improves productivity, job satisfaction, and safety partnerships.
- Development Opportunities: Provide targeted development opportunities that help workers refine their skills in leadership, critical thinking, and effective communication.

Benefits:

- Reduced Burnout and Turnover: Effectively managing and optimizing worker capacity can reduce burnout by preventing overwork and stress. This leads to lower turnover rates, as workers are more likely to stay with an organization that respects their capabilities and supports their well-being.
- Enhanced Worker Loyalty: Workers who feel that their employer values their ability to give are likelier to develop a solid loyalty to the organization. This loyalty can translate into higher engagement, productivity, and advocacy for the company.
- Greater Innovation and Creativity: When workers are not constantly operating at or beyond their capacity, they have more mental and emotional energy to devote to innovation and creative problem-solving. This can lead to developing innovative ideas, products, and services that drive organizational growth and success.
- Continuous Improvement: Leveraging the workforce's collective knowledge and experience fosters an environment of continuous improvement in safety practices.
- Organizational Engagement: Involving every worker in the organization in developing and leading specific initiatives to broaden their part ownership of the safety process leverages cultural growth and partnership.

ELEVATING

Functional leadership often comes from designated roles, such as your role as a safety practitioner or leader, but it should not all be lodged there. Safety champions and second-hat roles form the backbone of an influential workplace safety culture that extends the safety practitioner's reach very deep in the organization. Groups of people are keen to develop their capability and capacity to lead safety if they see the value of their contributions. Champions are known to be the organization's chief safety ambassadors, working with the safety practitioner, leading by example, advocating for safety protocols, inspiring their peers to prioritize safety in every aspect of their work, and fostering a proactive safety environment. They are trained and vital communicators between management and workers, ensuring that leaders hear and address issues promptly. In addition, the second hat role is a persona that supports a specific area necessary for critical safety control, such as activities that support compliance, inspections, training, and consultation. Both roles are supplemental to a front-line worker's primary duties but are crucial for embedding safety values within the organization's culture and operations.

Strategies:

- Clear Role Definition: Clearly define the responsibilities and expectations for champion and second hat roles, ensuring they have the authority and resources they need to be effective.
- Leadership Development: Provide training and development opportunities for those in safety leadership roles to enhance their effectiveness in driving safety initiatives.
- Recognition and Empowerment: Identify and nurture champions and second hats within the workforce. Empowering these individuals through recognition, training, and leadership opportunities can enhance their ability to influence their peers and the organization positively.

- Balanced Feedback Mechanisms: Establish mechanisms that allow champions and second hats to express their views and contribute to decision-making processes, ensuring a balanced approach to innovation and problem-solving.
- Creating a Synergistic Environment: A productive work environment leverages the strengths of front-line champions and second hats, fostering a culture in which enthusiasm for innovation is balanced with critical analysis and thoughtful consideration.

Benefits:

- Advocates for Change: Champions and second hats serve as the front-line supporters of change, embodying the organization's values and pushing forward initiatives with enthusiasm and dedication. They are the driving force behind innovation, leading by example and inspiring their peers.
- Enhancing Collaboration: Encourage collaboration between champions and second hats, facilitating discussions that harness their diverse perspectives for more comprehensive and practical solutions.
- Grassroots Engagement: Engaging workers in safety roles promotes a sense of ownership and responsibility toward workplace safety at all levels.
- Extension of Safety Leadership: A healthy organizational ecosystem includes champions and second hats. It encourages a culture that values constructive dialogue and different perspectives to improve outcomes.

HIRING

Incorporating safety into hiring practices signals an organization's dedication to fostering a safe work environment from the onset of a worker's journey. Beyond evaluating technical abilities and professional experience, gauging a candidate's safety and risk management approach is critical. The recruitment process is a pivotal platform for assembling a team that values and actively embraces workplace safety. By weaving safety considerations into the hiring framework; organizations ensure that new workers bring the requisite technical prowess and a deep-seated commitment to upholding safety standards and an organization's safety values.

Strategies:

- Safety-Focused Job Descriptions: Emphasize the significance of safety within job postings, detailing expectations for adherence to safety protocols and contributions to a safe culture.
- Behavioral Assessment in Interviews: Deploy behavioral interview strategies to delve into candidates' safety philosophies, prior engagements with a safety emphasis, and capacity to act safely under pressure.
- Safety Competency Testing: Introduce pre-hiring assessments to measure a candidate's ability to recognize potential hazards and problem-solving skills in safety-critical scenarios.
- Comprehensive Skill and Trait Evaluation: Seek a balanced combination of technical knowledge and essential soft skills, such as effective communication, flexibility, and the ability to empathize, which indicate a proactive approach to safety.
- Alignment with Safety Culture: Evaluate how well a candidate's values and behaviors align with your organization's established safety culture, ensuring that new hires are predisposed to contribute positively to the workplace safety environment.

Benefits:

- Cultivation of a Safety-Conscious Workforce: By prioritizing safety from the hiring phase, organizations nurture a team inherently aligned with safety values, leading to a marked reduction in workplace incidents and a proactive stance on high safety expectations.

- Heightened Safety Engagement: Selecting candidates with a strong safety mindset encourages a broader engagement with safety initiatives, fostering an environment of continuous safety improvement.
- Foundation for a Robust Safety Culture: Starting with safety-focused recruitment lays the solid groundwork for an enduring safety culture, making safety a shared priority across all levels of the organization.
- Improved Incident Response and Prevention: Workers selected for their safety awareness and problem-solving skills are better equipped to prevent accidents and respond effectively when incidents occur.
- Alignment with Organizational Values: Hiring workers whose personal safety philosophies align with the organization ensures a cohesive workforce that maintains and enhances workplace safety standards.

MOTIVATING

Maintaining worker motivation in the context of workplace safety is a multifaceted challenge. Motivational strategies should recognize and reward safe behaviors, create meaningful consequences for non-compliance, and foster intrinsic motivation by connecting individual actions to broader organizational safety goals. Motivation is what drives workers to apply their knowledge and skills consistently. It encompasses intrinsic and extrinsic incentives encouraging adherence to safety protocols and active participation in safety initiatives.

Strategies:

- Safety as a Core Value: Embed safety into the organizational culture, making it a core value supported and reinforced by all levels of leadership.

- Career Development Opportunities: Link safety training and education to career advancement within the organization. Demonstrating that investment in safety can lead to personal and professional growth significantly enhances motivation.
- Lead by Example: Model the behaviors, work ethic, and attitudes you wish to see. Demonstrating commitment, resilience, and integrity in your actions inspires front-line workers to emulate these qualities.
- Cultivating Intrinsic Motivation: Embed safety into the organizational ethos, making it a core value everyone, including leadership and workers, can embrace and champion.
- Recognition Programs: Implement programs that recognize and reward workers for exemplary safety behaviors and contributions.

Benefits:

- Enhanced Safety Culture: A motivated workforce contributes to a positive safety culture in which safety becomes a shared value.
- Continuous Improvement: Leveraging the workforce's collective knowledge and experience fosters an environment of continuous improvement in safety practices.
- Sustained Safety Engagement: Motivated workers are likelier to remain engaged with safety practices without supervision.
- Enhanced Job Satisfaction: Enabling workers increases job satisfaction as workers feel their contributions are meaningful and important. They go from making a product or delivering a service to helping lead the business.
- Proactive Safety Participation: High motivation levels encourage workers to actively participate in safety discussions and initiatives, leading to a more dynamic and responsive safety culture.

THRIVING

The well-being of workers is intrinsically linked to the effectiveness of an organization's safety culture. Stress and overall health significantly affect workers' ability to perform safely and efficiently, making the management of those factors pivotal in fostering a robust safety environment. A crucial aspect is the relationship between management and front-line workers.

Strategies:

- Implement Comprehensive Wellness Programs: Develop and offer wellness programs that address physical and mental health aspects, including stress management courses, fitness memberships, and mental health days. Tailor these programs to meet the diverse needs of the workforce.
- Promote Work-Life Balance: Encourage a healthy work-life balance through flexible work schedules, feasible remote work options, and policies allowing workers to take time off when needed without fear of repercussions.
- Foster Open Communication: Create channels for open communication that make workers feel comfortable discussing stressors, health concerns, and safety issues. Regularly check in with workers to gauge their well-being and provide support.
- Provide Access to Mental Health Resources: Offer access to counseling services, stress reduction programs, and mental health support tools. Educate managers and supervisors on recognizing signs of stress and mental health struggles in their teams.
- Encourage Worker Engagement and Participation: Involve workers in decision-making processes related to health, safety, and workplace improvements. Empower workers to contribute ideas and feedback, fostering a sense of ownership and belonging.

Benefits:

- Reduced Workplace Accidents: Workers who are mentally and physically healthy are more alert and aware, reducing the likelihood of accidents and enhancing workplace safety.
- Increased Productivity: Workers with lower stress levels and better health are more focused and efficient, leading to increased productivity and a better quality of work.
- Enhanced Worker Morale: A supportive work environment that prioritizes well-being boosts worker morale, leading to a more positive workplace atmosphere and more robust team cohesion.
- Reduced Absenteeism and Turnover: When employers appreciate and support their workers, it proactively addresses stress, lowers absenteeism rates, and reduces turnover.
- Strengthened Safety Culture: Organizations reinforce the importance of safety and well-being by demonstrating a commitment to worker health and stress management, strengthening the overall safety culture, and fostering a closer link between management and front-line workers.

REASONING

Worker intelligence and reasoning encompass emotional and cognitive abilities and play a vital role in safety. Emotional intelligence (EQ) enables workers to manage their own emotions and understand those of others, facilitating better communication and teamwork. Cognitive intelligence contributes to problem-solving and decision-making, which is crucial for identifying and mitigating risks. Both mental and emotional intelligence are vital components in creating a safe work environment. Elevated levels of EQ among workers and leaders can lead to better stress management, more effective communication, and more collaboration, all of which are critical for identifying and mitigating safety risks.

Strategies:

- Cognitive Skill Development: Based on the complexities of the work environment, incorporate exercises and training that boost cognitive skills, especially hazard recognition, risk assessment, and creative problem-solving.
- EQ Training Programs: Implement training sessions focused on developing emotional intelligence skills, such as self-awareness, self-regulation, social awareness, and relationship management. These programs can help workers better manage their own emotions and understand the feelings of others, contributing to a safer and more supportive work environment.
- Communication Workshops: Conduct workshops focusing on effective communication strategies, active listening, and empathy. These skills are essential for building trust and communicating safety concerns openly and effectively.
- Stress Management Techniques: Provide resources and training on stress management techniques that leverage emotional intelligence, such as mindfulness, emotional regulation, and positive reframing. These techniques can help reduce the effect of stress on decision-making and behavior.
- Intelligence Assessment and Development Plans: Assess workers' emotional and cognitive intelligence levels during ongoing professional development. Tailor development plans to individual needs, strengthening workers' contributions to workplace safety.

Benefits:

- Improved Agility and Responsiveness: Enabled organizations can respond more quickly to changes and opportunities, as decisions can be made at the level closest to an issue.

- Greater Sense of Ownership: By having a say in decision-making, all workers develop a stronger connection to their work and the organization, driving them to perform at their best.
- Enhanced Team Collaboration: Emotional intelligence fosters better teamwork by improving communication and empathy among team members, which is essential for identifying and addressing safety issues.
- Effective Conflict Resolution: High-EQ individuals are better equipped to resolve conflicts in ways that maintain safety and respect for all parties involved. This skill is precious in high-stress situations, in which clear, calm communication is crucial.
- Resilient Response to Emergencies: In emergencies, individuals with high emotional intelligence are more likely to remain calm, think clearly, and take effective action, thereby enhancing the overall response to safety incidents.

CLOSING

The front line is critical to driving service excellence, supporting operational efficiency, and keeping everyone safe and healthy. By effectively empowering, supporting, and capitalizing on the talents of those on the front lines, organizations can significantly improve worker job satisfaction and, consequently, elevate customer satisfaction and operational achievements. This approach to understanding the people element underscores the importance of an ongoing commitment to understanding and addressing the dynamic needs and capabilities of the workforce. Incorporating people-centric practices at the core of organizational strategies enables businesses to fully harness their frontline workers' potential. This transforms challenges into opportunities for advancement and creativity and fosters an environment where continuous improvement and innovation are part of the organizational DNA. As such, making the people element a lever in your operational and service strategies is essential for any organization aiming to excel in today's competitive landscape.

Chapter 15

The Culture Element

For individuals, character is destiny. For organizations, culture is destiny.

— Tony Hsieh

A successful organization is the result of an intricate dance between culture—the collective values, beliefs, and practices that define the daily life of a company—and the more specialized notion of safety culture. This latter concept focuses on the facets of the broader culture that prioritize safety, underscoring a dedication to health, well-being, and preventing harm. Though these two cultural dimensions share a common ground, they diverge in their focus, with organizational culture providing the canvas on which the specific patterns of safety culture emerge and flourish. For those immersed in the world of safety practice, this intersection becomes a crucial area of engagement and influence.

Let's tackle a contentious issue head-on. The concept of "safety culture" often sparks debate among safety practitioners. Another safety practitioner once confronted me after I repeatedly mentioned "safety culture" in a presentation and insisted that the idea did not exist. Despite his enthusiasm, he didn't win the debate. The truth is that perspectives on safety culture vary widely, even among those with similar backgrounds. Some view it as an attribute an organization has or lacks, while others, drawing from organizational culture research, see it as the confluence of general cultural practices and specific safety management strategies. The important lesson in this situation is not to listen only to the loudest voice, even though both viewpoints provide insightful information. It is about embarking on your journey to understand and shape the culture within your organization, drawing on various perspectives to find what best suits your context. Safety culture often eludes a precise definition, but everyone knows it when they see it in action. At its heart, it is a mindset—a collective commitment to safety that permeates every level of an organization. It is visible in the actions and attitudes of individuals who prioritize safety, embedding it into the organization's essence. The challenge lies in fostering a culture that balances accountability with a learning-oriented approach to safety, a theme I've discussed in previous chapters.

This chapter explores eight key actions:

- Partnering
- Involving
- Mentoring
- Coaching
- Embracing
- Ensuring
- Disciplining
- Recognizing

These actions provide a roadmap for building better safety, enabling culture, and navigating the delicate balance between aspirational safety culture ideals and the practicalities of fostering a just culture.

In the previous chapter, we moved further from shore. Now with our focus on bettering culture, let's focus on swimming in a direction that further propels the organization.

PARTNERING

In the tapestry of organizational culture and safety, "partnering" is a key thread, weaving together the strengths and capabilities of various stakeholders to forge a united front to achieve and sustain safety success. That is why I used it as the title of this book. It underscores the significance of collaboration among workers, management, and external partners in nurturing a safety-centric and culturally robust organization. By championing a partnering ethos, organizations transcend traditional hierarchical boundaries, fostering a climate of mutual respect, shared goals, and collective responsibility. Such an environment amplifies the efficacy of safety initiatives and cultivates a sense of belonging and purpose among all participants. It develops interdependence. Organizations can harness their entire ecosystem's collective insights, expertise, and energy through strategic partnering, setting the stage for innovative safety solutions and a thriving organizational culture.

Strategies:

- Clear Communication Channels: Implement systems for accessible information and feedback exchange across all levels. Communication should be bidirectional.
- Joint Safety Initiatives: Encourage deep collaboration on safety projects to reinforce the importance of safety and demonstrate organizational commitment to a culture of care.
- Cross-functional teams: Create teams across the organization to share best practices and insights, embedding safety into the organizational culture.
- Global Thinking, Local Action: Engage with external safety experts, benchmark leading safety programs, and read forward-thinking safety culture data to bring fresh perspectives and expertise. Then, deploy what your organization will endorse and implement.

- Organizational Engagement: Involve every worker in the organization in developing and leading specific initiatives to broaden the worker's ownership of the safety process. This is a significant lever for fostering an interdependent culture.

Benefits:

- Better Safety Outcomes: Collaborative efforts lead to more robust safety solutions and reduced workplace incidents.
- Improved Worker Morale: A culture that relies on partnerships fosters a sense of belonging and value among workers, boosting morale and interdependence.
- Increased Innovation: Diverse perspectives encourage innovative solutions to safety and cultural challenges.
- Remarkable Commitment to Safety Goals: Shared responsibility ensures that safety becomes a collective priority.
- Sustainable Safety Practices: Collaborative development and implementation of safety practices ensure that those practices are more sustainable and embedded in the organization's culture.

INVOLVING

"Involvement" as an action plays a pivotal role in creating a cohesive and proactive workplace. It means engaging every front-line worker in safety initiatives and cultural development, fostering a sense of ownership and partnership among workers. This inclusive approach ensures that safety and culture are not merely top-down directives but are embraced and lived values across all levels of the organization. Involvement enables workers, encourages open communication, and leverages diverse perspectives and experiences within the workforce to identify areas for improvement, innovative solutions, and a safer, more positive working environment. By prioritizing involvement, organizations can unlock the full potential of their people, driving meaningful change and reinforcing a culture where safety and well-being are paramount.

Strategies:

- Worker Safety Committees: Form committees that include workers from various levels to participate in safety planning, decision-making, and strategy setting.
- Safety Surveys and Feedback Mechanisms: Regularly conduct perception surveys to gather worker feedback on safety and suggestions for improvement.
- Safety Training Programs: Comprehensive safety training is a cultural driver that better enables workers with knowledge, skills, and the capacity to expand the learning environment.
- Open-Door Policy for Safety Concerns: Encourage workers to report safety concerns without fear of retaliation, ensuring they feel heard and valued.
- Recognition Programs for Safety Contributions: Implement recognition programs that acknowledge and reward workers for significant safety contributions and innovations.

Benefits:

- Increased Safety Awareness: Direct involvement raises worker awareness and understanding of safety issues.
- Empowerment: Front-line workers feel empowered and responsible for their safety and the safety of their colleagues.
- Improved Safety Performance: Active worker involvement improves adherence to safety protocols and practices.
- Enhanced Problem-Solving: Involvement encourages creative problem-solving by bringing diverse perspectives to safety challenges.
- More Robust Safety Culture: Worker participation reinforces a culture where safety is a collective responsibility.

MENTORING

Mentoring, a beacon of guidance in organizational development, stands out for its profound effect on cultivating a safety culture and improving the workplace environment. When experienced individuals impart wisdom, skills, and insights to their less experienced counterparts, it fosters a continuous learning and growth cycle. In the context of safety and organizational culture, mentoring transcends mere knowledge transfer; it is about building relationships that nurture confidence, encourage risk awareness, and instill a deep-seated commitment to upholding the highest safety standards. By embedding mentoring into its core practices, an organization not only elevates its safety protocols but also strengthens the fabric of its culture, creating a supportive and dynamic environment where every worker is empowered to contribute to the collective well-being and success.

Strategies:

- Formal Mentoring Programs: Develop structured mentoring programs that pair mentors and mentees based on skills, interests, and safety goals.
- Safety-Specific Mentoring Objectives: Set clear objectives for safety awareness, protocols, and behaviors within the mentoring relationship.
- Mentor Training: Train mentors to ensure they have the skills necessary to guide mentees effectively, focusing on communication, teaching techniques, and safety knowledge.
- Monitoring and Feedback: Establish mechanisms to monitor the mentoring relationship's progress and provide regular feedback to mentors and mentees.
- Integration with Safety Initiatives: Integrate mentoring programs for broader safety initiatives to reinforce their importance and ensure alignment with organizational safety goals.

Benefits:

- Accelerated Learning: Mentees quickly acquire safety knowledge and skills, reducing the learning curve.
- Improved Safety Culture: Mentoring fosters a culture of continuous learning and safety consciousness.
- Increased Worker Engagement: The personal connection in mentoring relationships increases overall engagement and commitment to safety.
- Improved Communication: Mentoring enhances communication across different levels of the organization, promoting a more open, safety-focused dialogue.
- Leadership Development: Mentoring prepares future leaders with a strong foundation in safety leadership and culture.

COACHING

A dynamic and personalized approach to coaching is pivotal for elevating safety and fostering a positive culture. Unlike traditional training methods, coaching focuses on individual growth and performance enhancement through tailored guidance, goal setting, and feedback. It bridges the gap between potential and achievement, empowering workers to refine their skills, embrace safety protocols, and actively contribute to the cultural ethos of their workplace. Through the lens of safety and organizational culture, coaching transforms theoretical knowledge into practical wisdom, enabling workers to navigate complex challenges with confidence and competence. By integrating coaching into its developmental strategies, an organization can cultivate a proactive and resilient workforce adept at meeting and exceeding the evolving demands of safety and excellence in the workplace.

Strategies:

- Goal-Oriented Coaching Plans: Develop coaching plans with clear, measurable safety goals to focus efforts and track progress.

- Regular Coaching Sessions: Schedule consistent coaching sessions to review progress, address challenges, and adjust goals as necessary.
- On-the-Job Coaching: Implement on-the-job coaching to provide real-time feedback and guidance in actual work situations, enhancing the practical application of safety practices.
- Empowerment Through Coaching: Encourage coaches to identify solutions and make decisions about safety improvements, fostering a sense of ownership.
- Coaching for All Levels: Offer coaching programs for workers at all levels, including management, to ensure a comprehensive approach to safety culture.

Benefits:

- Improved Safety Performance: Direct coaching immediately improves safety practices and behaviors.
- Personalized Development: Coaching provides personalized feedback and development plans, addressing individual safety competencies.
- Enhanced Problem-Solving Skills: Front-line workers develop vital problem-solving skills to identify and mitigate safety risks.
- Increased Accountability: Coaching encourages individuals to take responsibility for their safety performance and contributions to organizational safety.
- Strengthened Safety Leadership: Coaching develops leadership skills, particularly in managing team safety and leading by example.

EMBRACING

Integrating diversity and inclusion practices into workplace safety represents a pivotal shift toward creating a more resilient, understanding, and comprehensive safety culture. Effective cultural leadership in this area goes beyond mere compliance with safety regulations; it involves recognizing a diverse workforce's unique contributions and needs and leveraging these differences to improve safety. This approach acknowledges that workers from varied backgrounds bring distinct perspectives, experiences, and ideas that can significantly enrich safety initiatives. By prioritizing diversity and inclusion in safety practices, leaders can unlock innovative solutions to safety challenges, improve worker engagement and morale, and cultivate a workplace where safety is a shared responsibility and value.

Strategies:

- Foster an Inclusive Culture: Create an environment that values all workers regardless of background, role, or experience. Ensure that everyone can access safety meetings and communications, including those with language barriers.
- Encourage Diverse Perspectives in Safety Planning: Actively involve workers from various backgrounds in safety planning and decision-making processes. Diverse perspectives can lead to more innovative and effective safety solutions.
- Address Unconscious Bias: Train leaders and workers to recognize and mitigate unconscious biases affecting safety practices, such as assumptions about individuals' abilities or risks.
- Promote Equity in Safety Equipment: Ensure that all safety equipment and PPE are available in sizes and styles that accommodate diverse body types and cultural needs, ensuring everyone's protection.
- Conduct Regular Safety Climate Surveys: Regularly assess workers' perceptions of the inclusiveness of the safety culture and the effectiveness of diversity and inclusion, initiatives in safety practices. Use feedback to make continuous improvements.

Benefits:

- Enhanced Safety Innovations: Diverse teams bring various experiences and ideas, leading to more creative and practical safety solutions.
- Improved Safety Compliance: Tailoring safety training to accommodate diverse learning styles and languages can improve understanding and compliance with safety protocols.
- Reduced Accidents and Injuries: Inclusive safety cultures that value diverse perspectives and address potential biases can more effectively identify and mitigate risks, reducing accidents and injuries.
- Strengthened Trust in Leadership: Leaders who champion diversity and inclusion in safety practices earn trust from their teams, strengthening overall leadership effectiveness.
- Higher Job Satisfaction: Workers who feel safe, respected, and valued are more likely to experience higher job satisfaction and morale.
- Stronger Talent Recruitment and Retention: Organizations known for their commitment to diversity, inclusion, and safety are more attractive to potential workers and tend to retain their workforce longer.
- Better Risk Management: A diverse and inclusive approach to safety can uncover potential hazards and risks you might not have identified through a more homogeneous lens, leading to better overall risk management.

ENSURING

Ensuring accountability to do the right things is a fundamental pillar in the edifice of organizational integrity and is critical to enhancing safety and cultivating a vibrant organizational culture. It transcends mere responsibility, embedding a sense of ownership and commitment among individuals and teams toward upholding safety standards and cultural values. This attribute fosters an environment where actions and decisions are made with a profound understanding of their effect on collective well-being and the organization's ethos. By championing accountability, organizations create a transparent, trust-filled atmosphere where every member is empowered to act decisively, acknowledge mistakes, and celebrate successes.

Strategies:

- Clear Assignment of Responsibilities: Ensure every worker understands his or her safety and cultural responsibilities.
- Performance Measurement: Use key performance indicators (KPIs) and metrics to measure adherence to safety and cultural expectations. Balance KPIs between leading and trailing to offer comprehensive understanding.
- Constructive Feedback and Dialogue: Foster an environment where leadership regularly gives workers constructive feedback, focusing on improvement rather than blame.
- Recognition and Reward Systems: Implement systems that recognize and reward success with safety practices and cultural contributions.
- Corrective Action Plans: Develop clear procedures for addressing failures to meet expectations, including support and resources to improve. Do not shy away from helping the worker improve.

Benefits:

- Improved Safety Outcomes: A robust accountability framework improves safety outcomes as individuals uphold safety standards.
- Empowerment of Workers: Accountability enables workers to control their actions and contributions to safety and culture.
- Enhanced Trust and Transparency: Accountability practices enhance trust and transparency within the organization, which is crucial for a positive culture.

- Continuous Improvement Culture: An accountability culture encourages continuous improvement by learning from mistakes and successes.
- Stronger Organizational Commitment: When held accountable, workers are more likely to align with the organization's goals and values as they experience success.

DISCIPLINING

This is a more complicated action to write about, simply because I would not say I like it. With that said, not everything that happens is a free lesson. While I agree that much can be understood without blame, there will be occasions when discipline is required. Discipline in the context of safety is not merely about enforcing rules and administering consequences for violations. It is about creating a structured and consistent approach to safety that encourages accountability, reinforces standards, and fosters a culture of continuous improvement. Influential leaders understand that discipline should be constructive, aiming to educate and correct rather than merely punish. Applying discipline to promoting safety on the front lines requires a balanced, fair, and educational approach.

Strategies:

- Establish Clear Safety Expectations: Communicate safety protocols and expectations clearly and consistently to all workers. Ensure everyone understands what is expected and why it is essential. Use education and training programs to increase worker knowledge and skills to mitigate potential consequences.
- Organizational Engagement: Involve front-line workers in developing fair discipline programs and gathering and adding feedback to broaden their ownership of the disciplinary process. Though not often appreciated, this is a significant lever in fostering an interdependent culture.

- Encourage Self-Reporting and Accountability: Foster an environment where workers feel comfortable self-reporting mistakes or near-misses without fear of punitive action, emphasizing learning and prevention for the future.
- Implement a Progressive Discipline Policy: Develop a fair and transparent progressive discipline policy for safety violations, such that the consequences escalate reasonably with repeated offenses, focusing on education and correction at the initial stages. Conduct thorough investigations to understand the root causes and factors involved in safety incidents rather than rushing to assign blame.
- Ensure Consistency in Enforcement: Apply safety rules and disciplinary actions consistently across the board, regardless of position or tenure. This fairness reinforces the importance of safety and the impartiality of safety protocols. Tailor disciplinary actions to the individual and the specific situation, considering the worker's history and the circumstances of the violation to find the most constructive approach.

Benefits:

- Improved Safety Compliance: A structured approach to discipline helps improve overall compliance with safety protocols, reducing the likelihood of accidents and injuries.
- Increased Worker Engagement: Workers who see leadership enforce safety rules fairly and consistently are likelier to feel engaged and invested in the safety program.
- Greater Respect for Safety Guidelines and Rules: Clear and consistent discipline reinforces the importance of safety protocols, encouraging more profound respect and adherence among the workforce.

- Fostered Trust and Transparency: Encouraging self-reporting and focusing on corrective actions rather than punitive measures fosters trust and transparency within the organization.
- Customized Learning Opportunities: Using disciplinary moments for targeted education allows customized learning, addressing specific gaps in understanding or practice.

RECOGNIZING

Recognition, a vital component in the mosaic of organizational dynamics, is indispensable in reinforcing safety and nurturing a vibrant culture. It transcends mere acknowledgment, embodying a strategic approach to valuing and celebrating the contributions, achievements, and behaviors that align with and advance the organization's safety and cultural aspirations. A valid consideration, however, is that recognition should never be a proverbial carrot dangling in front of the workers since this approach is often viewed as a bribe for acting a certain way and is not a sustainable recognition process. By implementing a thoughtful recognition system, organizations can tap into the profound human need for appreciation, motivating individuals and teams to strive for excellence, adhere to safety protocols, and embody the desired cultural values.

Strategies:

- Align Recognition with Organizational Goals: Ensure the recognition program is designed to reinforce behaviors supporting safety and positive cultural values.
- Diverse Recognition Methods: Use a variety of recognition methods (e.g., personal acknowledgment, group recognition, written documentation) to meet the diverse needs and preferences of workers.
- Timely and Relevant Recognition: Provide recognition close to the time of achievement to reinforce positive behaviors and their connection to safety and cultural goals.

- Peer Recognition Programs: Implement peer recognition programs to foster a culture of appreciation and support among workers.
- Transparency and Consistency: Apply recognition programs transparently and consistently across all levels of the organization to ensure fairness and support credibility.

Benefits:

- Motivates Positive Behavior: Recognition is a powerful motivator for workers to continue engaging in safe and culturally positive behaviors.
- Enhances Worker Satisfaction and Retention: Acknowledging efforts and achievements can significantly increase job satisfaction and retention rates.
- Strengthens Culture: Recognition programs emphasizing safety achievements strengthen the organization's overall safety culture.
- Encourages Peer Support: Peer recognition initiatives support a community where employees feel appreciated by their co-workers, which improves teamwork and collaboration.
- Boosts Overall Performance: Recognizing and rewarding safety and cultural contributions can boost organizational performance, as workers feel more connected and committed to the organization's goals.

CLOSING

As we intertwine the various strands of actions we have discussed, we are crafting a comprehensive and dynamic framework—a blueprint aimed at bolstering safety measures and nurturing a culture that flourishes with them. Each action is unique but also part of an interlinked system that is pivotal in laying a robust foundation, one in which safety transcends mere compliance or procedural obligations, becoming a core value deeply embedded in the organization's ethos. This transformation elevates the organizational culture from standard safety practices to a vibrant, living principle that resonates throughout the organization.

The harmonious combination of these actions weaves a resilient structure that is durable over time and drives the organization toward future growth and success. The journey to ingraining these qualities into the organization's essence is a formidable challenge and a rewarding venture. It calls for a steadfast commitment to ongoing improvement, an openness to embrace change, and a deep-rooted dedication to ensuring the welfare and well-being of every organizational member. This path extends beyond the mere enactment of policies; it is about cultivating meaningful connections, encouraging personal development, and fostering an environment where every voice is valued and every effort recognized.

In the next chapter, we will delve into the critical roles and responsibilities of leaders and managers and their place in supporting the safety system and embodying the tenets of a safety-first culture within the organization.

Chapter 16:

The Leadership Element

Great leaders love to see people grow.

— JACK WELCH

When I started my safety journey years ago, I delved into the intricacies of safety management systems, intrigued by how they evolved alongside organizational growth. This journey was transformative, as it involved deep dives into critical elements and enhanced control through targeted actions and the meaningful work to which we dedicated ourselves. Initially, my focus was on three core areas: refining the physical work environment, nurturing people's development to improve their performance, and fostering the growth of both organizational and safety cultures. However, I often encountered a palpable limitation: the missed achievement of desired success targets, primarily due to the management and leadership teams' lack of engagement in their pivotal roles. This disconnection, I came to realize, represented a significant gap in my chain of success.

My experiences have taught me that when leadership and management actively engage and partner across the organization—especially with the front line—the enhancement of safety performance is not just possible but assured. Conversely, the absence of this commitment often led to challenges in realizing our safety goals. My focus, therefore, expanded from three to four elements to bridge this gap and foster stronger partnerships from the front line to the senior leadership ranks.

Leadership in this context is defined not by position alone but by the ability to influence attitudes, behaviors, and the overall safety culture within an organization. Leaders, endowed with positional power, are crucial in nurturing a safety culture that prioritizes the well-being of every worker. They function as decision-makers and role models, embedding the organization's safety values through their actions, decisions, and communication. Leadership transcends formal titles, encompassing all who shape safety culture and practices, from the management team to front-line workers. The accurate measure of a leader's effectiveness in safety culture is not merely regulatory compliance but his or her capacity to cultivate an environment that proactively engages every worker, empowering them to contribute to a safe workplace.

By aligning the culture with the system's goals, leaders ensure the safety management system's vivacity and effectiveness across all organizational levels, setting the stage for enduring success and ongoing improvement. This chapter will explore eight pivotal actions:

- Guiding
- Monitoring
- Expecting
- Engaging
- Communicating
- Adapting
- Innovating
- Celebrating

Grounded in my firsthand experiences, this exploration will not cover every conceivable action but will highlight those I often encountered and the strategies I employed for enhanced safety oversight. Through the "leadership element," we aim to illuminate the critical role of influential leaders in elevating the intrinsic value of safety at the front line and throughout the organization.

At this point in your learning and as you reflect on this section of the book, you've studied three system elements along with their associated actions. In reality, they serve as the swim lane to keep you going straight ahead to victory. However, there are still dangers to success, so let's delve deeper into understanding and leveraging leadership and how this important element needs your consideration.

GUIDING

Leaders in positions of power need to lead effectively because promoting safety on the front lines is paramount. Leaders play a pivotal role in shaping and reinforcing a safety culture within any organization. Their ability to effectively guide safety at the front line is critical for ensuring their workers' well-being and overall operational efficiency and reputation. Guiding safety effectively requires clear communication, commitment, empathy, and strategic foresight.

Strategies:

- Lead by Example: Demonstrate a personal commitment to safety by adhering to all safety protocols and practices. Be on the front lines regularly to observe and participate in safety practices. Visible leadership demonstrates commitment and allows for real-time feedback and encouragement.
- Communicate Clearly and Consistently: Communicate all safety information, expectations, and changes clearly and consistently to all workers. Use multiple platforms and formats to accommodate different learning styles and language needs. Consistently communicate that safety is a non-negotiable core value of the organization.
- Enable Workers to Participate in Safety Decisions: Involve front-line workers in safety planning and decision-making processes. This empowerment encourages ownership of safety practices and leverages front-line insights for better safety solutions.

- Foster a Culture for Reporting Incidents: Promote a culture where workers feel safe to report safety incidents and near-misses without fear of blame or retribution. A just culture encourages openness and continuous improvement in safety practices.
- Invest in Safety Technology: Use safety technologies and equipment to enhance workplace safety. Technology can provide innovative solutions to traditional safety challenges and show a commitment to maintaining an innovative safety program.

Benefits

- Heightened Safety Culture: Strong safety leadership and guidance foster a culture where everyone values and prioritizes safety from the top down.
- Reduced Workplace Accidents: Leadership commitment to safety and proactive safety management can significantly reduce the frequency and severity of workplace accidents and injuries.
- Enhanced Worker Morale: A safe work environment and visible leadership commitment to safety enhance worker morale and job satisfaction.
- Improved Operational Efficiency: Fewer adverse events lead to more consistent operations and reduced downtime, enhancing overall efficiency.
- Stronger Trust Between Workers and Leadership: Open dialogue, empowerment, and visible leadership efforts to prioritize safety build trust and respect between workers and management.

MONITORING

Consistent monitoring and evaluation of the work system are essential for pinpointing areas that require enhancement, ensuring they align with the broader organizational goals, and improving overall performance. This crucial process entails assessing the effectiveness and efficiency of processes, policies, and practices within the organizational framework and making strategic adjustments to improve operations.

Strategies:

- Implement a Balanced Scorecard Approach: Employ a balanced scorecard system that includes safety leading and lagging metrics, financial and internal processes, and learning and growth metrics to assess organizational performance comprehensively.
- Use Technology for Real-Time Analytics: Leverage technology platforms that offer real-time analytics and dashboards, enabling immediate insights into operational performance and areas needing attention.
- Develop a Feedback Loop: Create a structured feedback loop that captures insights from workers at every level, especially from the front line, ensuring their experiences and suggestions inform continuous improvement efforts.
- Establish Regular Review Cycles: Schedule regular assessment cycles to systematically review the work system's performance, continuously identifying and implementing evaluations and improvements.
- Foster a Culture of Openness and Transparency: Encourage an organizational culture that values openness and transparency, in which assessments are shared and discussed openly with teams to foster a collective approach to improvements.

Benefits:

- Aligned Organizational Goals: Regular assessments align every element of the work system with the organization's strategic objectives, driving cohesive efforts toward shared goals.

- Enhanced Operational Efficiency: By finding and addressing inefficiencies within the work system, organizations can streamline processes, reduce waste, and optimize resource allocation.
- Increased Worker Engagement: Involving front-line workers in the assessment process and valuing their feedback boosts morale and engagement, as they feel their contributions are recognized and valued.
- Continuous Performance Improvement: Adopting a continuous improvement mindset facilitates the ongoing refinement of practices, leading to sustained enhancements in performance and outcomes.
- Informed Decision-Making: Clear metrics and gathering comprehensive feedback provide leaders with the data needed to make informed decisions, providing targeted and evidence-based adjustments.

EXPECTING

Setting lofty expectations and being inspirational are intertwined strategies that profoundly affect front-line workers. These approaches involve leadership communicating performance and behavior expectations to workers while motivating them to exceed them. This dual focus ensures that front-line workers know the standards they must meet and that leadership encourages them to reach and surpass them through their support and resourcing.

Strategies:

- Set Clear, Achievable Goals: Establish clear, measurable, and achievable goals aligning with the organization's safety vision and objectives. Communicate these goals effectively to all front-line workers, providing a solid foundation for their efforts and aspirations.

- Provide Resources and Support: Equip your team with the necessary tools, training, and support to meet and exceed the set expectations. This shows your investment in their success and motivates them to strive for excellence.
- Foster a Culture of Accountability: Create an environment where everyone values and practices accountability at all levels. Encourage open dialogue about successes and areas for improvement, ensuring that everyone takes responsibility for their actions.
- Encourage Innovation and Creativity: Inspire your team to think creatively and innovate within their roles. Emphasize that meeting expectations are about following procedures and finding better ways to achieve results.
- Build Trust and Inspire Confidence: Show trust in your team's abilities and inspire confidence by highlighting their strengths and potential. A leader's belief in their team can significantly boost motivation and effort.

Benefits:

- Improved Performance: Clear expectations and inspirational leadership lead to higher performance levels, as front-line workers understand what is required and feel motivated to achieve these standards.
- Enhanced Engagement: Front-line workers are more engaged and invested in their work when they have clear goals and when leadership supports and inspires them.
- Increased Motivation: Clear expectations and inspirational leadership boost motivation as workers strive to meet and exceed their goals.
- Strengthened Team Cohesion: Celebrating team achievements and fostering a culture of accountability promotes unity and a sense of shared purpose among team members.

- Greater Adaptability: Teams led by inspirational leaders who set clear expectations are better equipped to adapt to changes and overcome challenges, as they are motivated and understand what needs to be accomplished.

ENGAGING

Leadership involvement goes beyond merely overseeing operations; it signifies active engagement and participation in the day-to-day activities and challenges front-line workers face. Increasing the engagement of leaders with front-line operations is a strategic move that yields significant benefits for front-line workers and the organization. By implementing strategies that support this idea, leaders can bridge the gap between management and front-line workers, fostering a workplace environment that values open communication, mutual respect, and collaborative problem-solving. This hands-on approach enhances operational efficiency and team morale and builds a sturdy foundation for organizational success.

Strategies:

- Regularly Participate in Front-Line Activities: Dedicate time to collaborate with front-line workers and participate in their daily tasks and operations. This hands-on approach gives leaders a deeper understanding of their teams' challenges and realities.
- Host Regular Feedback Sessions: Implement open-door policies and regular feedback sessions, encouraging front-line workers to share their insights, concerns, and suggestions directly with leadership.
- Foster a Culture of Open Communication: Cultivate an environment that values open, honest communication. Encourage front-line workers to voice their ideas and concerns, demonstrating that their input is crucial for decision-making.

- Address Concerns and Provide Support: Address front-line workers' concerns and challenges. Offering timely support and solutions demonstrates a commitment to their well-being and success.

Benefits:

- Positive Organizational Culture: Increased leader involvement contributes to a positive organizational culture characterized by mutual respect, support, and collaboration, which attracts and retains top talent.
- Improved Communication: Regular interactions between leaders and front-line workers foster a culture of open communication, leading to better understanding and collaboration.
- Faster Problem Resolution: Actively involved leaders can identify and address issues more quickly, minimizing disruptions and maintaining operational efficiency.
- More Vital Trust in Leadership: Front-line workers develop a stronger trust in leaders and managers who understand their work and challenges, leading to a better work environment.
- Better Decision-Making: Leaders gain firsthand insights into front-line workers' operations and challenges, leading to more informed and effective decision-making.

COMMUNICATING

Effective communication is the foundation of successful safety management, especially at the front line, where direct risks exist. Leaders are crucial in shaping a culture and prioritizing safety through clear, consistent, and engaging communication. By adopting strategic approaches to communicating safety, leaders can ensure that workers hear, understand, and act upon safety messages.

Strategies:

- Tailor Communication to Your Audience: Understand front-line workers' backgrounds, roles, and responsibilities to tailor safety messages that resonate with their daily experiences and challenges.
- Use Multiple Channels: Employ a variety of communication channels (meetings, email, safety apps, bulletin boards) to disseminate safety information, ensuring that messages reach everyone, regardless of their preferred mode of communication. Encourage two-way conversations to get worker feedback and safety questions.
- Incorporate Visual Aids: Use visual aids such as pictures, infographics, and videos to make safety messages more engaging and easier to understand, especially for complex or technical topics.
- Regular Safety Meetings: Hold regular safety meetings that address current safety issues and reinforce ongoing safety practices and protocols. Ensure that all safety communications include clear, actionable steps workers can take to maintain safety.
- Reinforce Messages Regularly: Repetition is critical to retaining safety messages. Regularly reinforce key safety themes and protocols to keep them on the minds of front-line workers.

Benefits:

- Faster Identification and Resolution of Safety Issues: Open lines of communication ensure that workers report and address safety issues promptly, minimizing risks.
- Builds Trust in Leadership: Leaders who communicate effectively about safety demonstrate their commitment and value to the well-being of their workers, building trust and respect.
- Enhanced Safety Awareness: Regular and effective communication raises awareness about safety issues and protocols

among front-line workers. Clear, actionable safety instructions lead to higher compliance rates, as workers understand precisely what to do.

- Reduced Workplace Accidents: Better communication leads to a better understanding of safety practices, which can significantly reduce accidents and injuries.
- Improved Worker Engagement: Workers who feel their safety concerns are heard and addressed are more engaged and motivated to contribute to a safety-conscious work environment. Effective safety communication fosters a culture in which safety is seen as a shared responsibility, enhancing the organization's overall safety ethos.

ADAPTING

Adaptability in leadership refers to the ability of leaders to adjust their strategies, approaches, and behaviors in response to changing circumstances, challenges, and opportunities. This dynamic capability is critical in today's fast-paced and unpredictable business environment. Front-line workers are often the first to encounter changes in operational conditions, customer needs, and safety challenges, so having adaptable leaders can significantly influence the workers' performance, engagement, and adherence to safety protocols.

Strategies:

- Foster a Culture of Continuous Learning: Leaders can promote adaptability by embracing a culture of continuous learning within their teams. Encouraging front-line workers to engage in regular training sessions, workshops, and cross-functional learning opportunities prepares them to effectively manage diverse challenges and adapt to new situations.
- Implement Agile Decision-Making Processes: Adaptability requires the capacity to make quick, informed decisions. Leaders should establish agile decision-making processes that

empower front-line workers to respond swiftly to emerging issues, ensuring that these processes are flexible enough to adapt to changing circumstances.

- Encourage Open Communication: Maintaining open lines of communication enables leaders to gather insights and feedback from front-line workers about on-the-ground realities. This practice helps leaders adapt their strategies based on real-time information, grounding their decisions in the current context.

- Lead by Example: Leaders can model adaptability by demonstrating flexibility in their actions and decision-making. By showing a willingness to pivot when necessary and openly discussing the reasoning behind changes, leaders can inspire front-line workers to embrace adaptability as a core value.

- Develop Scenario Planning: Scenario planning allows leaders and their teams to anticipate potential challenges and changes. By considering various future scenarios and developing contingency plans, leaders can better prepare their teams to adapt quickly and efficiently to whatever situation arises.

Benefits:

- Enhanced Resilience: Adaptability fosters resilience among front-line workers by equipping them with the skills and mindset to navigate uncertainties and setbacks. This resilience is critical for maintaining productivity and morale in the face of challenges.

- Improved Problem-Solving: Adaptive leaders who encourage innovation and flexibility in problem-solving enable their front-line workers to develop creative solutions to complex problems, enhancing the team's overall capability to address issues effectively.

- Increased Engagement: When leaders adapt their strategies and approaches to reflect their teams' changing needs and circumstances, front-line workers feel more supported and understood. This relevance in the leadership approach increases worker engagement and commitment.

- Faster Response to Change: Adaptive leadership ensures that teams can respond more quickly to changes in the market, operational conditions, or safety requirements, minimizing disruptions and maintaining continuity in operations.

- Cultivation of a Positive Work Environment: Adaptability contributes to a positive work environment by signaling front-line workers that their leaders are proactive, responsive, and supportive of their needs. This positive environment fosters trust, encourages open dialogue, and promotes a more substantial alignment between leadership actions and front-line realities.

INNOVATING

Innovation in promoting safety at the front line is crucial for adapting to the evolving challenges of the work environment. Leaders are pivotal in driving this innovation, ensuring that safety practices are practical and align with technological advancements and behavioral insights. Leveraging technology for managing safety represents a significant shift toward more proactive and preventive safety measures. Leadership involvement in recognizing safety through innovation streamlines processes and significantly affects the effectiveness of safety programs on the front lines. By implementing innovative strategies, leaders can enhance safety outcomes and foster a culture of continuous improvement.

Strategies:

- Implement Safety Management Software: Use comprehensive safety management systems that track and analyze safety performance data and employ mobile apps to enable immediate reporting and bi-directional communication.

- Leverage Emerging Technologies: Explore and implement innovative technologies, such as IoT (Internet of Things) devices, wearables, and AI-driven analytics, to monitor workplace conditions and predict potential safety issues before they arise.
- Harness Prescriptive Analytics for Proactive Safety Management: Use prescriptive analytics to anticipate potential safety risks and prescribe targeted actions. This approach enables proactive interventions that address issues before they escalate, fostering a culture of safety excellence and continuous improvement.
- Adopt Wearable Safety Technologies: Integrate wearable technologies that monitor and alert workers to potential hazards. Recognizing workers who consistently adhere to safety protocols based on data from wearables can motivate others to follow suit.
- Establish Cross-Functional Safety Teams: Create teams that include members from different departments to collaborate on developing innovative safety solutions, ensuring a comprehensive approach to safety that leverages diverse perspectives.

Benefits

- Increased Visibility of Safety Efforts: Innovative digital platforms make safe behaviors and achievements more visible across the organization, raising awareness and setting benchmarks for safety excellence.
- Improved Reporting and Transparency: A culture that encourages the reporting of safety concerns fosters transparency and enables leaders to address potential issues proactively.
- Worker Expectations: An organization that leverages modern technologies for safety management is more attractive to prospective workers, especially as new generations of workers and organizations that embrace technology tend to retain their

workforce by demonstrating a commitment to worker well-being and innovation.

- Cross-Departmental Collaboration: Cross-functional safety teams promote a sense of unity and shared responsibility for safety, breaking down silos and integrating safety considerations into all aspects of the organization's operations.
- Broader Impact: Technology can reach a wider audience quickly, encouraging a culture of continuous improvement. Workers will be more motivated to innovate and to adopt best safety practices.

CELEBRATING

Leadership involvement in celebrating safety achievements is pivotal to embedding safety deeply within an organization's culture. By implementing diverse and meaningful strategies for celebration, leaders can effectively communicate the importance of safety, motivate continuous improvement, and foster a positive and engaged workplace. The benefits of such an approach extend beyond mere compliance with safety standards, contributing to a work environment that celebrates, values, and continuously embraces safety.

Strategies:

- Personalized Recognition: Tailor recognition to fit the individual or team you're celebrating. Personalized acknowledgments resonate more deeply and are more meaningful to recipients.
- Incorporate Peer Recognition: Encourage a peer recognition program through which workers can nominate their colleagues for safety recognition. This peer-to-peer approach fosters a supportive safety culture.
- Celebrate Safety Milestones: Mark significant safety milestones, such as meeting leading metrics, with celebrations that involve the whole team. These milestones highlight collective achievements in maintaining a safe workplace. Moreover,

celebrate misses when there was significant learning that offer an opportunity to improve.

- Use a Variety of Recognition Methods: Employ a mix of formal and informal, tangible and intangible methods to recognize safety achievements, from public acknowledgments during meetings to small tokens of appreciation recognizing efforts. A good approach for recognizing workers is focusing on leading indicators that drive positive lagging results. Diversity in recognition methods keeps the program fresh and engaging.
- Communicate Success Stories: Share stories of recognized individuals and teams across the organization through internal newsletters, meetings, or the company intranet. Highlighting these success stories promotes best practices and inspires others.

Benefits:

- Reinforced Safety Behaviors: Recognizing and celebrating safety achievements reinforces desired behaviors, encouraging workers to prioritize safety.
- Greater Visibility for Safety Initiatives: Highlighting safety successes raises the profile of safety initiatives, making safety a more integral part of the organizational dialogue.
- Improved Morale: Celebrations and recognition contribute to a positive work environment, improving morale and overall job satisfaction among front-line workers.
- Motivation for Continuous Improvement: Acknowledging safety efforts motivates workers to maintain high safety standards and continuously seek ways to improve safety practices.
- Strengthened Team Cohesion: Celebrating safety achievements as a team fosters a sense of unity and collective responsibility for maintaining a safe work environment.

CLOSING

In this chapter, I have elucidated a transformative safety journey that emphasizes the critical role of leadership in fostering a robust safety culture across organizational levels. I started this section of study with a focus on improving the physical work environment, developing people, and cultivating safety and organizational cultures. All of this is still heavily dependent on addressing the vital gap in leadership engagement. The expanded focus underscores the necessity for leaders, not just in formal positions but across the spectrum of your organization, to actively engage and partner with everyone, especially front-line workers, to enhance safety performance.

The elements I've discussed here outline specific strategies under themes such as guiding, monitoring, expecting, engaging, communicating, adapting, innovating, and celebrating, each contributing to a comprehensive approach to safety management. These strategies involve leading by example, fostering open communication, involving workers in decision-making, leveraging technology, and recognizing and celebrating safety achievements, all aimed at building a proactive, informed, and motivated workforce.

Leadership's role extends beyond traditional management, becoming pivotal in shaping safety culture through continuous engagement, communication, and recognition. By aligning organizational goals with the safety management system's objectives and adopting innovative practices, leaders ensure not only compliance but also a thriving environment where safety becomes a shared responsibility and core organizational value. This commitment to safety leadership guarantees that safety performance is not merely about preventing accidents but creating an environment that promotes worker well-being and operational excellence.

Let's move to the next chapter to see how we incrementally piece the safety process together. Since you are now swimming in a straight line in your swim lane, are you ready to learn the backstroke?

Chapter 17:

The Value of Incremental Safety Change

Slow and steady wins the race.

— AESOP

It is possible that you anticipated me discussing the prominent use of a pawn casting its shadow on the front cover at some point in the book. Indeed, those small, often insignificant game pieces that only move one or two spaces at a time are essential and have so much to give if only given a chance to contribute. Likewise, every role in an organization, no matter how small or seemingly insignificant, is integral and contributes to the overall success.

Chess is a hobby I enjoy, but I have never been particularly successful at it. The opposing player often determines the game's outcome, whether lengthy and complex or brief and decisive. My defeat usually comes from my impatient mistakes, but more often, it comes from a skilled chess player who has a profound understanding of the worth of each chess piece. Like many players, I've long understood the significance of each chess piece but always regarded the pawns as much less valuable than the other pieces. This underestimation of the pawns is a common mistake, as many novice players often opt to remove the pawns from the board's front line in the beginning, thinking it grants better control and access to the more critical pieces in the game.

To become a successful chess player, you need talent, unwavering dedication, strategic understanding, and psychological resilience. It requires a complete understanding of principles, including extensive knowledge of openings, middle-game strategies, and endgame tactics. When coupled with remarkable tactical vision, this mastery enables the chess player to anticipate opponents' moves, spot patterns, and take strategic action. The game requires not only intellectual prowess but also emotional and psychological resilience. The comparison is direct: great chess players don't ignore any piece, even the pawns, and safety practitioners had best not ignore the tremendous value they can find at the front line.

The pawns' strategic importance is a fitting metaphor when considering the role of front-line workers. Like pawns on a chessboard, front-line workers play a crucial role in your organization, often without the acknowledgment or support they deserve. Each deliberate step of the pawn on the chessboard captures the essence of incremental change. Given the proper environment, this seemingly insignificant element can become a matter of considerable importance. The transition from limited power to strategic advantage parallels the path of front-line workers, who play a vital role in your organization. The efforts of front-line workers highlight the significant effect of consistent, incremental, moves in a positive direction to achieve fantastic safety results.

By considering the role of the front-line workers and this idea of incremental change, we can better appreciate the significance of patience, persistence, and foresight in attaining long-term goals at the front line. In chess, the transformation of a pawn through promotion is a process that involves deliberate moves and strategic planning, not an instant change. Similarly, the influence of front-line workers on the organization is not limited to a single act but rather stems from their constant and gradual improvements in their work and environment. Much of this book is supported by the idea that doing small things consistently is vital in building your knowledge, developing a solid safety foundation, and leveraging the safety process to move in a positive direction through gradual improvement. I have found that safety is rarely the result of extensive, immediate moves; instead, it's a strategic, well-thought-out plan delivered along multiple facets. Even in chess, winning takes more than one move, and slow and steady progress positions you to win.

By appreciating and valuing the consistent efforts of workers on the front lines, whether in chess or leading safety, we can recognize the significant effect of fostering people's potential and encouraging gradual advancement.

This chapter examines how to become more effective through incremental safety change and taking everything you have learned so far in establishing partnerships at the front line.

THE VALUE OF INCREMENTAL CHANGE

We often attack big problems with big solutions. For example, suppose a worker sustains a severe injury or illness, or you identify the need for increased control, possibly because of an audit or an inspection, or you are just beginning your safety process and fear a substantial loss. In many of these cases, you jump on the problem with a sizable focus. Undoubtedly, some of the things I have shared are big and bold actions. However, as a safety practitioner, you will spend much of your energy on small yet significant problems that keep you from the safety performance you desire. The concept of incremental change embodies the principle that small, consistent improvements accumulate over time to yield substantial gains. This philosophy, rooted in the Japanese practice of Kaizen (Japanese for "a change for the better"), suggests that continuous, reasonable enhancements can often be more effective and sustainable than attempting large-scale transformations. The value of incremental change lies in its accessibility, sustainability, and cumulative effect. It is a powerful strategy for achieving the long-term performance improvements you desire as you move forward in your safety practice. Here are some considerations that support this idea of incremental change.

Accessibility and Manageability

One of the most significant advantages of incremental change is its ease of use. Small changes require less initial investment of time, resources, and energy, making changes more manageable and less daunting for your organization. Have you ever tried to get senior leadership to buy in on a large-scale project that consumes resources? I bet, at times, it has been a struggle. An incremental change approach democratizes improvement, enabling everyone, including the front-line workers, to contribute to performance enhancement regardless of their role or level of expertise. As I have discussed, this is especially vital to an interdependent work culture and authentic partnership. By focusing on attainable adjustments, incremental change fosters a culture of continuous improvement in which every worker feels empowered to identify and implement improvements.

Sustainability of Efforts

Incremental changes are inherently more sustainable than drastic overhauls. By gradually introducing new behaviors or processes, workers and organizations will likely adapt more quickly, reducing resistance and increasing the likelihood of long-term adoption. One of the biggest challenges with transformational safety change is that it is often challenging because it is time-consuming and requires ample resources; frankly, not everyone is likely to jump on board. A gradual adaptation process allows for continuous feedback and adjustment to integrate changes into daily routines and operational practices. Small-scale changes make culture more sustainable by quickly identifying and correcting negative safety consequences with minimal disruption.

Cumulative Effect on Performance

The true power of incremental change lies in its cumulative effect. While small improvements may seem minor, their effects compound over time, leading to significant performance gains. This principle is akin to compound interest in finance: small, regular investments grow exponentially because of the interest earned on both the principal and the accumulated interest from previous periods. In the context of safety performance improvement, each small change builds upon the previous, creating a snowball effect that can transform an organization's efficiency, effectiveness, safety culture, capability, accountability, leadership, and overall success.

Capability and Capacity Innovation

Incremental change encourages a mindset of constant learning and experimentation. Workers and organizations foster a culture of curiosity and innovation by continuously seeking improvement. Would an organization of workers who are always curious about making the work environment safer not be a good idea? This ongoing exploration of new ideas, tools, and methods leads to performance gains and keeps teams engaged and motivated. The iterative nature of incremental improvements provides valuable lessons from each attempt, whether successful or not, contributing to a deeper understanding of what works best in a given context.

Overcoming Challenges

Implementing incremental change is not without its challenges. Maintaining momentum and focus over time can be difficult, especially when the immediate effect of changes is not readily apparent. It requires persistent effort, clear communication of goals and progress, and mechanisms to celebrate small victories. Moreover, the cumulative effect of changes necessitates thorough tracking and measurement to ensure that improvements are moving in the right direction and contributing to the overarching goals. Remember your safety vision?

The value of incremental change in creating cumulative performance gains is profound. Workers and organizations can significantly enhance performance, efficiency, and innovation over time by making continuous, small improvements. This approach facilitates a more manageable and sustainable path to excellence and cultivates a constant learning and adaptability culture, essential for thriving in an ever-changing world.

SAFETY KAIZEN

The power of incremental change is evident through the lens of Kaizen. Kaizen goes back to the Toyota Motor Corporation, which implemented the concept to be more creative, drive innovation, gain better quality, and eliminate waste that hampered production. For the safety practitioner, it means removing or mitigating the risks in the work system that challenge safety performance and success.

A cornerstone of Kaizen is the belief that no day should pass without progress in the organization and that these small, daily changes can lead to substantial improvements over time. Central to Kaizen is the idea that everyone in the organization, from the senior leader's office to the front-line workers, contributes to the improvement process. In the organization where I work now, we fully embrace Kaizen. Even the company's CEO frequently leads his own Kaizen workshops and personally monitors much of this work throughout the organization because he has experienced the incredible value of Kaizen to improve how we operate and reach our lofty performance targets.

Kaizen democratizes innovation and enhances worker engagement and ownership. Kaizen values suggestions for improvement. It encourages a culture of persistent, attentive problem-solving and operational excellence, and the cumulative effect of minor adjustments leads to significant enhancements in efficiency, quality, productivity, and functional support areas such as safety and health. By fostering an environment where continuous improvement is part of the organizational DNA, Kaizen facilitates a sustainable path to excellence. It fosters team interdependence; everyone collectively takes part in the organization's ownership, driving it toward better practices, processes, and results. In the case of safety, people are getting home safely every single day.

Here is why you should consider employing Kaizen.

- Embraces the Idea of Continuous Improvement: At the heart of Kaizen is the belief that there's always room for improvement, no matter how efficient a process or practice may seem. This mindset encourages a culture of innovation in which you look for errors in the work system and regularly implement changes to enhance performance and efficiency.
- Promotes Worker Involvement: Kaizen emphasizes the role of every worker in the improvement process, encouraging contributions and ideas from all levels of an organization. This inclusive approach ensures various perspectives and fosters a sense of partnership and engagement among team members.
- Standardizes Successful Practices: Once you identify an improvement, you standardize it across the organization, ensuring every team or worker benefits. This cycle of implementing and standardizing changes ensures you sustain improvements over time.
- Takes Small Steps for Big Change: Kaizen focuses on small, manageable changes rather than large-scale transformations. This approach reduces resistance to change, making it easier to implement and sustain improvements over the long term.
- Increases Flexibility and Adaptability: The Kaizen approach fosters a culture of continuous learning and adaptability. Organizations become more curious, agile, and capable of responding quickly to changes in the market or operational challenges.
- Leverages Continuous Growth and Competitive Advantage: Organizations that practice Kaizen can achieve continuous growth and maintain a competitive edge. The cumulative effect of ongoing improvements can lead to significant advancements and innovations over time.

There are also challenges as you consider this process.

- Cultural Shift Required: Adopting Kaizen requires a significant cultural shift for those not accustomed to the continuous improvement mindset. It demands commitment from all levels of an organization, which can be challenging to achieve.
- Patience and Persistence: Kaizen's benefits may not be immediately visible, as it focuses on small, incremental, and often long-term changes that take time to see fully. Maintaining motivation and persistence in the face of gradual progress requires patience and a clear understanding of the philosophy's long-term benefits.
- Measuring Small Improvements: Tracking the effect of small, incremental changes can be complex. You must develop effective metrics and measurement tools to assess Kaizen's effectiveness and to ensure it drives meaningful progress.

Despite these challenges, the Kaizen approach to incremental change offers a robust framework for achieving sustainable improvement. Its emphasis on continuous, small steps toward improvement provides a pragmatic path to significant transformations over time. By adopting Kaizen, workers and organizations are committed to an ethos of perpetual improvement.

DEPLOYING KAIZEN FOR SAFETY

Adopting Kaizen for safety improvement involves a systematic process for identifying opportunities, setting objectives, and implementing solutions with the entire team's involvement.

Here is a breakdown of applying a simple Kaizen practice to improve a problem.

1. Identify a Problem or Opportunity: The first step is to recognize an area within your organization that needs improvement. Break down the process and seek to understand and identify the root causes for anything that is causing safety concerns.

Logical areas include gaps within the safety management system, the work environment, workforce capability or skills development, waste found in safety process administration, or even activities that promote or allow substandard behaviors.

2. Analyze the Problem, Explore New Ideas, and Set Objectives: Build a team of everyone with interest, expertise, and investment in the problem. Assemble everyone to analyze and review data in brainstorming sessions to generate ideas to address the problem or opportunity. Encourage open communication and consider all suggestions, ensuring everyone's voice is heard and their expertise is leveraged. This collaborative approach fosters innovation and ensures team buy-in for any proposed changes early in the process.

3. Break the Objective Down into Deliverables and Sub-Objectives: Decompose the main objective into smaller, manageable sub-objectives or deliverables. Develop a detailed task plan for achieving each deliverable and sub-objective if necessary. This planning phase should include defining clear timelines, responsible parties, and required resources for each task. A well-structured plan helps avoid bottlenecks and ensures a smooth implementation process.

4. Test, Monitor Progress, Adapt and Standardize: Implement the changes on a small scale to evaluate their effectiveness. Monitor the progress closely, collecting data to measure the effect of the improvements. Be prepared to adapt the plan based on the outcomes of the testing phase. This may involve tweaking the approach, reallocating resources, or extending deadlines to accommodate unforeseen challenges. Remember, adaptability is key to overcoming obstacles and ensuring the success of your improvement process.

5. Move On to the Next Objective: After successfully implementing the improvements and achieving the set objective, standardize the new processes to ensure you apply the steps

consistently. Then, move on to identify the next problem or opportunity for improvement, starting the Kaizen cycle anew.

This continuous loop of identifying opportunities, setting objectives, implementing solutions, and standardizing successful practices drives organizational growth and efficiency. It is a practical, sustainable way to remove or mitigate safety risks in the work system.

The cycle looks like this in Figure 1.

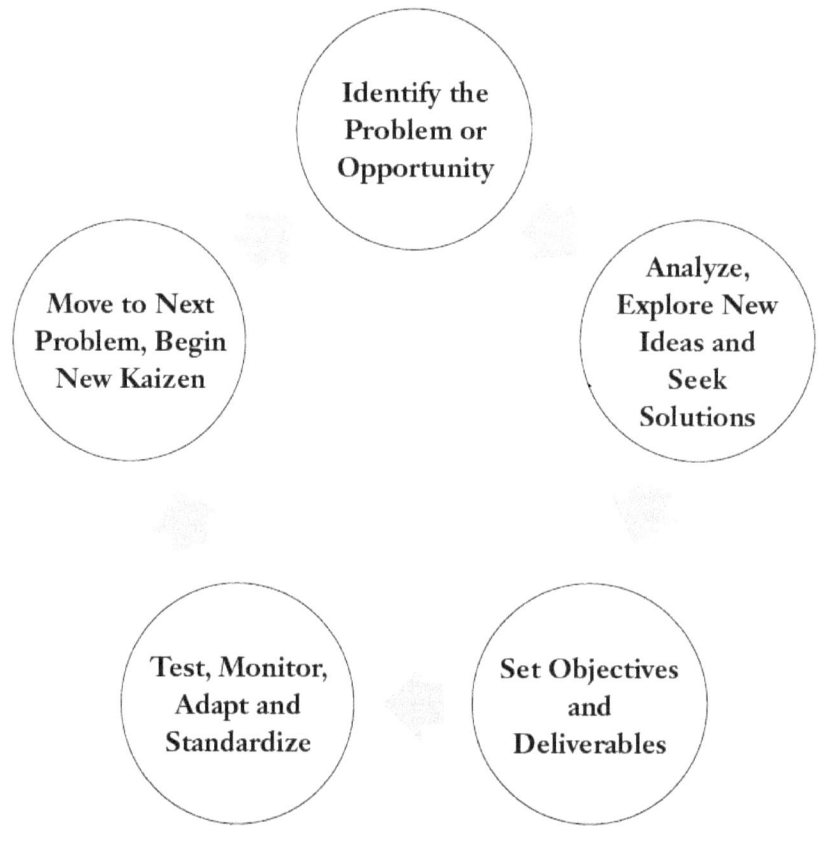

Figure 1

Another tool that supports Kaizen is the PDCA (plan-do-check-act) cycle, also known as the Deming Cycle. This cycle is a continuous loop of planning, doing, checking (or studying), and acting. It provides a systematic method for gaining valuable learning and knowledge to continuously improve a product or process. You can apply the PDCA cycle to various changes and processes within organizations or even individual projects.

Here is a look at each step:

Plan: This phase is the foundation of the cycle, where you define the objectives and processes necessary to deliver results and outputs. During this stage, you:

- Identify and Define: Clearly define the problem or improvement opportunity and understand its nature.
- Set Objectives: Establish objectives for what you hope to achieve.
- Develop Hypotheses: Predict the changes that could lead to improvement.
- Plan Actions: Devise a detailed plan for change, including the steps needed, resources required, and timeline for implementation.
- Establish Metrics: Decide how to measure success, choosing relevant metrics to indicate whether the change has achieved the desired improvement.

Do: The plan is implemented in this phase, but on a small scale if possible. This stage is about experimentation and application:

- Implement the Plan: Execute the steps in the Plan phase in a controlled setting.
- Document Everything: Keep detailed records of what you did and what data you collected.

- Begin Data Collection: Gather data for analysis in the next phase.

Check: This phase involves evaluating the results of the Do phase, analyzing data, and comparing the outcomes against the expected objectives to identify any discrepancies:

- Analyze Data: Look at the data you collected during the Do phase to see what it tells you about the effectiveness of your plan.
- Learn from the Results: Determine whether the change caused an improvement.
- Report Findings: Summarize findings, capturing lessons, successes, and failures.

Act: In this phase, you act based on what you learned in the Check phase. If the plan is successful, you can standardize and implement the new process on a broader scale. If not, you begin the cycle again from the Plan phase:

- Standardize Improvement: Implement the successful strategies on a broader scale.
- Adjust and Refine: Make necessary adjustments based on feedback and learning from the cycle.
- Plan for Next Cycle: Identify further improvements and continue the cycle with a new plan.

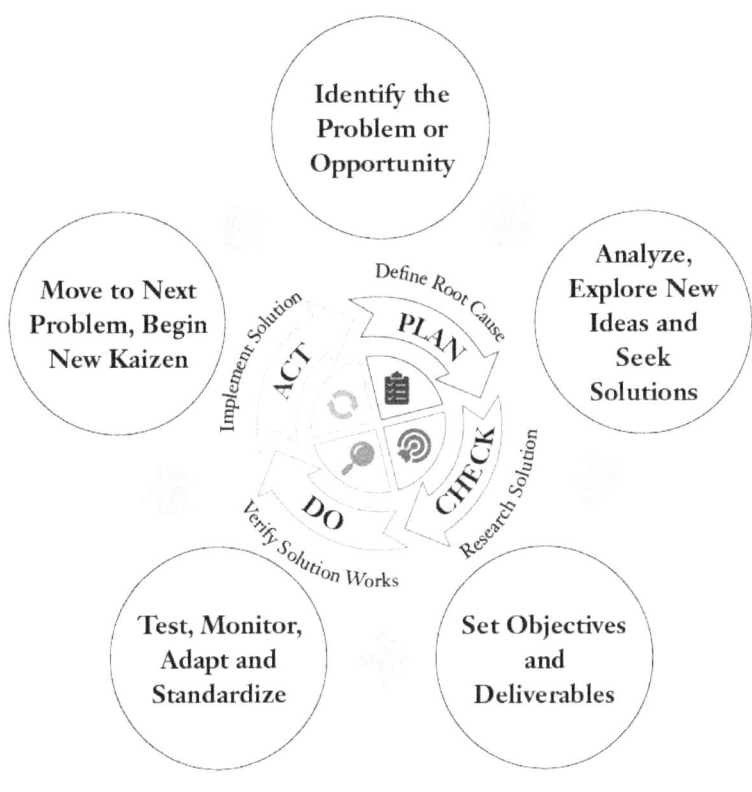

Figure 2

HOW KAIZEN AND PDCA WORK TOGETHER

Using Kaizen and the PDCA cycle is a comprehensive and practical approach to problem-solving and continuous organizational improvement. This combination, shown above in Figure 2, leverages the strengths of each method to create a culture of ongoing enhancement, where small, incremental changes lead to significant long-term benefits. Here are the critical values of integrating Kaizen with the PDCA cycle in problem-solving efforts:

1. Systematic and Structured Approach

- PDCA provides a structured, iterative framework that ensures organized and systematic problem-solving efforts. It guides teams through planning, implementing, checking, and acting on changes.
- Kaizen, with its emphasis on continuous improvement, complements PDCA by embedding a structured approach into the daily activities of all employees and fostering a proactive environment for identifying and solving problems.

2. Empowerment and Engagement of Employees

- Kaizen encourages the involvement of all employees, from top management to the front-line workers, in the problem-solving process. This inclusivity boosts morale, as employees feel that leadership values their contributions and that they have a stake in the organization's success.
- Integrating PDCA within this inclusive culture ensures that you collect and act upon employee suggestions in a disciplined and measurable way to support continuous improvement.

3. Focus on Continuous, Incremental Improvements

- Kaizen's philosophy of small, continuous changes ensures that the organization constantly moves forward without waiting for breakthroughs. This approach can lead to significant improvements without needing large investments or overhauls.
- The PDCA cycle complements this by providing a mechanism to systematically assess these small changes, evaluate their effectiveness, and standardize successful practices throughout the organization.

4. Data-Driven Decision Making

- The Check phase of the PDCA cycle ensures that decisions are based on data and analysis rather than assumptions. This scientific approach to problem-solving minimizes risk and increases the likelihood of successful outcomes.
- Kaizen promotes a culture in which feedback from all levels of the organization informs decisions, grounding improvements in real-world insights and experiences.

5. Building a Culture of Continuous Improvement

- Together, Kaizen and PDCA embed continuous improvement in the organization's DNA. This culture encourages constant vigilance for improvement opportunities and fosters an environment where change is embraced rather than feared.
- This continuous improvement culture helps organizations stay competitive, adapt to changes quickly, and continuously enhance their processes, products, and services.

6. Efficient Problem-Solving

- The combination of Kaizen and PDCA enables organizations to tackle problems efficiently by identifying root causes and implementing solutions in a controlled, measurable way. This efficiency saves time and resources and increases the chances of solving problems permanently.

CLOSING

Safety success is both a shared endeavor and an individual covenant. It requires collective effort and collaboration at all levels of an organization to create a safe environment, while also demanding personal responsibility and commitment from each individual. By working together and upholding our commitments to safety, we can achieve a culture of mutual care and continuous improvement. Within the spectrum of the actions I've discussed, a dynamic interaction among leaders, mid-level management, and front-line workers lays out a strategic blueprint for success. It spans four key elements: physical environment, person, culture, and leadership. There are ample pathways to consider across this metaphoric chessboard. Still, as I have shared in this chapter, your journey significantly involves working in incremental steps, considering Kaizen and PDCA as tools to actualize the cumulative effect of these small changes and create transformative results.

You might have noticed that as we explored the four elements and their thirty-two actions in this part of the book, certain strategies and benefits consistently appear across them all. You're absolutely right. There are indeed a few common, repeatable behaviors and actions that are crucial to your understanding and key to moving your safety process forward, no matter the actionable subject area.

Your task now is to evaluate each element and its associated actions, perhaps against a more extensive list of your own, and determine how to intricately weave this fabric of control in a manner that fosters greater safety and cultivates a culture of collective responsibility—from senior leadership to the front-line worker and across all organizational levels.

In the final chapter, I will share my insights on the future of safety and health, outlining what lies ahead and how you can best prepare for the evolving landscape of your professional development. Let's embark on this final leg together, with an eye toward the future and a commitment to lifelong learning and adaptation in safety and health.

Part IV:
Looking Forward in Occupational Safety and Health

Chapter 18:

The Future of Occupational Safety and Health

The only thing we know about the future is that it will be different.

— Peter Drucker

As we stand on the threshold of a new era, a confluence of factors molds the future of occupational safety and health. Technological innovations, from digital data collection, automation, and robotics to artificial intelligence, the Internet of Things, and wearables, are revolutionizing how we monitor safety, identify hazards, and protect workers. Technologies such as these promise a better understanding of the workplace that will further opportunities for better control of the work environment. However, they also introduce new challenges, including the need for rigorous data privacy protections, policies, training, and skills development.

Simultaneously, the demographic composition of the workforce is changing. Millennials and Generation Z will become the majority in a few years, bringing different workplace safety, health, and well-being expectations. These younger generations will demand more from their organizations, seeking physical safety, mental health support, work-life balance, and a commitment to sustainability characterized by the pillars of environmental, social, and governance (ESG) measures. Their influence will catalyze a prominent shift toward more holistic approaches to safety and health that consider the worker's whole person and place within the broader ecosystem.

Moreover, the nature of work itself is changing. The rise of remote work, the gig economy, and flexible working arrangements are redefining the traditional workplace, expanding the scope of safety and health to encompass the home office, shared workspaces, and beyond. These changes will require reimagining safety controls and practices to address these new working methods' unique risks and challenges.

Additionally, the global nature of the workforce and the interconnectedness of economies will take a step toward international collaboration in developing and implementing safety and health standards and practices. As we embark on this journey into the future of leading safety and health, the stakes have never been higher. The well-being of workers is not just a moral imperative but also a critical component of sustainable, productive economies and societies. By embracing change, fostering innovation, and prioritizing the health and safety of all workers, we can likely forge a future in which every individual can work in a safe, healthy, and supportive work environment.

This chapter invites you to envision that future, exploring the trends, challenges, and opportunities that will define the following occupational safety and health era.

THE EXPANDED FOCUS ON WORKER WELL-BEING

The change in thinking toward an expanded focus on worker well-being within safety and health is a critical evolution in how we conceptualize and prioritize care of the workforce. Historically, managing safety has concentrated on minimizing physical risks and preventing accidents and illnesses directly tied to the workplace. While undeniably important, this conventional approach no longer fully addresses the multifaceted nature of work and its effect on an individual's health and well-being. The changing dynamics of work, the workforce, and the workplace demand a broader, more holistic perspective that acknowledges the full spectrum of factors influencing worker safety and health.

There will be an expanding focus on leading safety to include worker well-being, which will stem from recognizing that today's workforce's challenges extend beyond physical hazards to encompass a range of psychosocial factors. These include workplace stress, job insecurity, work-life balance issues, financial stressors, and the effect of organizational culture on mental health. The rise of digital technologies and the increasing prevalence of remote work further complicate these dynamics, introducing new stressors and blurring the boundaries between work and personal life. Addressing these psychosocial hazards is imperative to safeguarding worker well-being, as they can significantly affect mental health, job satisfaction, decision-making, and overall quality of life.

Here are the areas that will require your attention:

Work-Life Balance and Flexibility

The overall quality of work life has become crucial to workers' well-being and will continue to grow in importance. This encompasses not only the absence of negative factors, such as stress and job insecurity, but also positive elements, such as job fulfillment, a sense of purpose, and opportunities for growth and development. Enhancing the quality of work requires attention to job design, organizational practices, learning, team culture, and the overall work environment, all of which are pivotal in influencing worker satisfaction and well-being.

This expanded focus on worker well-being acknowledges that the health and safety of workers are not separate or isolated issues but are deeply interconnected with broader societal and environmental factors. Economic inequality, knowledge of world events, and societal well-being directly and indirectly affect worker health and safety. For example, social or climate change can introduce new work risks, while economic inequality can exacerbate stress and mental health issues among workers. Addressing these complex challenges will necessitate a transdisciplinary approach to safety that draws on insights from public health, psychology, sociology, environmental science, and other fields. Such an approach recognizes that creating safe and healthy workplaces is part of a more significant effort to build a sustainable, equitable work team.

Workforce Demographic Evolution and Expectations

The composition of the modern workforce is undergoing a profound transformation as millennials and Generation Z quickly become the predominant demographic segments within the workplace. This generational shift is not just a numerical change but a fundamental alteration in the ethos and expectations that workers bring to their professional environments. These younger workers will prioritize better work-life balance, demand greater flexibility in their work arrangements, and significantly emphasize cultivating a positive and supportive organizational culture. Grasping the nuances of these demographic changes is essential for crafting safety and health strategies that resonate with the evolving aspirations and values of the new workforce.

The demographic shift will also influence the expectations for workplace safety and the overall safety culture within organizations. Engaging younger workers in safety initiatives will require a shift toward more collaborative, transparent, and technology-driven approaches. This includes leveraging social media and digital platforms for data collection, supporting microlearning opportunities for safety training and knowledge transfer, supporting strong bi-directional data exchange and communication, and adopting a more holistic view of health that encompasses mental well-being. Organizations will need to foster a more engaged, proactive, and safety-conscious workforce by aligning culture with the values of millennials and Gen Z. By acknowledging the values of younger workers while also recognizing the changes that workers of older generations will need to make, the safety practitioner can foster a safer and more inclusive workplace. Furthermore, all groups will see the benefits of this approach as a mature path toward better team interdependence and workforce partnership is promoted.

TECHNOLOGICAL ADVANCEMENTS IN WORKPLACE SAFETY

The landscape of safety and health is undergoing a seismic shift driven by the relentless pace of technological advancements. This growth will be expansive in the future. However, I am not sure we can predict the pace or level of technological advancement in the next decade with certainty. With that said, the transformative impact of technology on safety practices, the pivotal role of AI, machine learning (ML), digital safety management systems, mobile applications, wearable technology, and connected network devices will be rampant. There will also be further advancements to already well-adopted technologies, such as automation and the use of robots. Safety practitioners should think about and plan for these significant paths of advancement. As these technologies redefine management control, hazard detection, risk assessment, and safety training paradigms, they offer a glimpse into a future in which safety becomes more proactive, predictive, and prescriptive to address specific workplace problems. However, embracing such innovations also introduces complex challenges for the safety practitioner, including data privacy concerns, the need for digital literacy, and integrating new tools into existing safety frameworks. The technology area is critical for preparing safety practitioners, employers, and workers alike for the next era of workplace safety, ensuring that technological progress translates into tangible benefits for worker well-being supported by a solid management system.

Here are the areas that will require your attention:

Digitalization of Safety Management Systems

The shift toward digital safety management systems is a pivotal change in occupational safety and health approaches. Traditional paper-based methods and disparate digital collection silos are giving way to digitally connected platforms offering real-time tracking, analysis, and reporting capabilities. These systems will facilitate a more dynamic approach to safety management, enabling organizations to respond swiftly to emerging risks and compliance requirements and supporting bi-directional data engagement. Some key benefits include streamlined incident and event reporting, job safety analysis, concern reporting, action planning, and a toolbox filled with risk management and control of work tools, improving the ability to use data to identify, collect, and analyze where you should apply controls. Future advancements will continue integrating more sophisticated analytics, artificial intelligence, and machine learning to predict incidents and automate safety compliance tasks.

Mobile Applications

Mobile applications are poised to transform the rapidly evolving safety and health landscape and connect safety to the front line. These applications, significantly supported by personal smart devices and tablets, will revolutionize safety practices by enabling real-time, bi-directional data exchange and communication, allowing instant reporting, access to safety program data, and a swift response to arising situations. With wearable technology, mobile apps can offer personalized safety and health monitoring, alerting users to substandard conditions and facilitating immediate intervention. Furthermore, mobile applications provide accessible training and microlearning opportunities directly to a worker's smart device, ensuring continuous learning and adherence to the latest safety instructions. A significant opportunity for mobile will be to place more of the safety management system in the hands of the front line.

However, the potential benefits of adopting mobile safety applications are significant. Overcoming challenges such as ensuring data privacy and security, addressing barriers to accessibility and digital literacy, and integrating with existing technology systems is crucial. We must also acknowledge the potential for worker distraction and the varying attitudes towards mobile applications. Overcoming these challenges is key to leveraging mobile apps to create a safer workplace. As organizations chart the future of safety, embracing mobile technology will be vital to fostering an integrated, informed, and proactive safety culture.

Wearable Technology

Wearable technology is at the forefront of innovative approaches to safety and health, offering a groundbreaking way to enhance worker protection and well-being. These devices, from smartwatches to fitness bands, specialized safety vests and belts, clip-on devices, and armbands, are equipped with real-time sensors that monitor the wearer's environmental conditions and physiological state. These wearable technologies can detect exposure to harmful substances and work environments, excessive noise, or extreme temperatures, monitor vital signs such as heart rate and stress levels, alert users to body posture, and even offer voice-to-text messaging that facilitates immediate communication and response if required. The data collected by these wearables is often connected to a comprehensive digital platform to gain even more invaluable insights through artificial intelligence and machine learning to identify patterns and predict future hazards, enabling proactive adjustments to work practices and environments.

Despite their benefits, integrating wearable technology into workplace safety requires addressing challenges such as privacy concerns, overcoming worker hesitancy, device comfort, user-friendliness, and maintaining the accuracy and reliability of the data collected. As this technology continues to evolve, it promises to play an even more pivotal role in advancing safety practices as the return on investment of these devices is better understood.

Artificial Intelligence and Machine Learning

AI and ML are increasingly becoming integral to advancing safety by offering sophisticated tools for data analysis, risk assessment, and predictive insights. These technologies analyze vast amounts of data from various sources, including workplace sensors, wearable devices, digital collections hubs, and even manual entries, to identify patterns and predict potential safety hazards and risks in the work system before they occur. AI-driven algorithms can automate routine safety checks, monitor compliance with safety protocols, and even customize training programs for individual workers based on their learning pace and style. Furthermore, AI and ML enhance decision-making processes by providing safety practitioners and other decision-makers with actionable insights, enabling them to implement more effective safety measures and interventions at the moment of need.

The predictive capability of AI and ML will also help prevent accidents and injuries and significantly reduce operational downtime and associated costs. However, successfully integrating AI and ML into safety practices necessitates addressing challenges such as ensuring the accuracy of predictions, ethical considerations regarding data use, and the need for continuous updating and training of AI models to adapt to changing workplace environments. As AI and ML technologies evolve, their potential to transform workplace safety is immense. They offer a proactive approach to identifying and mitigating risks, ensuring a safer and more efficient work environment.

Advanced Analytics and Big Data

Related to AI and ML, leveraging big data and advanced analytics transforms the landscape of managing safety and health by providing previously inaccessible insights. Organizations can identify hidden patterns by analyzing large datasets, anticipating potential hazards and risks, and implementing preventative measures. This predictive approach to safety will significantly reduce workplace accidents and illnesses. Moreover, data visualization tools will aid in communicating complex data in an understandable format, enhancing decision-making processes. Integrating real-time analytics will empower you as the safety practitioner to proactively address risks as this technology evolves.

Internet of Things and Connected Devices

The IoT introduces a new era of connected workplaces, where organizations continuously monitor and manage safety through a network of devices. For example, cameras and sensors can track environmental conditions, machinery can report maintenance needs before failures occur, and as mentioned already, wearable devices can monitor workers' health indicators. This interconnectedness enables a comprehensive approach to workplace safety, in which comprehensive, real-time data informs decisions. The potential for the IoT to improve safety is enormous, from smart personal protective equipment that adjusts to environmental hazards to automated emergency response systems. Integrating these devices will become more seamless as IoT technology advances, further enhancing safety measures.

Automation and Robotics

The advent of automation and robotics heralds a significant reduction in human exposure to hazardous work environments. Robots have been part of the work environment for a long while now. However, they will increasingly take on more roles that are not simply production-related but involve better control of repetitive tasks or dangerous jobs with increased risks of occupational injuries and fatalities. Automation enhances efficiency and safety in almost every business sector, including manufacturing, construction, transportation, mining, energy, and chemicals. The future will see a broader adoption of robotics, with technological advances making robots more adaptable and capable of performing complex tasks. This shift necessitates the safety practitioner reevaluating safety protocols and training programs to ensure workers can safely interact with and alongside automated systems.

ESG INTEGRATION INTO OCCUPATIONAL SAFETY, HEALTH, AND SUSTAINABLE DEVELOPMENT

Environmental, social, and governance criteria are set to fundamentally reshape the future of occupational safety and health within the broader context of bettering organizations' environment and social impact. By providing a framework emphasizing environmental stewardship, social responsibility, and governance practices, ESG is an ally to the practice of occupational safety and health for becoming a critical driver for how organizations will approach worker well-being and sustainable operations.

Here's a look at how these changes will affect the future:

Environmental: Sustainability and Safety and Health Integration

The "E" in ESG will be pivotal in aligning how we think about our broader work as safety practitioners. The safety practitioner will likely merge with the environmental side more often. Safety, long thought of as part of the larger EHS template, will be faced with sharing common sustainable development goals, particularly in addressing the escalating challenges posed by climate change regardless of our specific discipline. Environmental sustainability initiatives will increasingly affect workplace safety, such as reducing greenhouse gas emissions, minimizing waste, biodiversity, and resource efficiency. Integrating these environmental considerations into safety and health strategies will mitigate the direct effects of environmental factors that influence worker safety and health. As I discussed in an earlier chapter about management system integration, regardless of the business discipline, good work in this control category will likely lead to a safer, healthier, and more interdependent work environment that supports long-term sustainability goals.

Social Responsibility: Elevating Worker Well-Being

The social component of ESG will continue to gain prominence, highlighting the importance of worker well-being and fair treatment. There will be a growing emphasis on creating safe and healthy work environments, promoting diversity and inclusion, and supporting workers' rights. Safety practitioners and leaders will be pressed to prioritize the social aspects of ESG, ensuring that their organizations uphold high standards for workplace safety and health, address psychosocial hazards, support mental well-being, and enhance the overall quality of work life. In the future, social responsibility will also extend to community engagement and development, recognizing that worker health and safety are interconnected with broader societal well-being.

Governance: Strengthening Safety and Health Through Accountability

Governance within the ESG framework will become increasingly crucial in shaping corporate behavior, even in managing safety and health. Future governance practices will need to ensure compliance with safety and health regulations, foster transparency in reporting safety events, and promote ethical conduct throughout organizations. Effective governance structures will support the implementation of comprehensive safety and health strategies, ensuring accountability and driving continuous improvement in safety practices. This accountability will become a fundamental benchmark for evaluating and enhancing safety performance, setting a new standard for organizational integrity and responsibility.

INTEGRATING DIVERSITY, EQUITY, AND INCLUSION INTO SAFETY AND HEALTH

The imperative to weave diversity, equity, and inclusion principles into the fabric of safety and health practices is a significant evolution in occupational safety and health. It will undoubtedly be a new focus for the safety practitioner. This integration is not just about compliance or moral obligation; it is about enhancing the effectiveness of your occupational safety strategies to ensure they are genuinely effective for every worker, regardless of background.

Here are the areas that will require your attention:

Enriching Safety with Multiple Perspectives

Diversity in the workplace encompasses a broad range of differences among workers, including but not limited to race, ethnicity, gender, age, and socioeconomic background. In the context of safety and health, the safety practitioner will be pressed to acknowledge and value these differences, which are crucial for developing safety practices that are relevant and effective across the entire workforce. Diverse perspectives will lead to more innovative solutions to safety challenges, ensuring that safety protocols are not only universally applicable but also sensitive to the needs of various groups. For instance, safety gear designed to fit a diverse range of body types or considerations for cultural practices can significantly enhance the overall safety environment at the front line and foster greater team interdependence.

Fairness in Safety and Health Practices

Equity in safety means ensuring that the safety and health process is impartial, fair, and designed to provide equal outcomes for everyone. It involves recognizing and addressing systemic inequalities that may affect an individual's risk exposure, their perceptions of safety, or access to safety resources. Implementing equitable safety and health practices requires thoroughly assessing workplace policies, training programs, and emergency response strategies to identify and eliminate biases that may disadvantage certain workers. For example, providing safety training in multiple languages or accommodating work tasks for varying levels of physical ability ensures that all workers have the knowledge, skills, and tools they need to stay safe and feel valued.

Fostering a Culture of Belonging

Inclusion in the workplace is about creating an environment where all workers feel valued, respected, and supported. In the realm of safety and health, this means actively engaging with workers from diverse backgrounds in developing, implementing, and evaluating safety and health programs. Inclusive safety practices encourage participation and feedback from all workers, ensuring everyone has a voice in shaping the safety culture. Doing this well will lead to higher worker engagement, improved morale, and a more substantial and collective commitment to maintaining a safe work environment.

ENHANCING SAFETY AND HEALTH THROUGH POLICY AND REGULATION

Regulatory bodies play a critical role in shaping the future of occupational safety and health by setting standards and guidelines that drive the adoption of best practices. Regulatory action will continue to expand, and it will work to address the challenges of emerging technologies, remote work, and the gig economy to ensure comprehensive protection for all workers.

Here are the areas that will require your attention:

Future-Proof Regulatory Frameworks

As you move forward, regulations must evolve in tandem with the changing nature of work. This will involve crafting robust and adaptable policies that address the complexities introduced by technological advancements and new work models. For the safety practitioner, the goal will be to create a regulatory environment that balances the need for innovation with the imperative of safeguarding worker health and safety.

Global Collaboration in Advancing Safety Standards

In an increasingly interconnected world, occupational safety and health challenges will transcend national borders, highlighting the importance of global collaboration. International organizations, such as the International Labor Organization, the World Health Organization, and various country-specific safety organizations, will begin to play a more pivotal role in facilitating dialogue and cooperation between countries. Researching findings and developing technological innovations globally will be benchmark practices that help elevate safety standards worldwide, ensuring that advances in one region benefit workers everywhere.

Sharing Best Practices and Innovations

The exchange of best practices and technological innovations will be crucial to elevating occupational safety and health standards in a rapidly changing work environment. Organizations that successfully implement them in one region will be expected to adapt them for other regions, fostering a cycle of continuous improvement and innovation. Moreover, collaboration on research and development will accelerate the creation of solutions to everyday challenges, from mitigating the risks associated with emerging technologies to addressing the health implications of remote work and the gig economy.

STRATEGIC FORESIGHT IN OCCUPATIONAL SAFETY AND HEALTH

The work environment of the future presents a labyrinth of uncertainties shaped by the relentless pace of technological advancements, the fluidity of societal norms, and the unpredictable shifts in the global economic landscape. In this ever-changing terrain, safety and health practitioners will need strategic foresight. This will equip the safety practitioner with the ability to anticipate and navigate changes, ensuring that the safety and health of the workforce remain paramount.

Here are the areas that will require your attention:

Empowering Safety and Health with Strategic Foresight

Strategic foresight involves systematically exploring potential futures, including their challenges and opportunities. Safety practitioners must construct plausible future work environments using scenario planning and analysis techniques. This process will enable them to identify emerging risks and devise strategies that promote resilience and adaptability. It is a shift from a traditionally reactive posture to a decidedly proactive one, ensuring the safety process stays ahead of the curve.

The Critical Role of Scenario Planning

Scenario planning stands at the core of strategic foresight as a powerful tool for envisioning the myriad ways in which the future of work could unfold. Through scenario planning, you will be able to examine a variety of futures that are all influenced by the challenges mentioned in this chapter: technological advancements, the growth of the gig economy, demographic changes, regulation, and the evolving nature of the workforce. Each area is a concern, but they are not the only areas to consider. This exploration is not about predicting the future but about preparing for it and creating flexible strategies that can adapt to any number of potential scenarios. As the safety practitioner, you should understand your safety management and work system gaps today and how they may jeopardize your success going forward.

CLOSING

The future of occupational safety and health stands on the cusp of transformative change. Technological advancements, shifting demographics, global influence, new regulations, and evolving workplace norms present unprecedented challenges and opportunities. As safety practitioners, we can overcome many obstacles by embracing innovation, fostering inclusive and adaptive work cultures, and pursuing collaborative solutions that leverage a robust work system. The future of occupational safety and health is not without its challenges. Still, with proactive engagement from all stakeholders, including the front-line workers, it promises a safer, healthier workplace for everyone.

Chapter 19

Final Thoughts

"You can have brilliant ideas, but if you can't get them across, your ideas won't get you anywhere."

– Lee Iacocca

As I conclude and reflect on why I wrote *From Participation to Partnership: A Journey to Safety at the Front Line*, and why I ventured into the subject areas I asked you to consider, I realize this has been a journey of looking back over thirty-five years and seeing my personal values merge with my professional life. This book has explored the challenging areas in my safety practice, showing how facing those challenges has enabled me to serve better, lay a solid foundation for positively leveraging the safety management system, and establish genuine relationships at the front line. It has also helped me recognize the importance of partnering with people to achieve our goals while keeping an eye on future challenges and opportunities.

Each chapter has addressed a pivotal moment—an insight, a challenge, or an opportunity to improve myself and the safety programs I've led. These moments were threads weaving together programs and processes that have truly affected the front line. Early in this process, I told a friend that I aimed to write a letter to younger safety practitioners and new leaders with safety responsibilities. Indeed, this book has unfolded as a long personal letter, sharing the ingredients contributing to my safety success. Together, we've explored how to build a resilient self, cultivate a caring work culture, develop robust foundational processes, and make strategic adjustments to propel you toward success alongside your front-line teams.

I'm acutely aware that our profession has significantly changed since I started and will continue to evolve rapidly. I often visit my professional social media accounts and am amazed by some who are ready to disagree and present their opinion as the *one true* safety path. Possibly, it's my age, but more likely, my experience as a safety practitioner has taught me that there is no one magic way to achieve safety success. Plenty of information is available, but you and your teams will need to determine the path best suited for your organization. I advise staying curious, reading and listening, asking questions, and maintaining a keen sense of wonder. As you have gathered, I am pragmatic and lean on approaches that have worked well for me, even if they are not always seen as new. Some of the ideas I've shared in this book go back decades, but I've kept them in my practitioner's toolbox simply because they are robust and work. However, you should never stop learning and testing innovative ideas offered by others, deploying them if they help achieve safety success. What should be clear is that our core mission remains the same: as safety and health practitioners, it is our fundamental duty to ensure that all workers entrusted to our care return home safely to their families each day.

Allow me to conclude with an anecdote. After a particularly challenging day, an employee who had been part of a safety and health program I led approached me. He stopped me, gripping my hand firmly, and expressed his gratitude. He thanked me for providing a safe workplace and for investing time in his development, which ultimately ensured his safe return to his family every day. These moments, though rare, underscore the profound effect of our work and the reason we wake up every morning. If this episode had been the only positive response I ever received, it would have been enough to fuel my dedication as a safety practitioner.

You don't hear it enough, but thank you for protecting the lives of the workers under your care.

Bibliography

A Good Leader Gives Away Leadership | Manox
  Blog. 28 June 2019, https://manoxblog.
  com/2019/06/28/a-good-leader-gives-away-leadership/.

Brandon Rigoni, Ph D., and Jim Asplund. "Developing Employees'
  Strengths Boosts Sales, Profit, and Engagement." Harvard
  Business Review, 1 Sept. 2016. hbr.org, https://hbr.org/2016/09/
  developing-employees-strengths-boosts-sales-profit-and-engage-
  ment.

Greenleaf, Robert. "The Servant as Leader. 2007," Corporate Ethics
  and Corporate Governance. Springer, 2007.

Klau, Rick. "How Google Sets Goals: OKRs." Medium, 4 Dec. 2015,
  https://library.gv.com/how-google-sets-goals-okrs-a1f69b0b72c7.

Knowledge, HBS Working. "Why Isn't Servant
  Leadership More Prevalent?" Forbes, https://www.
  forbes.com/sites/hbsworkingknowledge/2013/05/01/
  why-isnt-servant-leadership-more-prevalent/.

Marsden, Eric. "The Heinrich/Bird Safety Pyramid: Pioneering
  Research Has Become a Safety Myth." Risk Engineering,

2 Mar. 2017, https://risk-engineering.org/concept/ Heinrich-Bird-accident-pyramid.

Maxwell, John C. "John C. Maxwell: How to Live Out Your Mission Statement." SUCCESS, 12 Oct. 2016, https://www.success.com/ john-c-maxwell-how-to-live-out-your-mission-statement/.

Memon, Dr Omar. "Part One: Exploring Aviation's Human Factors 'Dirty Dozen.'" Simple Flying, 25 Sept. 2023, https://simpleflying.com/aviation-human-factors-dirty-dozen-part-one/.

Petersen, Daniel C. "Human error reduction and safety management." University of Northern Colorado ProQuest Dissertation & Theses, 1980.

Sinek, Simon. Leaders Eat Last: Why Some Teams Pull Together and Others Don't. Penguin, 2014.

"The Science behind Why We Can't Look Away from Tragedy." NBC News, 6 Nov. 2017, https://www.nbcnews.com/better/health/ science-behind-why-we-can-t-look-away-disasters-ncna804966.

To Serve or Not to Serve. https://www.pmi.org/learning/library/ servant-leadership-cures-organization-9856.

Vaughan, Diane. The Challenger Launch Decision: Risky Technology, Culture, and Deviance at Nasa. University of Chicago Press, 1996.

"Yogi Berra: 'You've Got to Be Very Careful If You Don't Know Where You Are Going, Because You Might Not Get There.'" The Socratic Method, https://www.socratic-method.com/quote-meanings/yogi-berra-youve-got-to-be-very-careful-if-you-dont-know-where-you-are-going-because-you-might-not-get-there.

Zaleznik, Abraham. "Managers and Leaders: Are They Different?" Harvard Business Review, 1 Jan. 2004. hbr.org, https://hbr.org/2004/01/managers-and-leaders-are-they-different.

Afterword

By: Graham Freeman

When I was thirteen, I had a summer job in a factory that made fire logs from sawdust. The company was doing away with the excess packaging for their logs, so my job was to cut open the boxes, cut the old packaging off the logs, put the logs back in the box, tape up the box, pile the boxes on the pallet, and shrink-wrap the pallet, after which the warehouse manager would remove the pallet with the lift-truck and replace it with another pallet so I could start the entire process again. Much of the time, I was alone in the warehouse doing this work. There was no safety manager and no safety training. I was given a utility knife and some basic instructions about what to do. I remember inadvertently slashing my hands many times, but there was no process for incident reporting or corrective actions. I simply stopped the bleeding, taped up the wounds, and tried to be more careful next time.

Safety culture in that organization was little more than what they would have considered common sense. In other words, have the common sense not to get hurt, and if you don't have that common sense, go work somewhere else. That was typical of the period (late '80s) and the area (rural) in which I lived. I'm sure it's like that in similar workplaces such as farms and rural contracting even today.

Safety for me was mostly about luck and fortitude. If you're lucky, you won't get hurt. If you get hurt, keep going and don't let it get to you. Aside from my clumsy knife skills, the warehouse was full of hazards, any of which could have killed me, especially since I was alone much of the time. Pallets of logs were piled to the ceiling, flammable sawdust was everywhere, and I had no idea where to locate either a fire extinguisher or a first aid kit should they become necessary. My existence today is the result of sheer luck and nothing more.

My goal, aside from not slashing off my fingers, was to work for the summer and acquire enough money to buy my dream guitar, which a local seller was kindly holding for me while I worked to raise the funds to buy it. I wanted that guitar more than I wanted to stay safe. I certainly didn't make the connection between getting enough money to buy the guitar and the importance of retaining my fingers so I'd be able to play it. I was so focused on that guitar that I'm not sure I'd have done anything differently even if I had made that connection. I was paid by the hour, so if I slashed open my hand and had to take time off, there was no money in my pocket, and the date at which I could finally buy the guitar faded into the distance. I worked for the money with no regard for my safety. That was the first time I learned that workers in organizations with no particular interest in worker safety will take risks they wouldn't take in their personal lives because the threat of financial loss overrides their sense of self-preservation.

I thought a lot about this experience while I was reading Scott's book. Like all safety practitioners, Scott has dedicated his professional life to keeping people safe on the job. That's more than a job; it's a calling. More than making money for the company, experiencing the adrenaline rush of making a sale, or seeing leads come in from a marketing campaign, a safety practitioner's job success is measured in blood, fire, and lives. How much of the former can you avoid ensuring you preserve the latter? That's the currency of safety, and the fact that safety practitioners pursue that currency instead of mere profit and glory makes them—makes you—different. It requires passion, commitment, and, most of all, deep humanity and empathy for other people.

It's those qualities—humanity and empathy—that resonate most profoundly for me when reading this book. Much of what Scott describes here is hard work. Working with safety data and management systems can be difficult. It's complex, and the learning curve can be very steep. It would be easier for the company, and probably cheaper, if they simply didn't bother doing it at all. There are plenty of organizations that either don't do it or simply pay just enough lip service to the idea to make it look like they're doing it. Most of us could probably name companies we know that do exactly that.

But we've seen the consequences of that type of thinking. Scott begins the book with the story of Piper Alpha, the oil platform disaster off the coast of Scotland in 1988. Leadership didn't intentionally kill all those men. They didn't decide to sacrifice them for the sake of profit. At the same time, the possibility of a disaster of that scale wasn't unforeseeable. Any safety or risk professional could have looked at the myriad of design and process failures aggregating around the workplace and predicted the likelihood of an accident on some scale. But because they weren't looking for it, they didn't see it. What they did see they simply attributed to normalization of deviation. From the space shuttle disasters to Boeing, those incidents aggregated over time, giving off subtle warning signals to which no one was paying attention.

Scott's book is a masterclass in everything you need to know to be the best safety practitioner you can be. He's a master of his craft, and this book provides more knowledge and practical information than you could probably get in most university training programs, even more so because it's infused with decades of real-world experience in the workplace.

Yet underneath the practical wisdom is an even deeper message about humanity and empathy. The smartest, most disciplined person in the world could apply everything in this book and still not be a great safety manager if he or she lacks the humanity and empathy that makes safety practitioners unique. It's more than just a role or a job description; it's a way of seeing the world, one that puts people before profit and lives ahead of budgets. Every safety practitioner is probably familiar with leadership seeing safety practitioners as a burden or a source of red tape. That will probably always be the case. That doesn't always feel good. It can be tough when leadership doesn't appreciate the work you do. Nevertheless, safety is, at its foundation, a noble calling, even if you have to fight against the current of the organization's culture or leadership to do it.

Scott embodies all the best qualities of a safety leader. When you read this book again—as you should do several times if you want to squeeze every bit of wisdom from it you can—read beyond the words and the information to find Scott's voice as an empathetic human. If you can find the best parts of your humanity, if you can look at the workers for whom you're responsible and see your face or the faces of your children in theirs, if you can, when necessary, fight against complacency and power to protect the lives of those people, you will be on your way to becoming the kind of safety leader Scott has exemplified here.

About the Author

Scott Gaddis brings over three decades of dedicated leadership in safety, health, and environmental programs. His expertise and innovative thinking have made him a key figure in advancing the environmental, health, and safety (EHS) sector. Scott's efforts focus on fostering a global EHS community dedicated to sharing best practices and implementing strategies to minimize workplace risks. He plays a pivotal role at Intelex, seamlessly connecting product development, sales, and marketing teams to bolster the company's offerings in EHSQ and ESG solutions. His hands-on approach extends to providing tailored consultation to clients on EHS program management and strategic implementation.

Before his current position, Scott achieved significant milestones in the EHS field. His roles have included vice president of global environment, health, safety, and sustainability at Coveris High-Performance Packaging in Chicago, executive director of global EHS at Bristol-Myers Squibb in New Brunswick, New Jersey, and various senior safety and health leadership positions at Kimberly-Clark Corporation, culminating as global director of occupational safety and health in Roswell, Georgia. Scott's foundational experience in EHS was shaped during his early years as director of EHS in the Motors Division at General Electric.

Beyond his professional endeavors, Scott is actively involved in academia as a member of the board of visitors for the College of

Business at Athens State University, Alabama. In this capacity, he supports the university's mission by promoting education and advising on its advancement.

Scott's thought leadership in EHS is well-documented through his publications in trade journals and his contributions as a speaker at national and international conferences. His commitment to the field has been recognized through numerous awards and accolades. He is a graduate in Occupational Safety and Health from Murray State University.

With a career committed to improving workplace safety and health, Scott stands out for his ability to drive change through communication, collaboration, innovation, and visionary leadership. He has a unique talent for integrating EHS management deeply within organizational structures, enhancing safety and health outcomes by devising the best ways to develop partnerships between management teams and front-line workers.

For more information about Scott, find him on LinkedIn:
www.linkedin.com/in/gscottgaddis
To connect with Scott on a more personal level, visit:
MySafetyPartner.com
Alternatively, email him at:
Scott@mysafetypartner.com

www.ingramcontent.com/pod-product-compliance
Ingram Content Group UK Ltd.
Pitfield, Milton Keynes, MK11 3LW, UK
UKHW051605060225
454763UK00016B/103